A Hunter's Heart

Also by David Petersen

Ghost Grizzlies

Confessions of a Barbarian:
Selections from the Journals of Edward Abbey,
1951–1989 (editor)

Earth Apples:
The Poetry of Edward Abbey (editor)

Racks:
The Natural History of Antlers and the
Animals That Wear Them

Among the Aspen:
Life in an Aspen Grove

Big Sky, Fair Land:
The Environmental Essays of A. B. Guthrie, Jr. (editor)

Among the Elk

A
Hunter's Heart

HONEST ESSAYS ON
BLOOD SPORT

❧

Edited by David Petersen

A John Macrae / Owl Book
HENRY HOLT AND COMPANY
New York

Henry Holt and Company, Inc.
Publishers since 1866
115 West 18th Street
New York, New York 10011

Henry Holt® is a registered trademark of
Henry Holt and Company

Published in Canada by Fitzhenry & Whiteside Ltd.,
195 Allstate Parkway, Markham, Ontario L3R 4T8.

Library of Congress Cataloging-in-Publication Data

A hunter's heart: honest essays on blood sport / edited by
David Petersen.—1st ed.
p. cm.
"A John Macrae Book."
1. Hunting—Moral and ethical aspects. 2. Hunting—
Psychological aspects. I. Petersen, David.
SK14.3.H875 1996   96-13278
175—dc20   CIP

ISBN 0-8050-5530-4

Henry Holt book are available for special promotions and
premiums. For details contact: Director, Special Markets.

First published in hardcover in 1996
by Henry Holt and Company, Inc.

First Owl Book Edition—1997

A John Macrae / Owl Book

Designed by Kathryn Parise

Printed in the United States of America
All first editions are printed on acid-free paper∞

3 5 7 9 10 8 6 4

An extension of this copyright page
appears on page 331.

This book is for
Thomas D. I. Beck, who embodies all that's good in a hunter,
a wildlife manager, a conservationist, and a friend.

Contents

�-

Preface

"Hunting is one of the hardest things even to think about. Such a storm of conflicting emotions!"

In his two dozen books and scores of essays, that's one of the rare few times Edward Abbey ever used an exclamation point; we can safely assume he meant it.

Expanding on this theme, *National Geographic* senior editor John G. Mitchell points out the unfortunate truth that "in the matter of hunting or not hunting, everyone is so desperately eager to be considered correct. Yet there is such an overburden of dishonesty on both sides."

I was reminded of Abbey's and Mitchell's words recently while discussing hunting with H. Emerson "Chip" Blake, managing editor of that most literary of environmental journals, *Orion*. Blake and his comrades were looking to devote an issue to "the storm of conflicting emotions" surrounding hunting but, being personally unpracticed in blood, were a bit unsure how best—that is, most meaningfully and objectively—to approach this hot-potato topic. "When I think about the generally inept attempts at communication between hunters and antihunters," Blake told me, "I get this mental picture of a group of people sitting in a circle of chairs with the chairs all facing out."

Just so. "Singing to the choir" also comes to mind, as, sadly, does John Mitchell's unfortunate "overburden of dishonesty."

Unlike my urban *Orion* friends, I am rural and blooded to the elbows; I've been hunting and fishing—and thus, killing—for nearly four decades. Even so, I am no less torn and confused about so-called blood sport than they. It is an exceedingly complex issue and not, as self-appointed spokespersons for both sides would have it, simply right or wrong. Often as not, it's both; so much so that I sometimes think, were I not a hunter myself—lacking that intimate perspective, that hunter's heart—I suppose I could become an antihunter. The line is that fine.

As it is—being a hunter who writes and a writer who hunts, and possessed of sufficient objectivity (I flatter myself) to recognize at least the more obvious virtues and flaws in the arguments of both sides—I've long attempted to help promote a more open, honest, reality-based communication between hunters and antihunters; to turn at least a few of those out-turned chairs inward. How? By applauding the virtues of *ethical* hunting (and there are many) in general-interest and environmental magazines whose readers are primarily nonhunters with (it seems a fair assumption) likely antihunting leanings . . . then switching lecterns to condemn the sins of unethical *hunters* (and there are many) in hook-and-bullet publications. Singing against the choir, as it were. Or at least so far as my editors, on both sides, have allowed me to get away with it. But that's magazines.

Unburdened as they are by the advertiser (and, to a lesser degree, subscriber) influence that censors, rules, and ruins so many periodicals, books are different. As the late Pulitzer-winner A. B. Guthrie, Jr., once told me, "If you have something to say and can say it well, there's a book publisher willing to put it in print." The authors of the forty-one essays gathered here all have something to say about hunting—pro, con, often both, and by no means in universal harmony—and they say it well indeed. These are honest essays, written almost exclusively with hands stained red from personal experience and in a spirit more of soul-searching explication than defensive rebuttal.

After I experimented with various thematic groupings, it became apparent that while many of the essays do fit into categories, others don't, and most are so far-ranging as to defy definitive categorization. For that reason, I dropped all pretense of method in favor of offering the pieces in an order that seems both logical and pleasing (at least to me). If you're like most, you'll high-grade your favorite writers and topics anyhow, throwing order to the dogs. And why not?

"What can we say about hunting that hasn't been said before?" queries Abbey.

As I've discovered while editing this collection—a lot.

—DAVID PETERSEN

Acknowledgments

The editor expresses his deepest gratitude to Richard Nelson and John Murray, who conceived this collection and drafted me as its humble editor; Carl Brandt, a man as skilled and pleasant on a wilderness trail as in the literary jungle of Manhattan; John Macrae and Albert LaFarge, who have faith; Caroline Petersen, for editorial and spousal support; and the contributors, each of whom gave a lot for little in return.

A
Hunter's Heart

The world is not only watching, it is listening too. . . .
Other beings . . . do not mind being killed and eaten as
food, but they expect us to say please, and thank you, and
they hate to see themselves wasted.

—Gary Snyder,
THE PRACTICE OF THE WILD

Introduction:
Finding Common Ground

❧

RICHARD K. NELSON

I was always adamantly opposed to hunting. If I had known of anti-hunting organizations during my high school and undergraduate years, I would likely have joined; and if there had been public protests against hunting, I would have marched at the front. As an ardent conservationist, enraptured with animals and fascinated by all things natural, I thought hunting was entirely evil—no matter who did it, how they did it, or why. We lived in suburban Wisconsin, so I had many friends who loved to hunt and who regarded the fall deer season as practically sacred. But like most Americans, I had no experience with any kind of hunting, knew essentially nothing about it, and couldn't fathom why anyone would want to kill and eat a wild animal.

My first glimmers of understanding came through university courses in cultural anthropology, where I began to learn about Native American and other traditional hunter-gatherers. Then, at the age of twenty-two, I went to live for a year with Iñupiaq Eskimos on Alaska's arctic coast, where I studied how they subsist and survive—and they taught me about their hunters' way. We trailed caribou with dog teams over the tundra, tracked polar bears on a virtual continent of pack ice, and stalked seals among drifting floes. Once, as we approached a walrus herd far off the arctic Alaskan coast, an Eskimo companion advised me: "When you hunt walrus you must not act like a man. Do not be arrogant; be humble."

I continued this work intermittently over the next two decades, living with other Eskimo people and with their inland neighbors, the Gwich'in and Koyukon Indians—who hunted moose in the winter forest, sometimes crawled inside bear dens to see if they were occupied, and prayed to ravens for luck in pursuit of game. "For us, there's a really big law we have to follow, something like what you bring to the Supreme Court," a Koyukon woman once told me. "That law is respect—for the trees, for the animals, for everything."

Since those years in Native American communities, hunting has always been a centerpoint of my life, alongside a continued infatuation with natural history and a growing commitment to environmental activism. Hunting provides the most important staple foods in our home, deepens my sense of connection to the surrounding natural world, and sharpens my awareness that I am an *animal*, not separate from my fellow creatures but twisted together with them in one great braidwork of life. Hunting brings me into the wild and brings the wild into me.

If a particular moment stands out among my years of traveling and hunting with Native Alaskans, it's when an old Koyukon man said to me, "Every animal knows way more than you do." This is how he summarized the proper relationship between hunter and prey, and perhaps more broadly the vital conjunction between humanity and earth. Among the Koyukon and many other Native Americans, people understand—with a penetrating and almost intuitive clarity—that our fate rests completely with nature, our existence depends on what we take from the land, and ultimate power resides not within ourselves but within the world that nurtures us.

From my Native American mentors I discovered that a hunter's keenest edge is intimate knowledge of the animals and the surrounding environment; that hunting creates an acute awareness of being sustained by the plants and animals who necessarily die to feed us, whether we take those lives ourselves or delegate the responsibility to someone else; that hunters must show gratitude and respect toward every animal they take; and that hunting should be founded on a commitment to take only what we can use, to carefully practice conservation, and to protect the natural habitat we all depend upon.

The teachings of Claus Chee Sonny, a Navajo medicine man, were recorded by ethnographer Karl Luckert. In his account of instructions passed from the Divine deer-people to ancient Indian hunters, Claus Chee Sonny concluded: "And animals are our food. They are our thoughts." If we broaden this insight to all the living things arrayed on our table each day, we recognize a universal truth—that our life, our breath, and our thoughts are given to us by the plants and animals we eat. This is true not only for people like the Navajo, Koyukon, and Iñupiaq, but for every one of us, whether we get our food by hunting, fishing, gathering, farming, gardening, or shopping. The only difference is that we who inhabit the cities and suburbs and towns have *forgotten*.

And more than anything else, our forgetfulness is created by the supermarket, where we pluck from the shelves processed bits of plants and animals that are hidden inside boxes, cans, and packages— creating an illusion that we can have food without harvest, that life can be maintained without death, that our daily existence is separate from the land, and that we are fundamentally different from all other organisms.

Most of us are only dimly conscious of our own personal ecology—how we're rooted to the soil and water, forest and field; how we're affiliated with farmer and fisherman; and how we're connected even to wild animals and to hunting. Take the example of deer, which have become so abundant in many parts of the United States that they cause extensive damage to almost every kind of agricultural crop.

In Wisconsin, I asked a farmer what would happen to him if hunting were completely eliminated. "These deer would multiply so fast that we'd be out of the farm business in three to five years," he replied. After I heard similar opinions from other farmers, I put the question to a leading state deer biologist. "It's scary to think about the impacts that one wildlife species can potentially have on farming," he agreed. "Deer are already causing huge amounts of damage. But if that herd was allowed to grow statewide without hunting as a control means, I would agree with those farmers, and I'd say the farming economy in Wisconsin could be virtually eliminated, probably within three to five years."

How is this relevant to the vast majority of us who are not directly involved with farming? Every time we sit down to a meal, it's likely that deer were hunted to protect the fields where some of the food on our table was grown, no matter what sort of diet we prefer and no matter how we feel about hunting. All of us depend on a system that necessarily relies on the hunt. Foods that link us to deer and hunting include such ordinary items as bread, vegetables, salads, fruits, juices, and wine; specialties like tofu, soy sauce, almonds, and cranberries; and even staples like beef and chicken, as well as dairy products from animals fed on alfalfa, corn, and other grains often heavily damaged by deer.

Some folks might suggest we could solve this problem by reintroducing large numbers of wolves, mountain lions, and other four-legged predators to the farmlands of America, but such a plan would face enormous social and political barriers even if it were ecologically feasible, which it presently is not. Also, we might remember that people have long participated as active members of the North American ecosystem. Since Indians settled this continent at least 12,000 years ago and possibly much earlier, humans have been the single most important predators on deer and other wild ungulate populations.

Several million people—following a tremendous diversity of cultural lifeways and speaking about 175 different languages—inhabited these lands at the time of Columbus. And all of their communities were sustained, at least partially, by hunting. We seldom have this in mind when we speak of animals like wolves and mountain lions as North America's primary "natural" predators, or when we suggest that human hunting is somehow alien on this terrain. Indeed, humans must have influenced the very evolution of large mammals like deer, elk, moose, buffalo, antelope, and caribou; and so, we ourselves helped to create the qualities we love so deeply in these creatures: speed, grace, agility, elusiveness, strength, and wildness itself.

It was a crowning achievement of Native American cultures that a rich, diverse, and abundant array of wildlife still flourished here when the first Europeans dropped anchor along these shores. After all, every significant game species on this continent had been hunted intensively for millennia. Indeed, people from across the Atlantic were fairly overwhelmed by the New World's pristine beauty and richness; and, forgetting its long habitation by tribal peoples, they mistakenly called it a wilderness, as if no one had ever lived here.

The colonists brought a hunting tradition of their own, imbedded in a vastly different attitude toward land and wildlife. During the four centuries after Columbus, they spread and multiplied, cleared huge tracts of land, built thousands of new towns and cities, and killed untold millions of animals for subsistence and commercial markets. Between 1850 and 1900, Americans unleashed what Richard McCabe and Thomas McCabe have called "the period of greatest hunting pressure on wildlife *ever*." In the end, like revelers awakening from a binge, Americans beheld the havoc they had wrought: white-tailed deer all but extinct in much of the East, elk scarce in the West, buffalo essentially gone everywhere, passenger pigeons—once among the most prolific creatures on earth—now but a fading memory.

It may seem paradoxical, but as they emerged from this period of crazed overexploitation, Euro-Americans developed the modern conservation ethic, which is similar to the one evolved by our tribal predecessors here (perhaps after an earlier episode of excess and overkill). As history attests, and as several of this volume's authors point out, it was predominantly hunters who shaped and promoted the idea of conservation, the scientific principles guiding sustainable use of natural resources, and the concept of public wildlife preserves and national parks.

This is not to imply that hunters have been the paragon of reasoned and ethical behavior. Like any large and diverse community, North American hunters range from thoughtful and responsible to mindless and imprudent. Flagrantly delinquent "slob hunters," as they're aptly called today, make up a relatively small minority, but they cast a dark shadow over the American hunting community. If these misanthropes didn't exist, and if their behavior hadn't brought increasing pressure against the very idea of hunting, many of the essays in this book might never have been written. When David Petersen first discussed the project with me, his principal concern was to bring together a collection of thoughtful, openly critical, unblinkingly honest essays—written in clear, elegant prose, by people who are hunters, former hunters, or nonhunters intimately knowledgeable about the subject. His goal, I believe, was to directly confront the hardest issues and to nurture both ethical and environmental activism in an effort to preserve the hunt for future generations.

Of course, authors represented in this book are a minuscule fraction of the hunting community, but they speak to a very wide audience of people who hunt, their families and friends, readers with a sympathetic interest in the subject, and citizens who oppose hunting but want to educate themselves about it. These essays are filled with information about the hunt, drawn from personal, political, historical, and scientific perspectives. But more importantly, they give a rich sense of what hunting is "like" from the inside: how it feels to cross over the wild edge, to track and stalk game, to experience the mingled sadness and elation that accompanies a kill, to carry out the necessary business of dressing and butchering and storing meat, and then to cook, feast, and celebrate the profound gifts that come from an animal taken within its environment.

Many of these authors have tried to lay their own emotions bare—to explain who they are, why they hunt, what dilemmas they encounter, and why they consider hunting important to their lives. Their thoughts and experiences will be familiar to a very large number of people, because according to recent statistics there are about 15.5 million licensed hunters in the United States. This number is in slow decline—mainly because of urbanization, diminishing access to huntable land, and loss of opportunities for young people to learn hunting—but there are far more hunters today than the 1928 total of 4.3 million, and they comprise a larger percentage of our national population now than they did back then.

I suppose everyone who hunts has a somewhat unique background and a different set of motivations, but we can make some general statements by drawing from a bevy of sociological studies. First of all, researchers consistently find that hunters value the outdoors experience and closeness to nature above all other aspects of hunting. Their feelings are expressed in many ways, but perhaps seldom more eloquently than by outdoorsman and former U.S. president Jimmy Carter in his personal reflections on hunting, found among this book's chapters:

> I have never been happier, more exhilarated, at peace, rested, inspired, and aware of the grandeur of the universe and the greatness of God than when I find myself in a natural setting not much changed from the way He made it.

The social element also ranks very high as a motivation for hunting. Underscoring this point, sociologist Thomas Heberlein points out the simple fact that very few people hunt alone; almost all take to the field with family members, relatives, or other companions. In one study, three quarters of the respondents said they would rather hunt with friends in an area where chances of taking deer were slight than hunt alone where the chances for game were much higher. Among other incentives that might be considered "social," many hunters explain that they enjoy the temporary escape from pressures of city life, from work obligations, and from their normal daily routine.

Interestingly, the actual taking of game often ranks fairly low among hunters' stated motivations; but let's not forget that hunters *are* after an experience that cannot be gained just by camping, hiking, photographing, or wildlife watching. Hunters often mention a strong desire to at least *see* game animals and to feel they have a chance of bringing home their prey. Some are also motivated by the physical and intellectual challenges of hunting, as well as the sense of primal engagement with their environment. Only a small fraction of hunters (10 percent in a New York study, for example) say they're mainly interested in trophy animals.

Although taking an animal never ranks among the highest (or the lowest) of hunters' motivations, it's fair to say that most hunters have a strong interest in bringing home whatever game they've gone out after. Aside from the basic feeling of accomplishment this brings, a great majority of hunters are seeking game because they want to use the meat. The proceeds could amount to nothing more than a single, almost ceremonial meal—as in the case of ducks or grouse—or they could supply a year's worth of staple food for someone who takes deer, elk, or moose. Nowadays, many hunters (perhaps even most) bring the larger animals to butcher shops, where every bit of usable meat is processed and wrapped; bones and organs are delivered to rendering plants; hides are either given to the hunter or sold to tanneries; and even antlers are saved for commercial uses. Nevertheless, it's important to emphasize that very few hunters define a successful hunt as one in which they kill an animal, although studies show that taking game definitely contributes to their feelings of satisfaction.

As Thomas More concluded from his study of Massachusetts hunters: "I suggest that the pleasure of hunting comes more from the process than from the *product*." Putting the same thought in different words, an old friend from Wisconsin once told me, "Getting a deer is not important; going hunting is what's important."

Many critics of hunting base their objections on the belief that hunters are motivated by a twisted, singleminded pleasure derived from the act of killing an animal. No one familiar with hunting, and no credible sociological research, supports this notion. In fact, it runs directly opposite from the truth, as many of the following essays attest. The idea of killing for fun is nurtured, however, by such common terms as "sport hunting" and "recreational hunting," which do scant justice to an activity founded on a whole array of complex social, cultural, and personal aspirations.

This isn't to deny that the hunting experience, taken as a whole, rewards each participant with strong feelings of pleasure and satisfaction, and in this regard, Euro-Americans are no different from hunters in other cultures. I found that traditional Iñupiaq, Koyukon, and Gwich'in villagers were utterly possessed by the thrall and enjoyment of hunting, no less than the most fervent of Euro-American hunters. The pursuit of game was not just the basis for their economy and lifeway, but also something they passionately loved to do. During a year I spent in the arctic coastal village of Wainwright, I was struck by the fact that Iñupiaq men lived to hunt as much as they hunted to live.

Traditional communities like the Koyukon Indians also imbed in the hunt a strict code of moral behavior and ethical restraint, which not only regulates the kind and quantity of animals they take but also demands that every creature be treated with respect. Many essays in this book urge that we give strenuous attention to improving the moral and ethical standards that surround hunting in our own culture. Some of the authors take their compatriots to task for such practices as hunting over bait, pursuing game with dogs, and taking animals mainly for trophies. And they severely criticize hunting of depleted or threatened species—for example, some kinds of waterfowl, or grizzly bears in the mainland United States.

Most Americans recognize, to some extent at least, that problems related to hunting are much too complicated for a single, blanket solution. While a majority might oppose hunting grizzlies or shooting cougars chased up trees by dog packs, they do not feel that all hunting should be outlawed. A poll conducted by *USA Today* in 1992 indicated that 80 percent of Americans believe hunting should remain legal, while only 17 percent thought it should be made illegal. One New York biologist pointed out to me that many more citizens are antihunt*er* than are antihunt*ing*. Researchers have also found that people who know hunters are most likely to favor hunting, while people without any hunting acquaintances tend to lean the other way.

Not surprisingly, rural folks are far more likely to support hunting than are residents of cities or suburbs. This does much to explain the recent downturn in the number of hunters in our country, whose population was once predominantly rural and is now overwhelmingly urban. People tend to be most sympathetic toward hunting when they live close to the land, when wild animals and domesticated livestock are a part of their daily existence, and when they have direct experience with the organic processes that maintain their own lives. As our society has become less conscious of its earthly sources, we have increasingly begun to regard nature as nothing more than scenery, a backdrop to be admired as art or playground or sacred space, always viewed with a sense of detachment, and never a part of ourselves.

If my experience with Alaskan Eskimos and Indians is any measure, hunting gives us a powerful means to understand the error of such thinking. A community of thoughtful hunters could scarcely avoid recognizing that we are wholly dependent on the organisms who pass life along to us, that we are animals participating fully in the ecological network, that we hold membership in the environment no less than any other species, and that unrestrained or excessive use threatens the sources of our own existence.

We belong to an era marked by tremendous growth of concern for the natural world, but also an era of unparalleled threats from population growth, industrialization, land development, and loss of biodiversity. People who are deeply concerned about wildlife and the environment often disparage hunting and ignore the fact that hunters are perhaps their most important allies. In the United States, hunters are probably the largest, most diverse, and most important potential advocates for preservation of natural habitats and protection of wild animal populations. American lands set aside as parks, preserves, and refuges—totaling millions upon millions of acres—demonstrate the hunting community's early and continuing prominence as a conservation force.

After we've lost a natural place, it's gone for everyone—hikers, campers, boaters, bicyclists, animal watchers, fishers, hunters, and wildlife—a complete and absolutely democratic tragedy of emptiness. For this reason, it's vital that we overcome our differences, find common ground in our shared love for the natural world, and work together to defend the wild. The greatest potential of this book, I believe, is to nurture understanding of hunters by those who choose not to hunt, to encourage responsibility among hunters themselves, and to help us all toward that common ground.

These essays open a way into the heart of the hunter, and they show—more than anything else—that hunters can be guided by their hearts.

Blood Sport

❦

EDWARD ABBEY

What can I say about hunting that hasn't been said before? Hunting is one of the hardest things even to think about. Such a storm of conflicting emotions!

I was born, bred, and raised on a farm in the Allegheny Mountains of Pennsylvania. A little sidehill farm in hardscrabble country, a land of marginal general farms, of submarginal specialized farms— our specialty was finding enough to eat without the shame of going on "The Relief," as we called it during the Great Depression of the 1930s. We lived in the hills, surrounded by scrubby third-growth forests, little coal-mining towns down in the valleys, and sulfur-colored creeks meandering among the corn patches. Few people could make a living from farming alone: my father, for example, supplemented what little we produced on the farm by occasional work in the mines, by driving a school bus, by a one-man logging business, by peddling subscriptions to a farmer's magazine, and by attending every private and public shooting match within fifty miles of home—he was an expert small-bore rifleman and a member, for several years running, of the Pennsylvania state rifle team; he still has a sashful of medals to show for those years. He almost always brought back from the matches a couple of chickens, sometimes a turkey, once a yearling pig.

None of this was quite enough, all together, to keep a family of seven in meat, all the time, through the frozen Appalachian winters. So he hunted. We all hunted. All of our neighbors hunted. Nearly every boy I knew had his own rifle, and maybe a shotgun too, by the time he was twelve years old. As I did myself.

What did we hunt? Cottontail rabbit, first and foremost; we'd kill them, clean them, skin them, cut them up; my mother deep-fried them in bread crumbs and cooked and canned the surplus in Mason jars, as she did tomatoes, string beans, succotash, pork sausage, peaches, pears, sweet corn, everything else that would keep. We had no deep freeze; in fact, we had no electricity until the Rural Electrification Administration reached our neck of the woods in 1940.

So rabbit was almost a staple of our diet; fencerow chicken, we called it, as good and familiar to us as henyard chicken. My father seldom bothered with squirrel, but my brothers and I potted a few with our little Sears Roebuck single-shot .22s, out among the great ancient white oaks and red oaks that were still standing in our woodlot. Squirrel meat can be good, but not so good as rabbit, and a squirrel is much harder to kill; we missed about ten for every one we hit.

There were no wild ducks or other waterfowl in the hills; our only game bird was the ringneck pheasant, rising with a thrilling rush from the corn stubble. My father bagged a few of those with his old taped-together double-barrel shotgun. Not many. He didn't like to hunt with a shotgun. Wasteful, he thought, and the shells were too expensive, and besides, he disliked chewing on lead pellets. The shotgun was primarily a weapon (though never needed) for home defense. Most of the time he shot rabbits with his target rifle, a massive magazine-loaded .22 with a peep sight. Shot them sitting.

Was that legal? Probably. I don't remember. But he had a good eye. And he was a hunter—not a sportsman. He hunted for a purpose: to put meat on the table.

We kept a couple of beagle hounds on the place, but their job was to lie under the front porch and bark at strangers. Only when our Uncle Jack came out from town, with his sleek gleaming sixteen-gauge pump gun (as we called it), and the red bandanna and hunting license pinned to the back of his hunting coat, only then would our old man load his own shotgun and turn loose the dogs for some sport hunting through the fields and along the edge of the woods. What my father really liked about those occasions was not the shooting but the talk, the wild stories—Uncle Jack was a great storyteller.

And then there were the deer. The woods of Pennsylvania swarmed with deer, though not so many then as now, when many small farms, abandoned, have gone back to brush, thicket, trees. There were even a few black bear still wandering the woods, rarely seen. But deer was the principal game.

My father usually bought a license for deer, when he could afford it, but only because the penalty for getting caught with an untagged deer would have been a small financial catastrophe. In any case, with or without a license, he always killed his deer on the evening before opening day, while those red-coated fellows from the towns and cities were busy setting up their elaborate camps along the back roads, stirring the deer into movement. Our father was not a stickler for strict legality, and he believed, as most country men did, that fear tainted the meat and therefore it was better to get your deer before the chase, the gunnery—The Terror—began. We liked our venison poached. (As a result I find that after these many years I retain more admiration and respect for the honest serious poacher than I do or ever could for the so-called "gentleman hunter.")

My old man practiced what we called "still hunting." On the day before opening, about noon, when the deer were bedded down for their midday siesta, he'd go out with his gun, his cornfodder-tan canvas coat with its many big pockets, and his coal miner's oval-shaped lunch bucket full of hot coffee and sandwiches and Mother's stewed-raisin cookies, and he'd pick a familiar spot along one of the half-dozen game paths in our neighborhood, settle down in the brush with his back to a comfortable tree, and wait. And keep on waiting, sometimes into the long autumn twilight, until at last the first somewhat nervous, always uneasy deer appeared. Doe or buck, he always shot whatever came first. You can't eat antlers, he pointed out.

Usually he shot his deer with a "punkin ball" from the battered, dangerous, taped-up shotgun. But at least once, as I recall, he dropped a doe with his target rifle, like a rabbit. Drilled her right between the eyes with a neat little .22-caliber long-rifle bullet. Those deer slugs for the shotgun were expensive.

Then he'd drag the deer into the brush, out of sight, and wait some more, to see if anyone had noticed the shot. When nothing happened, he hung the deer to the nearest tree limb, dressed it out, ate the liver for supper. If it was a legal kill he would wait through the night, tag it, and take it home by wheel first thing in the morning. If not, he slung the carcass over his shoulders and toted it home through the woods and over the hills in the dark. He was a strong, large, and resolute sort of man then, back in the thirties and early forties, with a wife and five children to feed. Nowadays, getting on a bit, he is still oversize, for an old man, but not so strong physically. Nor so resolute. He works only four or five hours a day, alone, out in the woods, cutting down trees, and then quits. He gave up deer hunting thirty years ago.

Why? "Well," he explains, "we don't need the meat anymore."

Now that was how my brothers and I learned about hunting. My brothers still like to go out for deer now and then, but it's road hunting, with good companions, not "still hunting." I wonder if anybody hunts in that fashion these days. I did a lot of deer hunting in New Mexico from 1947 through the 1950s, during my student years and later, when I was living on seasonal jobs with the Park Service and Forest Service, often married, trying to write books. As my father had taught me, I usually went out on the day before opening. Much safer then, for one thing, before those orange-vested hordes were turned loose over the landscape, shooting at everything that moves.

Gradually, from year to year, my interest in hunting, as a sport, waned away to nothing. I began to realize that what I liked best about hunting was the companionship of a few good old trusted male buddies in the out-of-doors. Anything, any excuse, to get out into the hills, away from the crowds, to live, if only for a few days, beyond the wall. That was the point of hunting.

So why lug a ten-pound gun along? I began leaving my rifle in the truck. Then I left it at home. The last time I looked down the bore of that old piece there was a spider living there.

"We don't need the meat anymore," says my old man. And I say, Let the mountain lions have those deer; they need the meat more than I do. Let the Indians have it, or hungry college students, or unpublished writers, or anyone else trying to get by on welfare, food stamps, and hope. When the money began arriving from New York by airmail, those checks with my name on them, like manna from heaven, I gave up hunting deer. I had no need. Every time you eat a cow, I tell myself, you are saving the life of an elk, or two mule deer,

or about two dozen javelina. Let those wild creatures live. Let being
be, said Martin Heidegger. Of course, they're going to perish anyway, I know, whether by lion or wolf or starvation or disease—but
so are we. We are all going to perish, and most of us miserably, by
war or in a hospital, unless we are very lucky. Or very resolute. I am
aware of that fact and of our fate, and furthermore, I have no objections to it, none whatsoever. I fear pain, suffering, the likely humili-
ations of old age (unless I am lucky or resolute), but I do not fear
death. Death is simply and obviously a part of the process; the old,
sooner or later, have got to get out of the way and make room for the
young.

The subject remains: death. Blood sport. The instinct to hunt. The
desire to kill. Henry David Thoreau, notorious nature lover, was also
a hunter and fisherman, on occasion. And among the many things
that Thoreau wrote on the matter was this, from *Walden*:

> There is a period in the history of the individual, as of the race, when
> the hunters are the "best men," as the Algonquins called them. We
> cannot but pity the boy who has never fired a gun; he is no more hu-
> mane, while his education has been sadly neglected.

But he adds:

> No humane being, past the thoughtless age of boyhood, will wan-
> tonly murder any creature which holds its life by the same tenure he
> does. The hare in its extremity cries like a child. I warn you, mothers,
> that my sympathies do not make the usual *philanthropic* distinctions.

And concludes:

> But I see that if I were to live in a wilderness, I should become . . . a
> fisher and hunter in earnest.

In earnest. There lies the key to the ethical issue. Earnestness. Purpose. That sly sophist Ortega y Gasset wrote, somewhere, that "one
kills in order to have hunted." Not good enough. Thoreau would
say, one kills in order to eat. The killing is justified by the need and
must be done in a spirit of respect, reverence, gratitude. Otherwise
hunting sinks to the level of mere fun, "harvesting animals," *diver-
tissement*, sadism, or sport. *Sport*!

Where did the ugly term "harvesting" come from? To speak of "harvesting" other living creatures, whether deer or elk or birds or cottontail rabbits, as if they were no more than a crop, exposes the meanest, cruelest, most narrow and homocentric of possible human attitudes toward the life that surrounds us. The word reveals the pervasive influence of utilitarian economics in the modern mind-set; and of all the sciences, economics is the most crude and obtuse as well as dismal. Such doctrine insults and violates both humanity and life; and humanity will be, already is, the victim of it.

Now I have railed against the sportsman hunter long enough. I wished only to explain why first my father and then I have given up hunting, for the time being. When times get hard again, as they surely will, when my family and kin need meat on the table, I shall not hesitate to take that old carbine down from the wall and ramrod the spider out of the barrel and wander back once more into the hills.

❦

"Paw," says my little brother, as the old man loads the shotgun, "let me shoot the deer this time."

"You shut up," I say.

Our father smiles. "Quiet," he whispers, "both of you. Maybe next year." He peers down the dim path in the woods, into the gathering evening. "Be real still now. They're a-comin'. And Ned . . ." He squeezes my shoulder. "You hold that light on 'em good and steady this time."

"Yes, sir," I whisper back. "Sure will, Paw."

From *The Blue Hen's Chick*

❧

A. B. GUTHRIE, JR.

We were always poor, I guess, or, by generous appraisal, reduced in circumstances by illness and the undertaker; but if conscious of our state at all, I was not oppressed by it. Not many possessed much money then. We had enough to eat. Our clothes were stout though few. Our sometimes leaky roof sufficed. What more could people ask, except rarely for a nickel to buy an all-day sucker? I didn't see why Mother always wanted, in some glad and distant day that never dawned, to make structural changes in the house.

Our riches, felt rather than defined, lay at home, which the fragility of our family somehow made the dearer. Despite our modest means, despite bereavements or in their temporary absences, despite my forlorn soul, despite paternal plagues that I must come to later, we had our happy and abundant times. And whether poorhouse, hell, or heaven, home was home.

Added to our riches, though unreported by the bank, were the dividends the outdoors paid. Through my father's old field glasses he and I identified, with help from books, birds in our region rarely seen and more rarely recognized. We counted the Savannah sparrow, the olive-backed thrush, a brown thrasher that forsook ancestral acres in favor of the West and staked a homestead in a bullberry bush. We rejoiced at seeing these and others, at knowing more about the world around us. A weakened waxwing grew into a pet. So did a redpoll, and, when spring came on, a cottontail that at first my hand would hold. I found a mallard's nest and put the eggs beneath a hen, which followed her confusing brood along an irrigation ditch and was not seen again.

The joy of hunting was beyond accounting, once I was old enough to be trusted, if anxiously, with my father's old shotgun. I loved to bring birds down, to take quick aim at mallards, pintails, teal, and prairie chickens on the wing and feel the twelve-gauge bounce against my battered shoulder and see the flight stopped short and the broken target fall.

The season opened early, soon after the school year commenced, and I spent my classroom hours impatiently, straining for three o'clock and the hours that counted. Yonder, westward, were prairie chicken cover and beaver dams and potholes that blue- and green-winged teals frequented and, farther on, three little lakes well liked by bigger ducks.

My brother and I had done the chores at home, except for the evening milking, and that my father would attend to. There was chopped wood in the wood box, coal in the coal scuttles, no ashes in the stoves. My conscience was clear. The way was open, barred only by the crawling clock.

On dismissal I'd run home, change my clothes, and grab shotgun and shells and join, or be joined by, another hunter. Oftener than not it was George Jackson, my close friend then and now. . . . We'd start out happily afoot, not thinking of the ten miles or more we'd cover but of the birds we'd bag.

The days were yellow, tinted by September, and though shortened from high summer still were long. Across the valley, up the slopes, and on the benches the buffalo and bunchgrass had turned tan, cured on the stem. Along the river the cottonwoods were fading, revealing in their leaves the veins of age. The gophers had grown fat for winter. Jackrabbits began to show the change from brown to white, to match the coming snow. A meadowlark that should have flown south sooner sounded its fall song. Flushed by frost, bullberries sparkled in their silver thickets, red as Indian beads, and chokecherries hung in fat and purple clusters among despairing leaves. The sun and sky were kind, unwilling yet to yield to winter yet touched with a surrender that made the heart glad for this final, fleeting stand. The hunting season, the first, sad, gorgeous days!

Later the wild goose would cry, the snow goose and his grander kinsman, the Canadian, and still later I would drop four of the latter from a station in a homestead privy near a lake where I fired through a broken, foot-square window while crouching on the seat; but now we were laden, now we had spoonbills or mallards or widgeons or teals or butterballs or grouse or more likely a variety, and now night was closing in. Time to go home.

We were as tired as boys could be, but we sang as we slogged along, made vocal by our accompaniment, by the good, wild smell of blood and feathers and exploded powder. We sang "Heidelberg" or "La Miserere" or "Smile the While" or "The Rose of No Man's Land" or hymns like "Beautiful Isle of Somewhere." The themes didn't matter: they were all one and all glad. We sang in the listening silence or as the chinook wind moaned around us or as the north wind whistled, knowing we could make it home, knowing Mother would be waiting and have warmed and waiting for us the food our stomachs cried for.

Once with a .22 I shot down two coyotes. These wily little wild dogs are known to feed on chickens, lambs, and even calves, and so the rightful man destroys them. I had flushed the pair from a pigweed patch at the base of a butte. They sped angling up the slope, one to left and one to right, and I fired left and right, once each, and flattened both. Fine shooting, if by accident. Incredible marksmanship. I wished with pounding pride someone had seen me.

One of the coyotes wasn't dead, I found as I walked up to him. He lay without struggle looking at me, looking through and beyond me, with no fear of man now in his yellow eyes but only with the resigned and final wonder of death. I had to put another bullet in him, this time in his wondering brain.

No longer do I like to kill or see things killed. When slaughter justifies itself by simple economics, I yield, although reluctantly. Sometimes, rarely, even yet, for sake of pan and palate, I'll shoot a bird or beach a fish, but there's little sport in either act. And I'd as soon blast any trusting milk cow as fell an elk or deer. The watcher lives to see watched things again, and while life maybe isn't precious, to put an end to it is mournful.

But I would not give up my recollections, though touched with unease in thinking of my old blood-thirst and the crippled creatures that hid successfully and died in misery. Those days were great as of my time. I've long since said good-by to them, but never to remembrance.

Moose and Mangamoonga

❦

JOHN G. MITCHELL

My father shot and killed his first moose in New Brunswick in 1922. It was also his last, anywhere. The animal weighed eight hundred pounds after gutting and the antlers measured fifty inches across the full spread. The old man and his guide were a long portage from their canoe and a dozen miles out from the nearest roadhead when the big bull went down with a hole half the diameter of a man's little finger behind its shoulder. They gutted the moose in the shallow pond where it fell, quartered it, and carried everything edible or mountable to the canoe. The edible parts were long gone before my time. As for the moose's head, when I came of an age to notice such things, I found it mounted above the fireplace of our cottage in northern Michigan. Firelight flashed across the brown marbles of its make-believe eyes. Wherever I moved, the eyes seemed to follow. I spoke to the moose. I said: Moose, why do you watch me? Why do you look so sad when it no longer hurts? The moose did not answer. My father did not answer either, and I had asked him a more reasonable question. I asked him if killing moose is fun.

Perhaps there was no answer from the old man because he could no longer be sure how he felt about such things. Though he would live most of his life in it, he was not of the twentieth century. It seemed to me, for he was old enough to be my grandfather, that he was always back somewhere on the other side of the century, in a time of horses and bugles, among fresh memories of Cheyenne lances at the Little Bighorn and Krupp cannon at the Centennial Exposition in Philadelphia's Fairmount Park. He missed both of those events by three years, but not the great flights of passenger pigeons that still darkened the skies of Kentucky on summer mornings, or the diminishing herds of bison that would linger for decades in Texas, though the last of that breed in Kansas was dropped in its tracks on the Santa Fe Trail the month he was born.

He was a country boy, and he learned to shoot early and well and possibly with some confusion as to what was or was not decent and right in the slaughter of wild animals; confusion, because he came of shooting age at the interface between traditions, between the extirpative excesses of the western mountain man and newfangled restraints of the eastern aristocrat-sportsman. The bison were going fast then, and the pigeons would soon be gone forever, but not the old wrathy frontier appetite for killing. It would simply adapt itself to the law of the bag limit, so that in time most of my father's contemporaries would learn to be content slaying five of a species in a single day, instead of five hundred. My father was content with one moose for a lifetime.

I do not remember him especially as a hunter. There were occasional autumn trips after quail, and if you count the pursuit of fish with rod and reel a form of hunting, as I do, then there were summer trips in Michigan after trout and bass and walleyes as well. But he was not a hunter in the classic manner of those who are absorbed in guns and dogs and the vicarious fireside palaver of men impatient for the opening day.

Recognizing the old man's desultory attention to the blood sport, I am at a loss to explain my own early eagerness to taste of it. A country boy I was not, though woods and fields would be plentiful for a while yet in the suburbs where I grew up. I learned to shoot passably with a Daisy air rifle and a bolt-action single-shot .22, and later with shotguns of various gauges and vintages. I was about ten when I first shot a squirrel out of a beech tree in southern Ohio, and I was surprised how much lighter than human blood was the animal's as it splashed on the copper October leaves, and how sticky as it started to dry on the tip of my finger, and later how uncommonly tasty the thighs that came to table from the fat in the frying pan. I think I may have been sorry for the squirrel as I ate it, but only a little.

If I had stayed with it, I might have been more of a hunter. But somehow in the crucial years of postadolescence there seemed always to be other distractions on autumn weekends, such as chasing footballs. More lasting by far were the later distractions of jobs and children—female children who would acquire their mother's loathing of guns and would stare at their father with ill-concealed contempt as he ineptly explained how he had once enjoyed walking in the woods with a rifle in the crook of his arm. What did he kill with the rifle? they wanted to know. Rabbits and squirrels, he answered. And they were sure good to eat.

My friends of recent years tend to be the kind who object to the killing of anything. They speak of a reverence for life. Rifles and shotguns, not to mention handguns, give them a certain claustrophobic tremor in the viscera. They have lived their lives against a background of a constant gunnery—murder, hijacking, assassination, and war. Their most unpopular war is the one in the woods. They do not understand, or do not want to understand, how anyone could possibly derive joy from shooting at animals. They see the hunter as a bumbling sadist, and they speak sardonically of protecting their constitutional right to arm bears. "If you can't play a sport," the old antihunting advisory goes, "then shoot one." But of course they wouldn't. It might entail using a gun.

Not all of my friends frown on hunting. I have sat together with a few for and many against, partaking of the domesticated flesh of an animal killed in a slaughterhouse by a man with a blunt instrument, and listened to the two sides arguing. Pro-hunter says that he, too, has a reverence for life, but no hangups about death. "How can you eat this beef," he demands, "and say it is wrong to hunt deer?"

"But no one shoots cows for sport," says the anti.

"You mean for *fun*," says her friend. And there's an echo for my ear.

Pro-hunter throws up his hands. "Telling you about hunting," he says, "is like trying to explain sex to a eunuch."

On which analogy the anti pounces like a quick cat. "It's cigars all over again," she says. "The gun is a phallic crutch. Correct?"

(In the matter of hunting or not hunting, everyone is so desperately eager to be considered correct. Yet there is such an overburden of dishonesty on both sides.)

"And what side are you on?" It is my north country friend, the attorney from Bay City. We are standing before the stone fireplace of the cottage in Michigan. It is his place now, gone from my own family's clutches for half a lifetime, a third-party ownership having fallen somewhere between. I do not think the children of the third party had much esteem for my father's moose. They put curlers to its beard and left it festooned with red ribbons. The Bay City family, moving in, restored dignity to the threadbare head.

Whenever I am in northern Michigan, I make it my unofficial business to detour into the old place, take passing advantage of my friend's hospitality when he is around, or trespass a little when he is not. This time I am on my way to Gaylord for opening day of the hunting season and I am not even sure which side I am on. My friend, a man of strong opinions, is waiting for my answer. I look beyond his face and see the birch fire crackling on the undersides of the brown marble eyes. And I wonder: Why is it that the moose still watches me like this? Since it no longer hurts.

🌿

I was born and raised and I first hunted in Cincinnati, Ohio. When I left it, about 1950, it was the sixteenth-largest city in the United States. Now, there are twice as many cities ahead of Cincinnati in the statistical pecking order, and people no longer hunt game in any one of them, though they sometimes hunt each other.

My own game-hunting years fell into the forties. Even then, it was probably unlawful to discharge a firearm within the city limits of Cincinnati, but I do not recall any great fear of pursuit and arrest. There seemed to be little enforcement in my precincts, possibly because the excitable spinster sisters who lived next door were hard of hearing, and because the war sharply limited the availability of sporting ammunition and imposed on youthful wastrels a certain single-shot thrift. My other advantage was space. A great wooded hollow ran beside our place, with oak and maple and beech on its slopes and sumac and sycamore along the bottom. There was a grassy swale, too, always good for rabbit, and sometimes quail, too, though I was parentally forbidden to shoot the latter, bobwhites being a protected species in Ohio in those days.

If I have places to blame for my lingering inclination toward the out-of-doors, I suspect that the hollow of home should rank high among them. From the beginning of memory, it was a delicious place in every season, and it stirred my imagination hugely. Going back to a time before I was old enough to be entrusted with an air rifle, while death was still make-believe, the hollow with very little effort could be induced to assume the qualities of Cumberland Gap or Dodge City or the Little Bighorn or the Western Front, depending on what I might be reading at the time, or what I had seen at the picture show the previous Sunday at Hyde Park Square. I prowled the sumac thicket with a sumac stick snugged in the crook of my arm, stalking the Big Indian. And before that, I went to the hollow stalking the biggest game. The mangamoonga.

There was not a great deal known about the mangamoonga. Descriptions were sketchy and, as time went on, contradictory. My older brother was largely responsible for the confusion. At first it was said that the beast resembled a panther somewhat, though not very closely. Then came reports that it was not like a panther at all, but rather of the sort one might possibly mistake for a rhino, not armor-plated but long-haired in the shaggy fashion of the Pleistocene. In one version, it had fangs; in the next, flaring tusks. Its breath smelled of corned beef and boiled cabbage, which I detested. There were traces of smoke about its nostrils. Its paws were enormous, yet they left no tracks. It hadn't eaten since that Irish boy had vanished from O'Brienville in 1937. The reports grew more terrible each year. My brother and sister insisted that they had seen the mangamoonga on many occasions. Was something the matter with me? I tried harder and had not seen it once.

I suppose that trying was the best part of it. Day after day, with an astonishing lack of caution but no small measure of tingling dread, I slipped into the woods in hope of catching a glimpse of the surly beast, and possibly loosing a sumac shot at it. I kept watch on my belly in the darkest thickets. I climbed trees. I posted myself beside a rainwater pool, assuming that the mangamoonga must surely take a drink now and then in the heat of the day. I studied the rabbits and squirrels, the flickers and robins, seeking from their behavior some sign that the creature might be coming our way. And once, in a rage of imagined contempt, I stood at the edge of the hollow and shouted, "Moonga is *chicken*!" until the insult rolled back in echoes off a neighboring hill. If that doesn't bring him out, I thought, nothing will. And nothing did.

Exactly when or how it occurred to me that the mangamoonga and I were never to meet—all of that escapes remembrance. Possibly it was about the time I discovered that the hollow, after all, had limits; that there were streets and houses, and chain-link fences, on the other side. In any event, I do know that of the two discoveries, the more painful pertained to the creature I had sought in vain. It was as if all the rules of a wonderful game had suddenly been changed. However vast or truncated, the woods no longer seemed to crackle with excitement. Where there had been mystery, fantasy, danger, wildness, now there were solutions, facts, safety, domesticity. The effort to stay alert at all times was no longer essential. I grew languid and bored. But only for a while. Months or years later, a member of the family caught my eye at dinner and wanted to know if I had ever seen the mangamoonga. I replied that of course I had, and on many occasions. And what had become of the critter? I was asked. Dead, I said. Oh. And how had it perished? I replied that I did not know. Then, someone said, maybe the great beast simply curled up in its lair, gave a deep sigh, and died of old age. "Of *whose* old age?" said the wisest sibling.

I have been back to the hollow once or twice in recent years, if only to assure myself that it is still there. And it is. Most of it, anyway. Only the far northern end of it is a goner, all paved and buttressed under a cloverleaf interchange on I-71. We used to call that place Duck Creek. Now the creek runs through a sewer line and the old towering willows that furnished us switches are goners, too. There was one tree with a deep cavity in which we cached secret messages, and squirrels took the paper away for their nests. Now a public message hangs in steel above the expressway to inform the traveler, indirectly, that Columbus is less than two hours away.

The part of the hollow below our old place is as good a piece of country as it ever was. Maybe better. The sycamores are giants now; the swale, overgrown with brush and probably a lot better for songbirds than quail; the trail still winding through, on its way from what used to be Duck Creek to O'Brienville. Last time in there, I met a schoolboy on the trail. He seemed in a great hurry. He was carrying a baseball bat and catcher's mitt, and looked to be on his late way to some sandlot game in Hyde Park. On a perverse impulse, I said to

him as he passed, "Have you seen the mangamoonga?" He stopped
and said, "The *what*?" I said, "The mangamoonga." The boy stared
at me suspiciously for a while, shook his head, then resumed his way
along the trail. "I haven't even heard of that one," he called back to
me over his shoulder. "What channel—what night is it on?"

❧

The other city place I hunted was Hinkel's Woods. It was a fair-sized
piece of undeveloped country, probably thirty acres or more, with a
brook running through it and a good hilltop view of the eastern suburbs, though this, too, was well within the city limits, about a mile
from the hollow and only seven or eight from the heart of down-
town. I do not recall ever taking any game from Hinkel's Woods.
There were at any one time too many of us, in threes and fours, first
with air rifles and later with .22s, making too much noise together to
be at all effective in the pursuit of rabbits or squirrels. In that sense,
going to Hinkel's was like going to hunting camp—throwing up a
lean-to and building a fire in front of it, and stacking the rifles against
a tree, and roasting meat on sticks, and smelling wood smoke, and
being away for a while from family and other friends.

Other friends were not especially sympathetic to this kind of behavior. Other friends, then in Cincinnati, were of a kind who spent
their Saturdays with footballs (as I later would myself) or baseball
bats. To each his own. The others could have their sandlot talk of
Knute Rockne and Bucky Walters, the Redleg hero of Crosley Field.
We had our wet feet and smoky eyes and the lean-to talk of Daniel
Boone and Errol Flynn, who had just died with his boots on in the
last picture show at Hyde Park Square.

I have often wondered what might have made the difference between the two kinds of us, the jocks and the woodsboys. It surely
could not have been heredity. There were Germans and Irish and
English and Italians in both camps. Nor was it economic, for there
were rich men's sons and sons of men who were not so rich in both
camps. Nor was it parental guidance, in the sense of do-as-I-did, for
the fathers of some of my Hinkel's Woods colleagues had probably
never owned a gun, only golf clubs; while the fathers of some of the
jocks had grown up in the country with animal blood on their hands.
Among the latter cases, I suspect there may have been *some* gentle
guidance toward the playing fields, for in those days there was a ten-

dency for country folk to want to shed the rural heritage and citify themselves as fast as possible; and no doubt a few of the fathers must have felt somehow that it was more urbanely civilized to send their boys into violent bone-crunching gridiron battle than to encourage their participation in a desultory slaughter of squirrels. All of which is natural enough, and possibly appropriate. If humankind had not evolved as a hunting society, would we now have football? Of course not. In which case, Knute Rockne would never have invented the forward pass, the gridiron's longbow, though he might have become a heroic pitcher, like Bucky Walters.

Still, it is a puzzlement to understand what might have made the difference, turning some of us to Hinkel's Woods and others to the ball fields. No doubt a few of my woodsy fellows for a while were more or less motivated along malevolent lines, for there is no use denying the dark and scabrous bloodlust of the adolescent male in his earliest seasons of the hunt. He is insatiable. And some, burdened by a defect of mind or character, remain adolescent through the rest of their years, wondering why it is that so many people regard hunters in general as slobs.

Not so, I think, with my own hometown hunters, though I have lost touch and can vouch for neither their current sanity nor their continued interest in hunting. Not so because, then, on autumn Saturdays in Hinkel's Woods, emerging from the trace of atavistic grit within each one of us was something else that may have come close to the essence of hunting as it should be; if, indeed, it should be at all. I mean an appreciation of landscape, and an understanding of its parts in some small way approaching Aldo Leopold's perception. I hadn't heard of Leopold then and wouldn't read his writing for another twenty years. But I guess I would have liked what he had to say about the autumn landscape in the north woods, and how it all added up to "the land, plus a red maple, plus a ruffed grouse." In terms of physics, Leopold advised, "the grouse represents only a millionth of either the mass or the energy of an acre. Yet subtract the grouse and the whole thing is dead." Of course, there were no grouse in Hinkel's Woods in those years. And now, not even quail.

Perhaps what made the difference was our own perception. Not brains, or vigor, or a degree of aggressiveness, or anything that might have made us better or worse than our ball-field peers. None of those, but simply a way of looking at the land, and noting where the acorns fell, and which side of a tree the moss grew on, and how the prickly buckeye fruits split open in October, and why the stirred-up leaves and wisp of rabbit fur probably meant there was an owl nearby, dozing on a full stomach. Yet if land sense was truly the thing that set us apart, then how did we come by it in the first place? Had there been mangamoongas in the other boys' hollows, too? It never occurred to me to ask. And now it is too late to ask in any expectation of honest answers.

I do not go to Hinkel's Woods when I return as visitor to Cincinnati, though my brother now lives but a half block away. Hinkel's Woods is gone. All of it. All streets and houses, now. All trimmed and tidy, safe and domestic. All the facts and solutions of the twenty-five-year mortgage rolling down from the hilltop in tiers. I turn the corner near my brother's place and look across the street at the boys who are bound homeward from school. And I wonder if it will make any difference whatsoever to them, or to the world, that the things we saw and felt and knew in that place have been subtracted from it. The land is still there, yet the *whole* is dead.

Before the Echo

✤

PETE DUNNE

When I was young I was a hunter, walking wooded hillsides with confident steps and a gun in my hands. I knew the blur of wings, the rocketing form, and the Great Moment that only hunters know, when all existence draws down to two points and a single line. And the universe holds its breath. And what may be and what will be meet and become one—before the echo returns to its source.

The woods, my woods, lay behind my parents' house, and they were typical of New Jersey woodlots—second-growth tangles wrapped in catbrier, where rabbits made trails in the snow; stands of oak and hickory rich in wild grape and wildly flushing grouse. Some owner's stubbornness defended these acres from development. Some patience beyond the call of parenthood allowed me to wander them at will—with binoculars in spring and summer while lawns went uncut; with a shotgun in autumn and winter while homework went undone.

Through binoculars I learned the skills that would lead me to my craft as a professional birder. I learned the lore of wing bars and tail spots. I studied raptorial specks and conjured names for them. I watched hosts of migrating shorebirds and built identifications for them from scratch. With the shotgun I gained wisdom and understanding and a harvest of memories that have never dimmed.

There was a day, after the echo had passed, that I reached a trembling hand into the leaves and lifted a rabbit still warm as life and knew, and felt, and thought, *I did this.*

There was the drake wood duck, spawned by a misty dawn, that folded its wings at the report of my gun and arrowed into the lake without a ripple or sound. I stripped and swam to retrieve that bird, then carried it home in cradling arms so as not to spoil its feathers. Later, with the bird spread upon my desk—beside the homework that would not get done—I wondered how anything could be so beautiful.

There was the red fox, slung over my shoulder (the way I once saw such a thing depicted in a painting by Winslow Homer), that stopped rush-hour traffic along Old Troy Road and drew the praise and hands of strangers. My clothes were stained to the undergarments with blood by the time I reached home, and once again I stared and wondered at the life, now stilled, that had been absorbed by and become part of mine.

With these tools, binoculars and shotgun, I grew intimate with my woods. I came to know them the way a predator knows its territory, and my confidence grew in measure with my skills. This is what it takes to be an accomplished field birder. This is what it takes to hunt with confidence and clear purpose.

You will think, perhaps, that you see a contradiction here. You will wonder, maybe, how it is that a person can both appreciate wild, living things and kill them, too. I see your dilemma and I've faced this question before—from strangers and friends, in discussions with coworkers and at dinner parties where conversations turn serious and where truth is served. And there is an answer, if you'll have it, albeit an imperfect one.

Think of the natural world as a great play, an incredible drama held on a world stage in which all living things play a part. When I carry binoculars, I stand with the audience, an omniscient observer to all that goes on around me, and I enjoy this very much. But when I carry a gun, I become an actor, *become part of the play itself.* This I relish, too.

As I said, the answer is imperfect. It strikes deep into reason but misses the heart.

There is another answer—one that draws closer to the truth but in doing so becomes enigmatic and inexplicable. I cannot formulate this answer. I can only tell you where you might find it for yourself: it lies between the shot and the echo. It can be heard only by those who stand in the echo's path. This answer, which lasts only as long as the echo, is complete.

I hunted through high school. I hunted through college and into early manhood. I hunted right up to the morning in December when the line of my sight joined the point of my gun to a point that lies behind the foreleg of a deer—the place where its life is housed. I recall how the animal stopped where my will said "Stop." I remember how my finger found the trigger and how the cold touch of it set the world trembling. I remember how the animal stood. How the Great Moment came. How the universe held its breath, waiting—waiting for the sound of an echo that never came; the echo of a shot that was never fired.

Maybe it was the orange survey tape that was blooming throughout my woodlands, usurping my territory, sapping my resolve, forcing me to hunt elsewhere, without standing or confidence. Maybe it was the compounded uncertainties of that age: a president shot in Dallas, his brother who would be president dead in Los Angeles, a nation whose faith was being bled away by a conflict in Asia. Maybe it was the uncertainties of *my* age—that confused period in a person's life when questions are more common than answers and things that were *must* be set aside to make room for things that *might* be.

For whatever reasons, my heart and mind were no longer aligned along the barrel of a gun. My resolve had been breached, and without conviction hunting is a pantomime, a sham. And a person who cannot hunt with conviction should not hunt at all. So I put my gun away and found my place in the audience. I never stopped being a hunter, maybe. But I did stop hunting—until the day, if it ever was to come, that the rightness would return.

For nearly two decades now, my life has been directed toward fostering in others a greater appreciation of the natural world. I have listened to the war of words waged between those who defend hunting and those who decry it. Listened to the arguments mouthed by sportsmen—banal truths about "controlling the herd" and "harvesting the surplus" and "maintaining the balance," as if hunting were some sort of civic-minded cleanup. That's not why they hunt. I know that. Maybe they cannot articulate their reasons and so retreat behind the defensive arguments erected by game-management engineers. Their rhetoric bridges no gaps and does no service to the truth.

I have heard the arguments pushed by the gun lobby, who claim that they represent my interests but whose extremist stand against sensible legislation makes me ashamed to own firearms. I puzzle over the bumper stickers reminding me that guns, guts, and God are an American Trinity; that guns don't kill people (bullets do, right?); and that the owner of the vehicle ahead of me would sooner leave his wife than give up his guns. And I wonder what any of this nonsense has to do with hunting.

Similarly, I have listened to the impassioned accusations of anti-hunters who believe that hunting is synonymous with killing and that anyone who hunts is unfeeling and cruel. These people, at least, are not dishonest. They are sensitive people who feel the pain of others as if it were their own and are moved to stop it. They say what they feel and believe.

No, they aren't dishonest. They are merely wrong—and I have standing to judge. I know, where they could only guess, what hunting is, and I know that hunting is no more killing than the death of Julius Caesar is Shakespeare's play. I know, whereas they can only guess what my feelings are, and I know that I am neither unfeeling nor cruel. If they feel pain, I have felt the death. I have stood in the moment before the echo. They have not.

For twenty years I listened to the arguments. Weighed the words. Felt the conflict both within and without. And during that time I built a life, battled to keep orange flags at bay, schooled the public in the importance of protecting the natural world, and grew, as people do, in confidence and skill.

Then, in the last few years, as my life approaches midspan, a strange thing happened, a thing I did not expect. More and more I found myself paying heed to the choruses of geese on still autumn nights—found myself rising from my chair, edging onto the porch, turning my eyes to the sky and my mind upon memories. If while walking some woodland path I chanced to find a spent shot shell, I would reach into the leaves, cradle the empty casing in my hands, and attempt to reconstruct the drama that unfolded there—try to name the actors that took part in this ancient play. And if, as sometimes happened, a grouse flushed from beside the trail, a secret part of me would measure the distance. Judge the angle. Gauge the speed.

And estimate, based upon reflexes that exist only in memory, what my chances might have been.

I realized one evening, after the bird was gone, after the leaves had settled, after I had stood for what must have been a very long time, that I was waiting for something: a half-forgotten sound, a memory, an echo.

So it came to be, it came to pass, that one day last autumn I picked up my gun and I went hunting—excused myself from the audience and took up, once again, my old part, on a new stage, in a drama I recalled so well. I hunted all day with confidence and when the Great Moment came, discovered that both my heart and my mind were connected as truly as a line drawn between two points. I fired twice.

With what results?

The answer lies between me and the echo.

A Childhood Outdoors

❧

JIMMY CARTER

"Why do you hunt and fish?" I'm often asked.

The easiest answer is: "My father and all my ancestors did it before me. It's been part of my life since childhood, and part of my identity, like being a southerner or a Baptist."

I could add that, during the proper seasons, the urge within me to be in the woods and fields or along a stream is such a strong and pleasant desire that I have no inclination to withstand it. As a child and an adult, I would hunger for a chance to escape for a while from my normal duties, no matter how challenging or enjoyable they were, and to spend a few hours or days in relative solitude away from civilization. Such retreats have always been as much an escape *into* something delightful as *away* from things I wanted to avoid or forget for a while.

This impulse is not the same as laziness or abandonment of responsibilities. All my life, even from the early years, my dreams kept me hard at work: to attend the United States Naval Academy and become a submariner, to be a pioneer officer in the nuclear program, to develop a successful business back in Plains, to advance my political career from state senator to governor, to run for (and win) the presidency, then to build a presidential library and a center within which Rosalynn and I could work productively for the rest of our lives.

And yet, right through those busy years, there has never been any significant amount of time when I have stayed away from the natural areas that mean so much to me. During the most critical moments of my life I have been renewed in spirit by the special feelings that come from the solitude and beauty of the out-of-doors.

❧ .

I spent eleven years in the U.S. Navy, much of the time at sea, and still remember with nostalgia the feeling of liberation when we cleared the last channel buoy and headed for the open water. On long cruises the paperwork and routine family obligations were minimal or nonexistent. In the close confines of any ship, and particularly a submarine, personal privacy is carefully respected by all the members of the crew. Before submarines were equipped with nuclear power and snorkels, they stayed mostly on the surface. Our hours on the bridge, in the conning tower, or in the sonar room allowed each of us to know the ocean and the heavens in a unique way.

As sonar officer, I was expected to be familiar with all the sounds of the depths and could identify shrimp, dolphin and other fishes, and different species of whales as we recorded their chatter and songs on our extremely sensitive listening devices. Primary navigation was by sextant, and we most often had only a few seconds on the bridge or at the periscope to take a quick sight on a star or planet that might peep through an opening in the clouds. Underwater currents, temperature gradients, and the topography of the bottom were other factors crucial to our work—indeed, to our survival. But when our duties were done, there was plenty of time for sleep, reading, or long hours of quiet contemplation. Somehow the complexities of life seemed to sort themselves out, and my own priorities came into better perspective.

❧

Life on land, of course, is different, but not in the way it can affect the spirit. In forests, mountains, swamps, or waterways I also gain a renewal of perspective and a sense of order, truth, patience, beauty, and justice (although nature's is harsh). Even on one-day weekends at home during the frantic 1976 presidential election, my family found time together to hunt arrowheads in remote fields or to fish in our pond for a few hours. I probably know the inside of the Camp

David wooded compound more intimately than most of the permanent caretakers, and the nearby Hunting Creek—just six minutes down the mountain road from the main gate—saw Rosalynn and me regularly. We often landed in the helicopter at Camp David, changed clothes while the White House press corps departed to a nearby Maryland town, and then secretly took off again, to land forty minutes later in a pasture alongside Spruce Creek in Pennsylvania for a couple of days of secluded fly fishing. These jaunts were among our best-kept secrets in Washington.

As a president of the United States who enjoyed fishing, I realized that I was sharing a love of this art with several of my predecessors: George Washington, Chester Arthur, Calvin Coolidge, Herbert Hoover, Dwight Eisenhower, and, most notably, Grover Cleveland. In fact, they and I have fished in some of the same streams.

In the wintertime our family found a similar kind of isolation and pleasure on cross-country skis, exploring the many trails in the state forest areas around Camp David. There were a number of summer camps in the region whose hiking and riding trails were never used during the colder months of the year. They stretched before us, pristine, and our cross-country skis made the first marks on the undisturbed open paths that wound up and down through these mountain areas of northern Maryland. Here we became avid students of the sport, largely self-taught.

In my eagerness I had two serious spills going down hills that were too steep for me, once slashing my face in a dozen places when I dived into a half-inch sheet of surface ice. Only heavy makeup saved me from embarrassment during the following week or two as I went about my presidential duties. Then, about a month before I left office, a submerged boulder caught my right ski. My left collarbone broke cleanly when I fell.

Several years later, when Rosalynn and I took up downhill skiing on the slopes of New Mexico and Colorado, we were careful to get expert instructors to help us master the technique more quickly and reduce the danger of serious accidents. Both kinds of skiing, quite different in character, let us savor a new relationship with nature.

❦

I have never been happier, more exhilarated, at peace, rested, inspired, and aware of the grandeur of the universe and the greatness of

God than when I find myself in a natural setting not much changed from the way He made it. These feelings seem to be independent of the physical beauty of a place, for I have experienced them almost equally within a dense thicket of alders or rhododendron alongside Turniptown Creek in North Georgia and in the high mountains of Alaska or Nepal.

Although actually carrying a gun or rod has become increasingly unnecessary as a motivation for my sojourns into remote places, I still go on hunting and fishing expeditions several times a year. There is special pleasure not only in these moments but also in my thoughts and conversation in the months before and afterward.

To find game and to become a proficient wing shot or to be able to present the proper fly to a rising fish demands the greatest degree of determination, study, planning, and practice; there is always more to discover. In the woods or on a stream, my concentration is so intense that for long periods the rest of the world is almost forgotten. I also immerse myself in books and magazines to acquire an understanding of nature, plants, insects, birds, fishes, and mammals, and the complicated interrelationships among them. I will read almost anything on these subjects, they interest me so much.

But reading is never enough. Books and articles must be supplemented continually by personal experiences, shared when possible with more accomplished friends who are willing to teach what they know—preferably in a kind, not overbearing, manner! When I was a boy, my daddy provided this instruction as though it were his natural and pleasant duty. I would have considered it inappropriate and somewhat disloyal to seek advice or information elsewhere unless Daddy specifically asked someone to take me hunting or approved of my fishing with another adult. However, instruction by others was frequently available to me without my having to ask.

During the summer months I sold boiled peanuts every day in the town of Plains, near our home. When I had served my regular customers and pretty well covered the town, there was often time before returning home to hang around the checkerboards, whittling benches, or barbershop and listen to the never-ending discussions and arguments about farming, weather, philosophy, town gossip, and hunting and fishing. The few acknowledged masters of the woods and fields had solidly established reputations, and everyone was more inclined to listen when they spoke. Those who trained the best bird dogs, observed the niceties of hunting etiquette and still brought home the most quail, were consistently successful in a dove field, caught fish when others couldn't, or were wise in the ways of the fields and swamps were usually treated with respect no matter what their financial or social status. Thinking back on it, I don't remember any really prominent citizens who were in the master class of outdoorsmen. Perhaps the persistent recounting of exploits, for which only a loiterer could spare the time, was also a necessary component in the establishment of a notable reputation. In any case, a great number of leisure hours were a prerequisite for developing the outstanding skills a person could boast about.

And yet, over the years, no one could get away with inflating his accomplishments; there were too many witnesses to the actual performance in this tiny community. For instance, a special string of fish or a trophy bass had to be displayed or weighed in the local grocery store in order for a claim to be believed. Performance on a dove field could be observed by as many as a dozen other hunters in the immediate vicinity. Although it was expected that some ultimate secrets were withheld, the storytelling and debates were entertaining and sometimes helpful. For me they became a kind of classroom. Daddy was usually busy and seldom joined these bull sessions, but later I would ask him to confirm some of the more questionable statements and claims or to assess the veracity of the participants.

As a voracious reader, I searched for adventure books by Zane Grey, Jack London, and others, and liked, too, the flowery writing of John Muir. Thoreau's memoirs were fascinating and sometimes disturbing—he was against honest labor, seemed to have no religion, and favored civil disobedience. Thoreau had lived almost all his days in cities but wrote beautifully about two years spent at Walden Pond. In contrast, my own early years were spent in the country, and I had no knowledge of city life.

I also read a lot of the hunting and fishing magazines but never remember buying one when I was a boy. The Plains drugstore had a good stock, and I was a frequent visitor to the home of the druggist's son, Pete Godwin, where dozens of magazines were always available, stripped of their covers which had been returned for credit. At the end of each month a few of the dated periodicals circulated within a small circle of Pete's friends. Among those we enjoyed were *Field and Stream, Outdoor Life, American Sportsman, Boys' Life,* and many nature articles in the *Saturday Evening Post* and *Collier's.*

I was always eager to test this new information or advice in the woods and streams nearby. When there was no opportunity to hunt, I used my BB gun or .22 rifle to hone my shooting skills. Shotgun shells were too expensive to waste, but a dime would buy a giant cylindrical container with five hundred shots for the air rifle. My friends and I would spend hours throwing up tin cans for one another to shoot at, varying the distance and direction to simulate as best we could the explosive rise of quail or the swift passing flight of doves. An open bucket in the yard was an excellent target for bait casting. I would vary the distance and my arm delivery to correspond with the circumstances we would face in the creeks and ponds.

❦

I learned these skills as a boy, but there is no age limit to the enjoyment of outdoor excursions. Some of my most memorable moments have been spent teaching my own children and grandchildren how to catch their first fish at the age of three or four. On the other hand, among my cherished fishing and hunting companions is D. W. Brooks, who as an octogenarian still demonstrates his personal superiority in inducing wary fish to take a well-placed fly or in successfully following up a beautiful bird-dog point.

The joy of fishing was well described more than three hundred years ago by Izaak Walton, when he referred to angling as "that pleasant labour which you enjoy, when you purpose to give rest to your mind, and divest yourself of your more serious business, and (which is often) dedicate a day or two to this recreation."

As for the lives of those who are not fishermen, this best known of all piscators deplores their lot:

> Men that are taken to be grave, because nature hath made them of a sour complexion; money-getting men, men that spend all their time, first in getting, and next in anxious care to keep it; men that are condemned to be rich, and then always busy or discontented; for these poor rich men, we Anglers pity them perfectly, and stand in no need to borrow their thought to think ourselves happy. No, no, sir, we enjoy a contentedness above the reach of such dispositions.

Such "contentedness" can be attained in the company of others or alone; I am thankful that it is not necessary to choose between those states. There are times during the fall and winter hunting months when my only desired companions are my two bird dogs. Fly fishing in a small mountain creek requires solitude; Rosalynn may be upstream or down, in a separate pool, often out of sight. But there are other times. Sitting in a small bateau in our own farm pond, choosing for our supper the mature bluegills and bass we've caught and returning the others to grow some more, give us long and precious hours of uninterrupted conversation about all kinds of things, an opportunity quite rare in the lives of many married couples. Usually, on hunting trips or when fishing from a boat on large streams or lakes, I am with family and friends, and it is good to share with them the frustrations and successes, the hardships and delights, the plans and memories. Outdoor people constitute a close fraternity, often international in its membership. Like music and art, love of nature is a common language that can transcend political or social boundaries.

✼

What about the taking of life? Every hunter and fisherman, I am sure, sometimes has twinges of uneasiness when a beautiful and swift quail or waterfowl is brought down, or when a valiant trout finally is brought to the net. Those of us who habitually release trout know that on occasion even a barbless hook will kill. For people who might find these feelings overwhelming, my advice would be: "Don't hunt or fish." Indeed, if someone has a moral or ethical objection to taking an animal's life for human use, it is logical that he or she be a dedicated vegetarian and not require others, perhaps in a fish market or slaughterhouse, to end lives for their benefit; many make that decision.

Although these sentiments are admirable, I have never suffered from such compunctions, except on one or two occasions during my younger childhood days. I was brought up in an agricultural society, where chickens, hogs, sheep, goats, and cattle were raised for food. There was no real distinction in my mind between those animals and the quail, doves, ducks, squirrels, and rabbits that also arrived on our table after a successful hunt. Nevertheless, there were limits on hunting activities, observed and imposed by my father.

Even before I had my first gun, Daddy made me a flip. With rubber bands, cut from an old inner tube, connecting a leather pouch to the two prongs of a forked stick, I could propel small projectiles with considerable velocity. I practiced regularly, shooting small pebbles and chinaberries at various targets, including birds, with no effect except that a few of the green glass telephone-pole insulators around our house were shattered. One day, while my mother and father visited on the front porch with a friend, I aimed at a robin sitting on a fence that surrounded the yard. The chance shot killed the bird, and I approached the adults with the dead robin in my hands and tears running down my cheeks.

After a few awkward moments, Daddy didn't help by saying, "We shouldn't ever kill anything that we don't need for food."

Mama partially salvaged my feelings by adding, "We'll cook the bird for your supper tonight."

When I grew older, it would have been considered effeminate, or even depraved, to discuss such feelings with my friends. As an adult, however, I became aware of debates on the subject. I'll always remember how surprised most hunters were at the storm of protest that arose early in 1972 when a photograph was published of a smiling Senator Ed Muskie in hunting clothes, holding a gun in one hand and a dead Canada goose in the other. He was bombarded with criticisms and threats; the photo may have contributed to his defeat during the subsequent presidential primary season.

On my first Christmas home as president, I went quail hunting on our farm with one of my sons. That night our family enjoyed a nice quail supper, a fact that the ever-present White House reporters included in their routine news articles. The following Sunday morning as we approached the entrance to the First Baptist Church in Washington, I was amazed to find the sidewalk populated with demonstrators protesting my murderous habit.

In the church, I answered some questions about it from my Sunday School students by referring them to biblical references about God's sending manna and quail to the people of Israel, who killed and ate them. Even more pertinent was the intriguing account in the twenty-first chapter of the Gospel according to John, when our resurrected Lord advised his disciples on how and where to catch fish, cooked some on a charcoal fire and ate with them, and presumably joined in counting their catch: 153 large ones.

I have been made to feel more at peace about my hunting and fishing because of my strict observance of conservation measures, including the deliberate protection of overly depleted game and the initiation and support of programs to increase the population of species that seem scarce. It was because my father liked to hunt that he was an active worker in the Chattahoochee Valley Wildlife Conservation program, directing my work as a child in this effort. We planted feed patches, controlled burning, and attempted to improve habitat in our woods and along fencerows and terraces. I also know that many of my fellow hunters and fishers, in personal practice and through formal organizations, are the very people most dedicated to these same worthy goals; they are the prime founders and supporters of Ducks Unlimited, Trout Unlimited, and similar institutions whose purpose is to protect habitat and increase the population of their quarry. Working with professional game and fish specialists and donating substantial time, influence, and funds, they have been quite successful. For instance, when I was young we seldom saw a white-tailed deer in Georgia, but now there are more of these animals there than at any time in history; wild turkeys, too, are making a remarkable comeback.

It is the strict circumscription of hunting and fishing—those unwritten rules of ethics, etiquette, and propriety—that define the challenge. Therefore, the game sought must be abundant enough that your gun and rod do not deplete or permanently reduce a desirable population of the species. At the same time, there should be a relative scarcity or elusiveness of the game or fish, and not too much disadvantage for the prey in that particular habitat, so that both skill and good fortune will be necessary in achieving your goal. Our home is in an area well populated by deer, turkey, quail, doves, ducks, fish, and other animals of many kinds, but I have often spent many hours without any success whatever, either because I did not encounter any game or because bad luck or my lack of skill led to failure. These experiences, still enjoyable despite the results, only enhance the pleasure of my times of success.

Success, when it comes, must be difficult and uncertain. The effortless taking of game is not hunting—it is slaughter. My only experience in hunting the rail, or marsh hen, happened to be at the time of a maximum spring tide near one of Georgia's coastal islands. Much of the marsh grass was covered with water, and the birds had little cover. I soon reached the legal limit without missing a shot and still remember the facile experience with distaste. I've never wanted to shoot another rail.

On the other hand, I have hunted and fished with neophytes who shot fifty embarrassing times without touching a feather or who cast a fly thousands of times without much likelihood of a strike, while others around them were repeatedly demonstrating their prowess. And yet the newcomers were undeterred, eager for some private advice and another chance. I finally took my first Atlantic salmon after three and a half days of steady and fruitless casting; that year I was one of the few successful East Coast salmon fishermen. Curt Gowdy, my fishing partner, and I timed the number of our casts in a ten-minute period and then estimated that I had caught that fish after presenting a fly more than eleven thousand times, mostly while balanced perilously on large slick boulders in a rushing torrent or shivering in a boat during extended cold and steady rains. In all that time, I don't remember a dull or unenjoyable moment!

Even in the best of times there is an element of difficulty, doubt, discomfort, disappointment, and even danger involved in such pursuits, and often great distances must be covered during very early hours, even in the dark of night. It is almost inherent in the seeking of wild things in their native habitat that you must forgo many of the comfortable trappings of civilization. Although sporting goods stores offer adequate supplies to substitute for many of the normal conveniences, there is a limit to what you can tote, and living without some of the manufactured luxuries is a necessary part of being absorbed within a woodland or wilderness.

Even ancient records show that there has almost always been a scarcity of available game near centers of human habitation, and that for many centuries hunting and fishing were considered the unique privileges of the rich and powerful. The historic accounts of national revolutions, as well as the delightful tales of Robin Hood and his merry men in Olde England, indicate that these special rights were both jealously guarded by a few and deeply resented by common people who were deprived of both food and pleasure. I have been fortunate all my life to live in a community where working people have had almost unlimited access to game and fish, and later to have the means to travel when my interest was aroused by distant places.

Not that you must hunt or fish in order to enjoy unknown regions and new adventures. During the time I was governor, Rosalynn and I lived fairly close to the North Georgia mountain streams. It was not long before some of our younger friends asked us to join them in canoe trips through the whitewater areas. We started off on the Chattahoochee River above Atlanta, just to get acquainted with the paddle and learn how to handle moderate turbulence. Then we graduated to the much more challenging Chattooga, a truly wild river on which the movie *Deliverance* was being filmed—a story by James Dickey about the devastating encounter of four Atlanta businessmen with terrible rapids and some grotesque mountain hoodlums.

As we proceeded down the river, the rapids became increasingly challenging. Soon we were taking the more difficult "section two" and "section three" rapids in open two-person canoes. One day my partner and I successfully traversed what is known as Bull Sluice, a double five-foot waterfall where the canoe descends almost vertically at times. This unprecedented achievement was written up in a nationwide magazine for canoeists. Eventually Rosalynn and I even tackled the lower "section four" in a small rubber raft. We made it, but I was covered with bruises and had trouble walking for several days afterwards!

Then we graduated to kayaks, spending several evenings in an Atlanta university swimming pool learning how to roll all the way over and continue on without "bailing out." Unsurprisingly, this proved much more difficult in a moving stream with a shallow and rocky bottom, but we persisted and greatly enjoyed this new sport and an opportunity to see parts of our state that would otherwise have been inaccessible.

❦

My recently gained knowledge and pleasure are never at the expense of my earlier memories or habits. I've hunted mallards in the rice fields and pin oak of Arkansas and fished for steelhead in the Queen Charlotte Islands, for Atlantic salmon on the Matapédia River in Quebec, for giant rainbow trout in Alaska and New Zealand, and for bonefish and marlin in the Caribbean, but I still find the same excitement ten minutes from my home in Plains, perhaps with renewed pleasure and a deeper gratitude.

Now, as my bird dog strikes the scent of a covey on the edge of a deep gully in Webster County, I remember my father taking me there as a little boy, and my own son Chip bringing down his first quail on the same spot. With the rise of a largemouth bass or the slow but steady disappearance of my cork on a bream bed below the Pond House in May, I can almost hear my mother's voice at the other end of the boat as she chortled over catching the most and biggest fish in spite of my best efforts. In my early life she would say, "You always pull too soon, Jimmy, when you get behind." Later: "You may be president, but you still haven't learned how to catch fish." Some of the memories are painful because my parents and other dear companions are no longer with me, but they're still especially vivid and will always be precious.

Although we hope to be active for many years, Rosalynn and I are already making careful plans to enjoy the final years of our lives. One of our most important priorities is the opportunity to spend more and more time in interesting and beautiful places—places that are quiet, simple, secluded, and relatively undisturbed.

We won't have to go far to observe the beauties of nature. In our own yard we see gray and flying squirrels, rabbits, chipmunks, opossums, raccoons, quail and many other birds, snakes and other reptiles. Deer frequently graze within fifty yards of our front door, and without going farther we regularly harvest wild plums, peaches, mulberries, black and white muscadines, cherries, blackberries, persimmons, and mayhaws.

Wherever life takes us, there are always moments of wonder. I remember going to the roof of the White House to watch the thrilling flight of Canada geese overhead, their weird calls barely penetrating the night sounds of Washington, and their breasts illuminated by ghostly reflection of the city lights. A few years earlier, we and our children had lain on our backs on the governor's mansion lawn in Atlanta to watch millions of monarch butterflies on their southward journey to distant Mexico.

When I look at how fragile and lovely the natural world is, I can understand the feeling of Henry David Thoreau: "The earth was the most glorious instrument, and I was audience to its strains." In the late twentieth century, his conviction that "in the wilderness is the salvation of mankind" is more true than ever.

The Call of the Climb

❧

RUTH RUDNER

My father shot a black bear in the Adirondacks before I was born. I grew up with it, its face as familiar to me as any in my family. For years I crawled around the house on hands and knees with the bearskin over me, believing I had become the bear. I've never known whether I was playing or participating in some private ritual of spirit. But the bear has never left me.

By the time I was born, my father hunted only pheasant. When he and the dog took off for the golden autumn fields I could so easily imagine, I longed to be included, to tramp about the fields with him as we did in other seasons, to engage day-long in the crispness of the air, to wade the high, shimmering grasses, to watch the dog work the fields as perfectly as my father always described the point, the flush, my father taking aim, the shot, the dog retrieving in her gentle mouth that beautiful bird of autumn. It seemed so holy an offering on our dinner table, each pheasant we ate, a celebration of the life of wildness, of our connection to it through my father, the hunter.

Mankind began as hunters. Making up in tools and technique what we had already lost in our descent from wildness, we assumed our rightful place in the scheme of things, one link in the chain of nature. If, for us, the price of civilization has always been the loss of instincts that make us kin to all that is wild (the more improved our

47

tools, the farther we come from kinship), the instinct toward kinship remains.

The hunter, entering the environment of the hunted, seeks this relation. To enter that world where the wild is at home, and where success—however one measures it—depends on the hunter's ability to be at home as well, is to claim our birthright to wildness. Hunter and hunted are partners, the presence of each honing the instincts and senses of the other. The hunter possesses the skills to chase; the hunted the skills to evade. Each provides the other with an energy carefully balanced. Life, through death, provides life. The predator is integral to the prey.

"There is hardly a class or phylum in which groups of hunting animals do not appear," writes José Ortega y Gasset in *Meditations on Hunting*. "The cat hunts rats. The lion hunts antelope. The sphex and other wasps hunt caterpillars and grubs. The shark hunts smaller fish. The bird of prey hunts rabbits and doves. . . ."

For many people, hunting plays an important part in providing a family's food. Subsistence hunting is real, although there are critics, especially in urban areas, who cannot comprehend this. "Supermarkets are full of meat," they say. "Why kill an innocent animal?"

But do they also ask what the ease of buying food has done to our awe of the animals that feed us? How awed is anyone by a cow? How many people, for that matter, cutting into a piece of cow, remember its life or have much interest in ingesting its spirit? How many ask its forgiveness? (Yet the cow is dead and we may as well eat it. Eating it does it more honor than allowing it to rot, whether we ask its forgiveness or not.)

The hunter who kills the meat he or she means to eat at least allows the animal its natural place in the life chain, allows it not to have been raised for the slaughterhouse where the animal, smelling and hearing death, waits in terror. The hunter, allowing the animal to die in its own world, as it has lived, confronts his or her own responsibility for the animal's death. It is a death with honor and with love, for there is no true hunter who does not love the animal. (I am, throughout, not talking about that person who calls himself a hunter, then goes out to prove his manhood in a world he neither cares about nor understands. "He" is deliberate. Most women who hunt—and their numbers are steadily increasing—hunt with reverence.) I have been told by a number of hunters of the intense self-doubt and questioning that sometimes happens before letting go an arrow or bullet. Sometimes the hunter does not shoot. Sometimes he does not ever shoot again.

❦

My father never took me hunting. He took my brother and, before I was born, my mother, and he took me hiking from the time I could walk. But he did not teach me that thing I longed to know, to seek out the animal in the animal's world, to seek it on nature's terms, to be in responsibility for its death, responsible for my own life. By taking food in the full awareness of what it is you take, you participate in some ultimate spirit of the earth. I think my father did not mean to deny me access to that spirit, but to allow me my own route to it. He knew how hard it would be for me to kill an animal. Much later, when it was time for me to leave home, he said to me, "You must find your own way now."

I found my way in mountains. I think what I—and most climbers and mountaineers—find in mountains is what my father found in hunting. The ultimate quest for hunter and climber is the same. Hunter and climber both enter an intimacy with the earth at the cost of often enormous physical and mental effort. It is an intimacy that challenges, demands, exhausts; that leads you on when you can go no farther; that presents a triumph as immense as it is private.

In a climb, all your faculties—eyes, mind, body, your will, and your soul—come into play. You examine the mountain from a distance, on the approach, and again and again as you climb. Your muscles push you, pull you upward. Your chest expands with air, with the necessity of breathing, and your breathing sets a rhythm for the climb. Your feet feel every nuance of earth, the soft places, the pebbles, the rocks, the tiniest of ledges, the slippery twig that rolls beneath your boot, the cushioning of pine needles, the tiny descents where a creek babbles across your route, the centuries of boulders on boulders that teeter and shift as you present your weight to them. Every part of you is poised for the next move and the next. Your hands feel the mountain as your feet do, the rock cold where it lies in shadow, warm in the sun, jagged rock, smooth rock, the little niches for your hands or fingers that make the next move possible. Your eyes search the places for your hands and feet. Your body, or your will, moves them. You smell and feel and breathe the mountain.

There is nothing on earth that is not you and the mountain. Completely focused, you are aware of everything.

"The hunter knows that he does not know what is going to happen," Ortega y Gasset writes. "Thus he needs to prepare an attention of a different and superior style—an attention which does not consist in riveting itself on the presumed but consists precisely in not presuming anything and in avoiding inattentiveness. It is a 'universal' attention, which does not inscribe itself on any point and tries to be on all points. . . . The hunter is the alert man . . . life as complete alertness—is the attitude in which the animal exists in the jungle. Because of it he lives from within his environment."

❧

On the mountain the sun shifts. The shadows slant longer across the face. A stone falls, arcing out, away from the mountain, to land on eons of fallen stones below. It is so easy to let go, to fall. A sound of water issues without stop into your thirst. A tiny flower grows in a crevice just above your foot. The rock eases into dirt. A tuft of goat hair clings to a scraggly twig. A cloud hovers over the sun, then passes by. You reach the top. The mountain holds you. You have come to that place where you were going.

The hunt is the same whether the goal is the top of the mountain, the honorable kill, a philosophical problem, or the quest for peace. One must enter absolutely into the process to be capable of enduring to the end. To engage in the presence of the earth, of nature; to seek what is never easy; to fail as well as to succeed; to grow weary and ragged in the search and yet to persevere because the mountain does, indeed, have a summit, the war an end; to enter a depth and a distance that go so far beyond the ordinary routines of a day, or a life, that they bring you to the beginning, is to hunt.

❧

I no longer have the bearskin. No one in my family knows what happened to it. It just disappeared somewhere in the many moves we all made. But in my soul I know the spirit of the bear has not gone from me. It is renewed with every moment I spend in wild country, every moment I spend finding my own way. The black bear my father shot was never a trophy. It was the beginning of my life.

Deerskin

✣

Terry Tempest Williams

I remember, as a small girl, waking up one morning to the wild enthusiasm of my father and brothers. They were outside my bedroom window, and I could vaguely hear them talking about some sort of tracks they had found. Their voices conveyed a sense of awe as well as excitement. Not wanting to miss anything, I ran out to see.

The front door had been left open, and through it I could see all four of them crouching in the snow.

"Deer tracks . . ." my father said, touching them gently.

"Deer tracks," I said. "So?"

"Deer tracks," my brother restated emphatically.

"Deer tracks," I said again under my breath. No, something was missing when I said it. Feeling out of place and out of touch, I went back inside and shut the door. Through the glass I watched the passion that flowed between my father and brothers as they spoke of deer. Their words went beyond the occasion.

Many years have passed since that morning, but I often reflect on the relationship my brothers and father share with deer. Looking back and looking forward into the Navajo Way, I have come to realize the power of oral traditions, of stories, even in our own culture, and how they color our perceptions of the world around us.

Nowhere is this relationship of earth and story more poignant than in the Navajo perception of living things, *nanise*. The Dine have been told in their origin histories that they will receive knowledge from the Holy People, from plants and animals. As with other Indian peoples, the Navajo do not "rank-order" animals. Barry Lopez writes:

> Each creature, from deer mouse to meadowlark, is respected for the qualities it best seems to epitomize; when those particular qualities are desired by someone, then that animal is approached as one who knows much about the subject.

And elsewhere:

> In the native view, each creature carried information about the order of the universe—both at a practical level (ravens might reveal the presence of caribou to hunters), and at the level of augury. Moreover, each creature had its own special kind of power, and a person who wished knowledge in those areas—of patience, of endurance, of humor—would be attentive to those animals who possessed these skills.

Gregory Bateson points out in *Mind and Nature* that "the very word, 'animal,' means endowed with mind and spirit."

This idea of animal mentors is illustrated in the Navajo Deerhunting Way. The Deerhunting Way is a blessing rite, a formula for corresponding with deer in the appropriate manner. Traditionally, hunters would participate in this ritual as a means to a successful hunt and their own personal safety.

Claus Chee Sonny, a Navajo medicine man who lives in the Tunitcha Mountains near the Arizona–New Mexico border, tells the following story, which is part of the Deerhunting Way. He learned the Deerhunting Way from his father, who had obtained it from his father—Claus Chee's grandfather—and the many teachers who preceded him. The First People who taught the Deerhunting Way were the Deer Gods themselves. The Deer supplied the first divine hunters with the knowledge that was necessary to hunt them. And so the story begins:

> There was a hunter who waited in ambush. Wind had told him, "This is where tracks are. The deer will come marching through in single

file." The hunter had four arrows: one was made from sheet lightning, one of zigzag lightning, one of sunlight roots, and one of rainbow.

Then the first deer, a large buck with many antlers, came. The hunter got ready to shoot the buck. His arrow was already in place. But just as he was ready to shoot, the deer transformed himself into a mountain mahogany bush, *tse esdaazii*. After a while, a mature man stood up from behind the bush. He stood up and said, "Do not shoot! We are your neighbors. These are the things that will be in the future when human beings will have come into existence. This is the way you will eat us." And he told the hunter how to kill and eat the deer. So the hunter let the mature Deerman go for the price of his information. And the Deerman left.

Then the large doe, a shy doe, appeared behind the one who had left. The hunter was ready again to shoot the doe in the heart. But the doe turned into a cliff rose bush, *aweets'aal*. A while later a young woman stood up from behind the bush. The woman said, "Do not shoot! We are your neighbors. In the future, when man has been created, men will live because of us. Men will use us to live on." So then, for the price of her information, the hunter let the Doewoman go. And she left.

Then a young buck, a two-pointer, came along. And the hunter got ready to shoot. But the deer transformed himself into a dead tree, *tsin bisga*. After a while, a young man stood up from behind the dead tree and said, "In the future, after man has been created, if you talk about us in the wrong way we will cause trouble for you when you urinate, and we will trouble your eyes. We will also trouble your ears if we do not approve of what you say about us." And at the price of his information, the hunter let the young Deerman go.

Then the little fawn appeared. The hunter was ready to shoot the fawn, but she turned into a lichen-spotted rock, *tse dlaad*. After a while, a young girl stood up from the rock and spoke: "In the future all this will happen if we approve, and whatever we shall disapprove shall all be up to me. I am in charge of all the other Deer People. If you talk badly about us, and if we disapprove of what you say, I am the one who will respond with killing you. I will kill you with what I am. If you hear the cry of my voice, you will know that trouble is in store for you. If you do not make use of us properly, even in times when we are numerous, you will not see us anymore. We are the four deer who have transformed themselves into different kinds of things.

Into these four kinds of things can we transform ourselves. Moreover, we can assume the form of all the different kinds of plants. Then when you look, you will not see us. In the future, only those of whom we approve shall eat the mighty deer. If, when you hunt, you come across four deer, you will not kill all of them. You may kill three and leave one. But if you kill all of us, it is not good.

"These are the things which will bring you happiness. When you kill a deer, you will lay him with the head toward your house. You will cover the earth with plants or with branches of trees lengthwise, with the growing tips of the plants pointing the direction of the deer's head, toward your house. So it shall be made into a thick padding, and the deer shall be laid on that. Then you will take us home to your house and eat of us. You will place our bones under any of the things whose form we can assume—mountain mahogany, cliff rose, dead tree, lichen-spotted rock, spruce, pine, or under any of the other good plants. At these places you may put our bones. You will sprinkle the place with yellow pollen. Once. Twice. Then you lay the bones. And then you sprinkle yellow pollen on top of the bones. This is for the protection of the game animals. In this manner they will live on; their bones can live again and live a lasting life."

This is what the little fawn told the hunter. "You will be able to use the entire body of the deer, even the skin. And we belong to Talking-god. We belong to Black-god. We are in his hands. And he is able to make us deaf and blind. Those among you, of whom he approves, are the good people. They will hunt with success and will be able to kill us. According to his own decisions he will surrender us to the people. The Black-god is Crow. But when you hunt you do not refer to him as Crow but as Black-god."

Then, referring to what the fawn had said, the other three deer said, "This is what will be. And this is what will be. And this is how it is."

So these are the four who gave information: the large buck, the doe, the two-pointer, and the fawn. Man was created later. All these events happened among the Gods, prior to the creation of man. All animals were like human beings then; they were able to speak. Thus, this story was not made up by old Navajo men. These events were brought about by Black-god. Then, after having obtained all this information, the hunter let the four deer go.

As final hunting instructions, Claus Chee Sonny shares the Deer People's knowledge:

> You will not throw the bones away just anywhere. Everything of which we are made, such as our skin, meat, bones, is to be used. . . . Anything that we hold onto, such as the earth from the four sacred mountains, the rainbow, the jewels, the corn, all the plants we eat, will be in us. Our bodies contain all these. And because of this we are very useful. . . . Needles can be made from the bones of the front and hind legs. This is what we use to stitch buckskin together. . . . A deer not killed by a weapon shall be used in the sacred ceremonies. All the meat is very useful. You can put deer meat as medicine on sheep, on horses, and on other domestic animals. All livestock lives because of deer.
>
> The usefulness of the deer is the foundation which has been laid. It serves as an example for other things. This is what is meant when we say that the deer are first in all things.

Through the Deerhunting Way one can see many connections, many circles. It becomes a model for ecological thought expressed through mythological language. The cyclic nature of the four deer's advice to the hunter is, in fact, good ecological sense. Out of the earth spring forth plants on which the animals feed. The animal, in time, surrenders its life so that another may live, and as its body parts are returned to earth, new life will emerge and be strengthened once again. Do not be greedy. Do not be wasteful. Remember gratitude and humility for all forms of life. Because they are here, we are here. They are the posterity of Earth.

It is this kind of oral tradition that gives the Navajo a balanced structure to live in. It provides continuity between the past and the future. They know how to behave. Stories channel energy into a form that can heal as well as instruct. This kind of cosmology enables a person to do what is appropriate and respect the rights of others. N. Scott Momaday tells the following story:

> There was a man living in a remote place on the Navajo reservation who had lost his job and was having a difficult time making ends meet. He had a wife and several children. As a matter of fact, his wife was expecting another child. One day a friend came to visit him and

perceived that his situation was bad. The friend said to him, "Look, I see you are in tight straits. I see you have many mouths to feed, and that you have no wood and that there is very little food in your larder. But one thing puzzles me. I know you are a hunter, and I know, too, there are deer in the mountains very close at hand. Tell me, why don't you kill a deer so that you and your family might have fresh meat to eat?" And after a time the man replied, "No, it is inappropriate that I should take life just now when I am expecting the gift of life."

True freedom is having *no* choice. In this case, the man knew exactly what he had to do with respect to the land. Behavior became gesture. "It isn't a matter of intellection. It is respect for the understanding of one's heritage. It is a kind of racial memory, and it has its origin beyond any sort of historical experience. It reaches back to the dawn of time."

My thoughts return to that winter morning—to the deer tracks—and then to a crisp day in October when finally, at the age of sixteen, my father invited me to go deer hunting with him in the Dolores Triangle of Colorado. We participated in the rituals associated with the season, clothing ourselves in yellow sweatshirts, fluorescent orange vests, and red caps. We polished our boots with mink oil and rubbed Cutter's insect repellent all over our bodies, so as not to be bothered by remaining insects. We rose before the sun, and stalked west ridges to catch the last of day's light. Finally, around the campfire, I listened to the stories my father told until the stars had changed positions many times.

It was only then that I realized a small fraction of what my father knew, of what my brothers knew about deer. My brothers had been nurtured on such tales, and for the first time I saw the context they had been told in. My education was limited because I had missed years, layers, of stories.

> *Walk lightly, walk slowly,*
> *look straight ahead*
> *with the corners of your eyes open.*
> *Stay alert, be swift.*
> *Hunt wisely*
> *in the manner of deer.*

I walked with reverence behind my father, trying to see what he saw. All at once he stopped, put his index finger to his mouth, and motioned me to come ahead. Kneeling down among the scrub oak, he carefully brushed aside some fallen leaves. "Deer tracks," he said.

"Deer tracks," I whispered.

Venison Sandwiches

❦

CRAIG MEDRED

The venison sandwiches Katie takes to school for lunch most days are viewed with suspicion by her friends. None of them want to try this foreign food.

Katie offered this revelation one night on the long drive home to the Hillside from Northstar Elementary School. She was confused by the behavior of her kindergarten peers. "They all say it's yuck," she said. "I told them it's good. They said, 'We don't like bear meat.' I told them it wasn't bear meat. They say, 'We've had it before. It's disgusting.' They're telling me lies. They don't like anything."

But their attitudes had a predictable influence.

"Can I have a peanut-butter sandwich tomorrow?" Katie asked.

Given the circumstances, the question came as little surprise, though Katie loves venison. Next to the McDonald's Happy Meal—the opium of the preadolescent—venison and Dall sheep are her favorite foods. Nobody ever told her these are health foods: high in protein, low in fat, and free of chemicals. All she knows is that these are things she has grown up eating.

It was the same for me. Venison, walleye, northern pike, grouse, pheasant, rabbit, squirrel, and duck stretched a tight budget for a family in a Minnesota poverty county. Some people think of these foods as exotic. They were far from that in our household. Wild game or fish were staples. We were hunters and fishers all, living off the land in large part or small, dependent on luck, laws, and need. It prepared me well for my flight from civilization to Alaska in the summer of 1973.

The first year here, home was a sleeping bag and meals consisted mainly of snowshoe hares, grayling, potatoes, and macaroni and cheese—separate or in various combinations.

Not all that much has changed over time. The years have taken me from the Alaska interior to southeast to south-central. I have gone through one wife and one life and begun again with a new family. But I have clung to the vestiges of older days. A fair amount of time is still spent in a sleeping bag, and all of the meat in our house—save for the bacon on the duck breasts—comes from the wild. It is collected in a deeply spiritual and personal communion with the land.

There are no easy kills. That idea itself is abhorrent. My father taught me that when a man engages in the natural struggle of predator and prey, he owes nature a special respect. No three-wheelers. No snow machines. No riding around in riverboats waiting for foolish moose to wander out onto riverbanks. No snagging or clubbing salmon in streams. No spring shooting of ducks on their nests or fall airboat chases to gun the birds down on the water.

These common methods of Alaska killing are a violation of the soul of the hunt. The venison, moose, caribou, sheep, duck, ptarmigan, salmon, grouse, or halibut that grace the table deserve to be paid for with sweat and cunning. The challenge, after all, is the cultural and spiritual significance of hunting and fishing. It is something difficult to explain to people.

Fewer and fewer are those who can identify. Greater and greater are the well-meaning but ignorant who debase what I do as unnecessary, who criticize my personal, spiritual activities as mere "sport." What part of *their* heritage, I wonder, should I demand they do without? What important aspects of their lives can I insist are unnecessary?

It is tough to avoid bitterness here, I admit, just as it is easy to recognize noble intentions. There are people in this state—thoughtful, intelligent, good people—who think the lives of animals are as important as those of people, and there are others who believe the best way to maintain the cultural ties of hunters and fishermen to the land is to limit the activities of hunting and fishing to a select few. They would give priority to rural residents and gamble that by further weakening a cultural fabric shared by all people who hunt and fish we can somehow save the hunting and fishing culture. I wonder about this all the time these days.

✻

Katie was sent to a school in the center of this city in part because of its cultural diversity. Robbie and I wanted our daughter immersed in the great American melting pot of ethnicity.

Now I worry that we have done nothing but expose her to the pressures of the great, urban homogeneity that crosses all class and ethnic lines in America. Few are the people familiar with the age-old bonds to the land. So many are those who see nature through the mind-numbing fog of a picture tube. Nature is to them a game show. It has no reality. It is something that exists in the fantasy of television. There is no blood and gore and life and death to it. Television sterilized the savagery of nature, and the logical reaction of people exposed to this subtle propaganda is a growing desire to sterilize— neuter might be an even better word—the pagan hunters and fishermen.

Which leaves me with one haunting question: Are we going to save the last vestiges of the old ways by limiting the number of people allowed contact with them?

Lord knows, I have enough trouble trying to explain to one six-year-old kid that it is OK to respect, worship, and partake of the land.

Climbing the Mountains After Deer

John A. Murray

The Perse owt of Northamberlande,
And a vowe to God mayde he,
That he wolde hunte inthe mountayns
Off Chyviat within dyaes thre,
In the mauger of doughte Dogles,
And all that ever with him be.

—Chevy Chase

It always came on a clear night in August when the stars were thick and the ranch windows were dark. The first to know about it were the hounds, sleeping outside the bunkhouse. You heard them pacing on the porch and whining and when you let them in it was like cracking the door on a meat freezer. The previous day it had been eighty degrees. Now the air was straight from Canada. An hour later, walking the footpath to the corral, you saw how the frost had painted the green summer woods with a cold white brush and how the water was frozen near the head gates by the fields. In the tack shed the saddles were stiff, and you had to warm the bit before putting the bridle on your horse. A week or so later a steady north wind arrived, and the bilberry patches on the high tundra turned a warm salmon red and there were soon bright streaks of yellow in the depressions where the alpine willows grew. One day there was a light dusting of snow that

brought out the sharpness and texture of the peaks and not long after that there was a heavy snow that closed all the gunsight passes to
the eternally young hikers of the Colorado Mountain Club.

Now it was October and the ducks and geese had passed through,
and the bull elk had no more bugle left in them, and the last of the
summer tourists had departed with the same storm that scattered the
quaker leaves. Somewhere another college football season was un-
derway, and downhill skis were being conditioned. For a time, the
mountains were empty. Opening day for deer season always fell on a
Saturday morning and down lower the hunters crowded the cattle
country, favoring the gentle ridges and ravines where unpaid-for
trucks could be safely driven. That was fine with us. We knew where
we wanted to be.

Into the back range, on trails too steep and narrow for steel-shod
hooves, we hiked, our backs bent under aluminum frame packs
crammed with baked beans and pots and pans and tents and sleeping
bags and everything else we needed to live for a week. We carried
bolt-action rifles, and hunted where the air was so cold and thin it
seemed we would soon be seeing caribou. We camped just below
timberline and hunted the cirques where the biggest bucks held fast.
These were smart old animals waiting for the drifts of November before moving down and they often outwitted us, and we always enjoyed testing our skills against theirs, especially later when we
evened the odds with archery. The places we hunted are secret,
known only to us and the deer. It would be heresy to share them
with anyone. They are still there as I write this, in places so remote
most would shake their heads, and in not too many years I will hike
up there on bad knees and show them to my son. Those places—
wild, beautiful, full of memories—are the greatest gift I could give
him.

How I came into this thing called deer hunting is an interesting
story, because I was not born into it. My family was from the city
and one full generation away from the land, my grandfather having
left the rural Ohio life after the 1937 flood. The only rifle my father
ever carried was as a paratrooper during World War II. He could not
teach me about hunting deer, and so I had to teach myself.

My first deer hunt occurred while Nixon was still president. I
hunted the Continental Divide west of Denver because it was close
to our new home. I was eighteen and my father loaned me the car

Friday afternoon on the condition that I return it unscratched Sunday evening. That gave me two days. I took my fifteen-year-old brother, and we packed in several miles Friday evening and set up a quiet camp near a grass park. Neither of us had ever hunted before, and our chances were statistically not good but we were cheerful in the way that natural-born optimists always are. Opening morning came and went without incident, and we slept most of the afternoon in pools of sunlight among the pines. It was very peaceful there, listening to the wind in the short-needled boughs and the idle chatter of the pine squirrels and the waterfalls making Debussey melodies in a little stream nearby. Just before last light a pair of deer, one a spike and the other a forkhorn, stepped from the timber two hundred yards away and, laying very still on the soft pine needles, I carefully aimed and put a bullet into the spike. With that the light went from the sky and it was suddenly so dark and the meadow so overgrown that we couldn't find the deer. Just when we were in despair at possibly losing the meat, nature intervened on our behalf. A full moon, the hunter's moon of October, rose over the massive crags of the Continental Divide and the light of the moon showed us where the deer lay.

When I reached him he lay relaxed on his side as if resting and still smelled of the fresh meadow grass. There was no blood on the side facing us and a part of me wanted to touch him and restore his life and watch him run off to join his comrade. But I had killed him, and I had work to do now, and death would forever be different to me. I would not fear it so much, as something strange and repugnant, as it is so often to people who reside from birth to death in the steel and concrete canyons of the city. Pulling loose his diaphragm, touching his heart, finding the mushroomed bullet in the tissue, I understood life in a new way. I had inflicted death on another large mammal and one day something similar, in one form or another, would happen to me. When it occurred, it would be like this. Silent and bleeding, on a gurney or beside a glacier, life continuing all around.

That winter I made a friend in the dorms at the University of Colorado, my first hunting friend, and, nearly a quarter of a century later, Greg and I are still as close as two men can be without being born brothers. The following autumn we hunted together during a blizzard west of Rocky Mountain National Park. We jumped a four point buck in a sage draw and I fired three times as the buck bounded off, hitting him once. We tracked his blood trail through the snow and Greg stood on the prow of a hill and directed me as I searched the dense brush by the river. When I found the deer I made a terrible mistake. I waited for my friend to arrive. While I was waiting the deer got up and ran away and only after another half hour of hard hunting were we able to put an end to the animal's suffering. I have always felt sick about that, and I write here as a form of public apology and so that readers will not commit the same unforgivable error.

After that I was in the Marines and when I returned I was more skilled with the rifle than I had been before. It was during this period that I began to work as a deer hunting guide each autumn. My first job was for Wally Sanders (fictitious names from here on for reasons that will become clear), a master sergeant in my reserve unit. Wally ran a camp in Routt National Forest near the Wyoming border. I was interviewed by the game warden in Walden as part of becoming licensed, and the interview consisted of tricky bar exam–type questions such as where the nearest hospital was and whether you could legally fill a tag for a client who was not physically present. Wally had already issued me a Red Cross first aid card for a course I had never taken, but which he was licensed by the state to teach. All through the bow and blackpowder season I worked for Wally, and he started out by serving pancakes every day, for breakfast, lunch, and dinner. There was a rather loud discussion about the menu on the third day and after that some adjustments were made. On the fifth or sixth day I saw my first black bear in Colorado. I was guiding a bowhunter from Pennsylvania and we were angling above four bucks as they browsed a raspberry patch. Suddenly I looked across the clearing and there was a bear standing there with fur the color of Ponderosa bark. When our eyes met the bear bawwed and took off in the other direction. I believe he had heard the coyotes singing in the swamp down the hill. The coyotes had found a gut-pile left by a hunter. They had sung over the remains all night.

While on this hunt I climbed a 12,000-foot mountain looking for deer sign and discovered a dead golden eagle. The young eagle had no wounds and I theorized it had been poisoned by woolgrowers and had flown to the top of the mountain to die. I left him there, poor magnificent creature, and when I returned to campus I told a friend, Oscar Night-Owl, about the eagle. Oscar was a Navajo Indian and was very excited to hear about the eagle. He told me his grandfather was a medicine man in Window Rock and that he was permitted to have eagle feathers, something non-Indians are not. He begged me to take him to the site and so I did, although he nearly suffered a heart attack on the way (Oscar was a two-pack-a-day-man). Oscar removed the wing and tail feathers and eventually disposed of them differently than he had originally indicated.

The most respected deer guide in Colorado during the 1970s was Bob Copenhaver. Bob operated several camps in Grand Mesa National Forest, all with private access, which meant that unless you paid him eight hundred dollars you couldn't hunt on that public land. Bob was something of a legend. He had flown torpedo bombers off a flattop in the South Pacific, pioneered the first outfitting business on the Western Slope, and had once been called in with his hounds to track and kill a homicidal bear. I first met him at a meeting of the Colorado Guides and Outfitters Association in Denver. He was a short, muscular man with a face permanently sunburned the color of red Utah sandstone. That was the meeting at which Kurt Schultz of Glenwood Springs taped a set of topographic maps to the wall and showed us what the proposed Beaver Creek Ski Resort was going to do to his trophy deer and elk business. After the meeting I told Bob about my background—by that time I had worked for Joe Jonas, Junior, as an apprentice taxidermist, had graduated from the Hillcroft School of Horseshoeing, and had learned horse packing at several jobs in Wyoming and Colorado—and asked him for work. He told me he would pay me twenty-five dollars a day, which was not a lot of money even then, but I was young and foolish and eager to study under a legend.

Bob hunted mule deer the way they hunt white-tailed deer back east—drives. In this method, the clients are put on stand around a patch of timber or along the rims of a canyon. The guides then tie off their horses and move noisily through the trees, pushing game out into the surrounding meadows and parks where the clients wait. Bob's veteran guides all used firecrackers, which are against the law and which I refused to do. I soon learned that the biggest deer and elk never left the timber during these drives. Sometimes I would walk near and they would be so preoccupied with some other driver they would not notice me. One night in the mess tent I mentioned this curious phenomenon. I suggested that the clients might be better advised to follow the guides into the timber. Bob laughed and called me a liar and suggested I take the next day off, as the guides were permitted one day of hunting, and kill one of those stationary trophies I was hallucinating. About ten o'clock the next morning, ghost-hunting a stretch of hellhole blow-down less than a mile from camp, I killed the largest nontypical mule deer taken in Colorado that year. The rack measured three feet across and had twenty-seven points. Bob was furious with the outcome of his scornful dare, especially when two clients offered me five hundred dollars and I turned them down.

Eventually I discovered the San Juans, which are the finest mountains south of Alaska. My favorite spot was the thousand square miles at the headwaters of the Rio Grande, a place where the last grizzlies roamed through the middle of the century. One summer Greg and I rented some horses from a ranch and explored the surrounding mountains and spotted the most incredible deer we had ever seen. He was atypical and looked to be forty or more inches wide. Opening day found me camped on the edge of the glacial bowl where he lived. The next morning I awoke to disappointment. In the spruce valley below a group of hunters had packed in with horses. I ignored them and went about my business and never saw the buck that morning but did find a full curl bighorn sheep skull, which I brought in my arms back to camp (the game warden in Creede subsequently told me the ram had probably died of lungworm disease contracted by domestic sheep).

Over lunch I noticed that the hunters were still in their camp and as I watched with binoculars something about the scene struck me as unusual and so I walked down with my rifle slung over my shoulder and introduced myself. There were three of them and they were all from west Texas and they told me that the fourth had died in his sleep the night before. Apparently the exertion and high altitude had been too much for his heart. My camp was just over 12,000 feet and theirs was only about 800 feet lower. He was a young man, in his thirties, and was their local minister. Someone said he had two preschool-age children. The hunters were in a state of shock and didn't know what to do and wanted my advice on whether they should leave the body where it was or pack it out and so I told them to pack it out and contact the sheriff from the valley ranch, which had a radio-phone. After that they needed some help securing the body, which was in a sleeping bag, over the saddle so that it would not roll off. That winter I wrote a short story about this incident entitled "One of the Nicest Ways to Die," but no literary magazine wanted a story about hunting.

What all these tales and rememberances have in common is love. A love for deer that also involves killing them. I was going to use the adverb "unfortunately" in the previous sentence but there is nothing unfortunate about it. Violent death is a daily part of nature and has been since the first fossil bed was laid. A man without vices is a man without virtues, declared Abraham Lincoln. Well, I guess one of my vices, at least according to its detractors, is hunting. I enjoy hunting, and ethical killing has never bothered me. My aim here, though, has not been to mount a philosophical defense for hunting, to talk about a more civilized era when the country was closer to nature and, a nation of farmers, hunters, fisherman, we had better things to do than massacre one another in the streets with assault rifles and machine pistols. Others are better prepared for that. All I have tried to do is to assemble a few "Sketches from the Hunter's Album," as the Russian hunter and novelist Turgenev called his own, for the amusement of my friends and readers.

Many stories have been left out of this essay. There is no mention of my time with Doc Dominick at the 7-D Ranch near Yellowstone, and how exciting it was to see a grizzly bear for the first time. Nor the day that Kyle Bergstad and I drove two dozen dude horses fifteen miles up a canyon near Trapper's Peak, and met some Basque sheepherders along the way who were trying to move a thousand head of sheep in the same direction. Nor the winter with Bill Koon in the Telluride country, and how we watched the wild horses feeding with the mule deer in Pony Draw as the sun set on the purple sage. Nor the 1978 hunt on Brush Creek in which someone forgot to bring the food and my brand-new two-hundred-dollar canvas wall tent burned down and the horses mutinied in the middle of the night and many other comical disasters occurred, too numerous to record. Nor is there any mention of my hunts for caribou, those giant deer, in the Arctic Refuge the half-dozen years I lived and worked in northern Alaska.

Those will all have to wait for another time. Until that time, I offer these few as a brief reminiscence and also as a historical testament of how it was to hunt deer in Colorado when deer and wilderness were still to be found in Colorado. So often it seems to me that what we are doing, as natural history writers, is providing a permanent record of how it was to live in the twilight years of the twentieth century. A hundred years from now, the western landscape will have changed beyond our capacity to imagine. It is perhaps not inaccurate to say that western Colorado will increasingly resemble Cisalpine France. What we write—the abundant game, the uncrowded land— will likely seem as amazing to posterity as the frontier records of a century past strike us now. Our grandchildren may say, as we do of our own, that the old ones lived in a better time, when a person could still kill the winter meat in mountains that were still wild and free. I, for one, am glad that I will never know a country where this cannot be done.

Hunting with Thoreau

❧

RONALD JAGER

[The] poet must, from time to time, travel the logger's path
and the Indian's trail, to drink at some new and more bracing
fountain of the Muses, far in the recesses of the wilderness.
—"Chesuncook," *The Maine Woods*

When Henry David Thoreau and his brother rowed a boat down the
Concord River and up the Merrimack in August of 1839—the trip he
memorialized in a book that didn't sell then but sells now, *A Week on
the Concord and Merrimack Rivers*—they took a gun along.

Thoreau doesn't mention the gun explicitly. He says that "beside
the provisions which we carried with us, we depended mainly on the
river and forest for our supply." Nor does he describe shooting any
game; it is likely that he left this to his brother while he went off to
buy food from the riverbank farmers. In chapter "Tuesday" he mentions passenger pigeons: "We obtained one of these handsome
birds ... and plucked and broiled it here with some other game, to
be carried along for our supper.... It is true, it did not seem to be
putting this bird to its right use, to pluck off its feathers, and extract
its entrails, and broil its carcass on the coals; but we heroically persevered, nevertheless, waiting for farther information."

The week is still young, and jaunty ambivalence is setting in. By
the time he published these passages he had given up hunting—this
favorite sport of his youth. A decade elapsed between the trip and
the book, yet the tone of voice speaks as eloquently as the words:
an uncertain mixture of the whimsical and the solemn. Thoreau is

both reporter and chaplain on this camping trip. The brothers had intended to live partly off the land, but by Tuesday there is a hitch.

> The carcasses of some poor squirrels, however, the same that frisked so merrily in the morning, which we had skinned and embowelled for our dinner, we abandoned in disgust, with tardy humanity. . . . If they had been larger, our crime had been less. Their small red bodies, little bundles of red tissue, mere gobbets of venison, would not have "fattened fire." With a sudden impulse we threw them away, and washed our hands, and boiled some rice for our dinner.

"If they had been larger, our crime had been less." So perhaps they hunted for a deer later? If so, we are not told.

The Thoreau who had been troubled as he broiled the pigeon while awaiting "farther information" got a message from the squirrels. However unsettling—or unsettled—the message, he took it to Walden Pond, and then into *Walden*, where he seasoned it with reflections on the moral meaning of hunting. Still unsatisfied, he collaborated on a Maine moose hunt and wrote a report on it. What we harvest from all this is an ambivalent game bag of insights into hunting—Thoreau's dialogue with himself.

It strikes me that today's conflicted public opinions about hunting parallel Thoreau's conflicted private views. His anxieties prefigure our own.

❧

Let me declare my personal interests here. As a youth I regularly hunted deer, birds, squirrels, and rabbits, especially rabbits; each winter game meat was an important part of our farm family larder, as was evidently true also in young Thoreau's household. On my eighteenth birthday I shot five rabbits, had an exhilarating day in the woods, and thought it as fine a milestone as anyone could want. I was earning my keep, a man among men, a steward of God's good earth. I imagined I would always be a hunter.

Today, when others wish to hunt rabbits, birds, deer, or raccoons on my rural property, I admit them but do not join them. Meanwhile, the memory of that former thrill is so keen that I can still sense the adrenaline surge at the sound of a beagle in full cry on the fresh trail of a snowshoe hare. The shift of values during the decades—forming new affections while old charms fade—is hard to analyze; but arguments and evidence played only a minor part. Most arguments about hunting are abstract, stalemated, inflamed with rhetoric, and some are solemn humbug. Talk of brutality and callous destruction of innocent and beautiful animals is met by ecological talk of food harvest, animal starvation, nature's bounties, and rural family economy. I know some of my rural neighbors warmly despise the easy morality of comfortable and inexperienced antihunters. Much piety is spilled on both sides.

Although Thoreau, in *Walden*, sometimes finds the entire sensual rigmarole of preparing and eating flesh, and of thinking about it, repugnant to his imagination (he may have had vegetarian impulses), he is usually on stronger ground. He thinks of hunting as a crucial *stage* in our education: hunting-up and gunning-down animals is finally incompatible with moral maturity. Yet he says flatly that he encourages parents to let their boys hunt, affirming that it had been one of the best parts of his own education. "Perhaps I have owed to [fishing] and to hunting . . . my closest acquaintance with Nature. They early introduce us to . . . scenery with which otherwise . . . we should have little acquaintance." It is a boy's best welcome to forest and field. "He goes thither at first as a hunter and fisher, until at last, if he has the seeds of a better life in him, he distinguishes his proper objects, as a poet or naturalist it may be, and leaves the gun and fishpole behind" (from "Higher Laws").

My young friends and I understood our introduction to hunting in terms almost exactly opposite to Thoreau's. In our minds, that first gun confirmed our new maturity and, like our masculinity, was never to be left behind. Without argument, Thoreau turns upside down the picture millions of us inherited: our rites of passage are his arrested morality. He hurries to conclude: "This was my answer with respect to those youths bent on this pursuit, trusting that they would soon outgrow it." But he surely knew well enough that most of them would not outgrow it, and within a page he concedes that "the mass of men are still and always young in this respect." Then why put trust in our outgrowing hunting, when most of us do not? He nowhere explains why he would adopt a position so nearly contradictory as that.

In fact, Thoreau has two axes to grind: one, his present revulsion with killing and eating the kill and hence with hunting—the legacy of those disgusting red carcasses on the Merrimack's bank; the other, his blunt unwillingness to repudiate the hunting of his own youth. In this bind, his suggestion that the love of hunting is a juvenile passion to be outgrown is a neat resolution of tensions tugging him apart. Yet it resolves his problem at a price, for it leaves him mute before those who are "still and always young."

But—and this is crucial—Thoreau has a strong hunch that society as a whole, if not the individual, is destined to give up, outgrow, the transient hunting stage through which it passes. "There is a period in the history of the individual, as of the race, when the hunters are the 'best men,' as the Algonquins called them." Is there evidence of outgrowing? Here we need a long view, maybe longer than he supposed. Game reports indicate that there had been large numbers of white-tailed deer in New England until after the land was well settled; that by the late nineteenth century deer were rare or nonexistent in all its regions of intensive farming, including Concord, Massachusetts. Farther afield, wholesale slaughter was common after the invention of the jacklight: railroad cars full of deer were shipped to Boston from northern New England. The youth of civilization?

And that was outgrown: the worst *is* out of our youthful system, though Thoreau did not live to see it. Under new legislation, changed mores, changed values, changed landscape, deer have bounded back to New England. Management of the deer herds today may represent as much social maturity as any environmental program we have booked. Is our stewardship of rivers, for example, as good as that of our deer herds? Not in my region.

Still, Thoreau does not enter sympathetically the imaginative life and mind of the dedicated hunter; nor does he ponder why many individuals do not outgrow it. He does not focus on the hunting experience as fed by fantasy, literature, and art; nor on the rich culture of the hunting mystique—its sporting fraternities, its ethic of nurture and harvest and providership, its machismo, its love of lore and the use of wits, its feeling for the raw outdoors, its ceremony of trophies, its celebration of firearms, its fantasies of the chase and suspense and dramatic triumph. All these symbolic resonances, though present in his day, have grown apace in our own time. Society outgrows some things; individuals grow into other things. If he thinks of hunting as only a form of spiritual immaturity, Thoreau will underestimate the ways it may be spiritualized by communities of adults. And he does tend to regard hunting through the inherited mythos of man and frontier.

But it was just this focus that enables us to follow him as he undertakes his longest and deepest musing on hunting—not in the calm clearings on Merrimack's bank or the shores of Walden Pond, but deep within the Maine wilderness.

❦

Prophets of old and sages, long antedating Thoreau, sometimes journeyed alone into the wilderness, later to return to their tribes with a vision clarified. We know little of what they did there. Some fasted and prayed. Some attended oracles or struggled with temptation or with the austerity of wilderness itself. Some waited upon God or their Muses. When they returned from mountain or desert or pond, it was with wisdom tested, sifted, refined, a vision made whole—else they were not prophets; but never made perfect—else they were not men.

In 1853 Thoreau journeyed to the Maine wilderness with two companions, a hunter unnamed and an Indian guide named Joe. The poet, he said, must "drink at some new and more bracing fountain of the Muses, far in the recesses of the wilderness" (from *The Maine Woods*). "Though I had not come a-hunting, and felt some compunctions about accompanying the hunters," he wrote, "I wished to see a moose near at hand, and was not sorry to learn how the Indian managed to kill one. I went as reporter or chaplain to the hunters." He took this trip while readying *Walden* for publication, including the section that lays a reproach upon hunting for its moral immaturity.

So Thoreau is now in the Maine woods, within the setting and ceremonies of an actual hunt, and his companions are intent on killing a moose? I imagine Thoreau foresees our arched eyebrows and neatly sidesteps: Joe is an Indian and a guide; hunting is his nature and the wilderness his habitat; the unnamed friend is, well, just a hunter. We are invited to suppose that it is *their* trip, not his; his only to "accompany" them. So he goes to confront wilderness untamed, and himself within it; he goes "as reporter or chaplain." And even at this distance we can hear the nervous whimsy in that phrase.

Arriving by steamer in Bangor, Maine, the nimrods travel next by canoe, watching for moose sign by day and hunting along the riverbeds by moonlight. Thoreau redeems the time by watching the Indian, inspecting the forest, comparing the flora with Concord's. The hunter searches for tracks; the Indian fashions a birchbark moose horn; the reporter takes notes on the wilderness. Several days into the wilds they meet an easy success. How did "the Indian manage to kill one"? Well, they saw a moose standing on the river's edge and shot it. What did Thoreau expect?

Thus the reporter got to see his "moose near at hand," to touch and measure it, describe it, marvel at its ungainly bulk. "Joe now proceeded to skin the moose with a pocket-knife, while I looked on; and a tragical business it was,—to see that still warm and palpitating body pierced with a knife, to see the warm milk stream from the rent udder, and the ghastly naked red carcass appearing from within its seemly robe." Indian Joe saved the hide as his trophy, took a few chunks of meat for camp use, and left the rest right there in the river where it had died. That evening they ate fried moose meat, which "tasted like tender beef."

The hunters, their blood up, wanted still more excitement that very night and paddled off down the river again. The chaplain stayed in camp, brooding about moose hunting. "I had not come to the woods for this purpose, nor had I foreseen it [not foreseen it?!], though I had been willing to learn how the Indian maneuvered; but one moose killed was as good, if not as bad, as a dozen. The afternoon's tragedy, and my share in it, as it affected the innocence, destroyed the pleasure of my adventure."

Surely Thoreau *had* foreseen it, yet he plunged ahead. He came to encounter the wilderness, to immerse himself in it, innocence and guilt and all, as resolutely as he had done in growing beans at Walden, woodchucks and sweat and all; the moose and the Indian and the hunter were part of the wilderness. And he knew when he met it face to face—maybe only then—that there was no way to reconcile himself to the idea of killing a moose for the sake of killing a moose. It is "too much like going out by night to some woodside pasture and shooting your neighbor's horses. These are God's own horses, poor, timid creatures . . . though they *are* nine feet tall." Indian Joe told him of hunters who had shot oxen, mistaking them for moose, and chaplain Thoreau asks himself how shooting moose differs from that: "Having killed one of God's and *your own* oxen, you strip off its hide,—because that is the common trophy . . . cut a steak from its haunches, and leave the huge carcass to smell to heaven for you."

Thoreau is in the wilderness to confront it, not to admire or deplore it from afar, not even to make peace with what happens there, but to assimilate it. He might have known he risked getting caught in his own philosophical crossfire, and, sure enough, the afternoon's experience shot down the trip's innocence. "As I sat before the fire on my fir-twig seat, without walls above or around me, I remembered how far on every hand that wilderness stretched . . . and wondered if any bear or moose was watching the light of my fire; for Nature looked sternly on me on account of the murder of the moose."

This brooding leads Thoreau to compare his own companions, the night hunters, to the lumbermen of the wilderness: "How base or coarse are the motives which commonly carry men into the wilderness." How appalling that we should come to think that boards are the true destiny of God's trees. "A pine cut down, a dead pine, is no more a pine than a dead human carcass is a man." Only the poet in us knows what pine trees are about. "[Lumbermen] have no more love for wild nature than wood-sawyers have for forests. Other white men and Indians who come here are for the most part hunters, whose object is to slay as many moose and other wild animals as possible." This is a black night.

And back in Concord the completed text of *Walden* lies on Thoreau's desk, including this easy speculation: "Fishermen, hunters, woodchoppers and others, spending their lives in the field and woods, in a peculiar sense a part of Nature themselves, are often in a more favorable mood for observing her . . . than philosophers or poets even." Ah, yes, chatting with Emerson under the shade trees in Concord, Thoreau indulges the idea that the world's hard laborers have the best rapport with Nature: "She is not afraid to exhibit herself to them," he wrote bravely. But now in Maine he declares that when she *does* exhibit herself to choppers and hunters, she stimulates not reverence or love but just lust. Here, among hunters and choppers near the wilderness fountain of the Muses, he finds his values grounded back in civilization with the philosophers and chaplains and poets! Thoreau's debate with himself.

And therefore his text seems at times aloof, spectatorial. The inner experience of his companions, hunting while he was reporting and hunting again while he is chaplaining, remains inscrutable. His sympathies reach out to the rich flora and fauna, to the remote stretches of the Maine vastness, to his predatory companions as objects in the wilderness; but seem to stop where their consciousness begins. We know nothing of what Thoreau and his companions *said* to each other about the shooting; the very dead and very large moose lying there in the riverbed has put a wall between them. Composing his notes and his soul in retrospect, he writes: "I already, and for weeks afterward, felt my nature coarser for this part of my woodland experience." Meanwhile, the hunters are off in the boat on the dark river trying to murder another moose, for which they cannot possibly have any use whatever. Thoreau and companions are afloat on different streams.

In imagination he propels himself farther into the woods: "It is true, I came as near as is possible to being a hunter and miss it, myself; and as it is, I think that I could spend a year in the woods, fishing and hunting, just enough to sustain myself, with satisfaction. This would be next to living like a philosopher on the fruits of the earth." Granted, he *could* have done it; but we know that in his first attempt at it, that fortnight on the Merrimack, he had flinched at the test: he discarded the first little squirrels he had prepared, convincing himself evasively that "if they had been larger, our crime had been less." Less? Very well, here in the Maine river lies a great dead moose, a thousand times larger than the Merrimack squirrel. Does the "crime" appear less? Not on his life! For he is no longer musing about it abstractly but confronting it concretely. Then, a "tardy humanity" protested the squirrels, but now all Nature gathers to testify about the moose.

And yet . . . although chaplain and hunters have put each other out of mind, probably glad to be apart, next day reporter and friends will jointly explore new territory side by side. They have to. They are on this voyage together; and tomorrow and tomorrow they are all in the same boat.

❧

Thoreau's journey to Maine was a pilgrimage for him and a parable for us. In the Maine woods a part of his vision is sifted and clarified, and a part is left quite unresolved and bequeathed to history, our history, there to be both ratified and amplified. His conflicts with himself echo our public ones; our current tensions about hunting are precisely his, writ large.

His mind is more permissive than his feelings. His intellect tells him that a philosopher, understanding and living within the harmony of the earth, may hunt food with impunity—the brothers had gone armed on that *Week* trip; but his imagination does not fully accept it. It is essentially the same tug-of-war that led him to posit a rationale for the hunting of his youth, of any youth, and yet find it spiritually repellent for an adult. He cannot reconcile the opposing impulses of intellect and heart. Remember the squirrels: beneath the surface of that excessively shrewd statement—"if they had been larger, our crime had been less"—may lie a worthy theory, one that may reasonably adjudicate the complex claims of harvesting nature and merely appreciating it. Fine; but it is not a theory Thoreau will ever reconcile with a particular blunt experience of the harvest. The ideas prompted by the squirrels will never be squared with the feelings aroused by the moose.

Halfway back from our own time to Thoreau's stands the representative figure of Teddy Roosevelt. He poses for pictures, high-powered rifle in hand, with magnificent but very dead animals deployed picturesquely around him. He has shot them. A dead moose does not disturb *his* innocence. It is unthinkable that a president would pose this way today, and there are few places in this country where one would run for high office with this sort of publicity. Something has changed; something matured; something lived through and outlived. Thoreau may be closer to us today than Teddy Roosevelt is, but the public sensibility is also more riven and perplexed than Roosevelt ever was. We have woven Thoreau's conflicted attitudes into our social fabric.

As Thoreau's head permits more than his heart approves, so too is today's official mind more permissive than the feelings of the body politic. Hunting is overtly encouraged by many state governments—the public mind at work. Each year my own state, New Hampshire, sells two or three licenses for every deer in the woods, and a dozen for every deer harvested. There is money in that for the state, and tourist business for the economy, and more tax money in that. Government promotes (for economic, hence rational, reasons) what office seekers would hesitate to exemplify (for emotional and moral reasons), and the gulf between public policies and public pieties grows. Policies of mind, pieties of feeling. Reporter and chaplain are at odds within us, as they were for Thoreau.

As a less urban nation, we were once closer to underlying consensus on these matters. Hunters and nonhunters spoke the same language, drew on the same background experience, most of which was rural, of the earth, earthy. Teddy Roosevelt, Big Game Hunter *and* Great Conservationist, typifies that larger unity of consciousness. It is harder to find today. The personal division within Thoreau—between mind and feelings, between reporter and chaplain, between hunter friends and himself—seems embodied now in public tensions and amplified in public actions. Conflict between what the political mind asserts and what the public sensibility endorses may become a permanent feature of our culture. All the more reason to recognize and contain it, to understand its sources; for today, and tomorrow again, we are all in the same boat.

❧

"Only that day dawns to which we are awake," declares *Walden*. After many generations, and just as Thoreau had hoped, white-tailed deer have returned to Concord, Massachusetts, without forever being shot on sight. Every year moose walk again over my own acres in New Hampshire; that's a new day, right there. He foresaw, dimly, the awakening of public sensitivities that was necessary and probably foresaw too that it would come not so much by quick polemic as by slow understanding. In that light we may see Thoreau's not engaging his hunting friends in debate. They were not awake. He knows how futile it is to combat or despise the feelings of others about hunting. He is a writer, not a propagandist; his words are a testimony, not an argument. What he writes about hunting—it is a kind of solitary consultation with the Muses—is by way of helping himself, and us, to get our heads and hearts together; to do so, we must stay on valid terms with the entire natural order that surrounds us, sustains us, whose misuse corrupts us. In Thoreau's eyes, our view of hunting is not separate from our view of forestry, of the land and its uses, or from a nature ethic generally.

Musing on hunting, Thoreau surely never saw himself an emblematic figure—as I do here. He would have thought his vision too fluid, too unresolved: sending the neighbor boys off to hunt, not countenancing it for himself; without inner sympathy for the hunting mystique, but outwardly commending it; siding now with hunters and choppers, now with poets; able to justify in theory what he could not accept in practice; serving as reporter *and* chaplain on a moose hunt that attracted *and* repelled him. Exemplary?

Indeed. Who else at the time was there to join a dialogue on hunting? Who else was awake? His are solitary reflections, a chaplain's debate within himself, not just a reporter's jottings and not a discourse with friends or even with his own era. Alone, he anticipates at one stroke and for the next 150 years both America's best wisdom on, and its most deeply conflicted experience with, hunting. When we hear his musings, we should know that they are ours.

Is Hunting Ethical?

✤

ANN S. CAUSEY

The struggling fawn suddenly went limp in my arms. Panicked, I told my husband to pull the feeding tube out of her stomach. Though Sandy had quit breathing and her death was clearly imminent, I held her head down and slapped her back in an attempt to clear her trachea. Warm, soured milk ran from her mouth and nose, soaking my clothes and gagging us with its vile smell. I turned Sandy over in my arms, and my husband placed his mouth over her muzzle. While he blew air into her lungs, I squeezed her chest as a CPR course had taught me to do for human infants in cardiac arrest.

After a minute or so I felt her chest for a pulse. Nothing at first, then four weak beats in rapid succession. "She's alive! Keep breathing for her."

My husband gagged, then spit to avoid swallowing more of the soured milk, and continued his efforts to revive Sandy. I kept working her chest, hoping that through some miracle of will she would recover. Come on Sandy, wake up. Please wake up!

Sandy never woke up. My husband, a wildlife biologist, and I had nursed over two dozen white-tailed deer fawns that summer for use in a deer nutrition and growth study he was conducting. Most of the animals were in poor shape when we got them. People around the state found them—some actually orphaned, others mistakenly thought to be abandoned. After a few days of round-the-clock feed-ings, the fun gave way to drudgery and frustration. That's when they would call their county conservation officer, who in turn called us.

All the animals we raised required and got from us loving care, at-tention, and patience, no matter how sick or recalcitrant they may have been. All were named, and we came to know each one as an in-dividual with unique personality traits and behavior patterns. Though most lived to become healthy adults, each fatality was a tragic loss for us, and we mourned each and every death.

The afternoon Sandy died, however, was not convenient for mourning. We were going to a group dinner that evening and had to prepare a dish. Through tears I made a marinade for the roast. While the meat smoked over charcoal and hickory, we brooded over Sandy's death.

When the roast was done, we wiped away our tears, cleaned up, and went to the dinner. Our moods brightened as our roast was quickly gobbled up, and the evening's high point came when several guests declared that our roast was the best venison they'd ever eaten. The best deer meat. Part of an animal my husband, an avid hunter, had willfully killed and I had gratefully butchered, wrapped, and frozen—a deer that once was a cute and innocent little fawn . . . just like Sandy.

❧

If any one word characterizes most people's feelings when they re-flect on the morality of killing an animal for sport, it is "ambiva-lence." With antihunters insisting that hunting is a demonstration of extreme irreverence for nonhuman life, thoughtful hunters must concede, albeit uncomfortably, the apparent contradiction of killing for sport while maintaining a reverence for life. Yet I know of few hunters who do not claim to have a deep reverence for nature and life, including especially the lives of the animals they seek to kill. It seems that this contradiction, inherent in hunting and increasingly the focus of debate, lies at the core of the moral conundrum of hunt-ing. How can anyone both revere life and seek to extinguish it in pur-suit of recreation? The opponents of hunting believe they have backed its proponents into a logical corner on this point, yet the pro-ponents have far from given up the battle for logical supremacy. Is ei-ther side a clear winner?

None who know me or my lifestyle would label me "antihunt-ing." Most of the meat in my diet is game. And many is the time I've defended hunting from the attacks of those who see all hunters as bloodthirsty, knuckle-dragging rednecks.

Yet I have on occasion found myself allied with antihunters. But it's an uneasy and selective alliance, my antihunting sentiments lim-ited to diatribes against such blatantly unethical behavior as Big Buck contests, canned Coon Hunt for Christ rallies, and bumper stickers proclaiming "Happiness Is a Warm Gutpile."

There is also a subtler reason for my concerns about hunting, stemming, I believe, from my disappointment with the responses of many hunters and wildlife managers to questions concerning the morality of hunting. In the interest of enlivening and, I hope, elevat-ing the growing debate, it is these moral questions, and their answers, I wish to address here.

❧

To begin, I should point out some errors, common to ethical reason-ing and to the current debate, that we should do our best to avoid. The first is confusing prudence with morality. Prudence is acting with one's overall best interests in mind, while morality sometimes requires that one sacrifice self-interest in the service of a greater good.

While thorough knowledge is all that's required to make prudent decisions, the making of a moral decision involves something more: conscience. Obligations have no moral meaning without conscience. Ethical hunters do not mindlessly follow rules and lobby for regula-tions that serve their interests; rather, they follow their consciences, sometimes setting their own interests aside. In short, ethics are guided by conscience.

Another important distinction is between legality and morality. While many immoral activities are prohibited by law, not all behav-ior that is within the law can be considered ethical. The politician caught in a conflict of interest who claims moral innocence because he has broken no laws rarely convinces us. Nor should hunters as-sume that whatever the game laws allow or tradition supports is morally acceptable. The ethical hunter is obligated to evaluate laws and traditions in light of his or her own moral sense. Conscience is not created by decree or consensus, nor is morality determined by le-gality or tradition.

Finally, it's all too tempting to dismiss the concerns of our opponents by questioning their motives and credentials instead of giving serious consideration to the questions they raise. Hunters do hunting no favors by hurling taunts and slander at their opponents. The questions raised about hunting deserve a fair hearing on their own merits. Consideration of antihunting messages must not be biased by personal opinions of the messengers, nor should hunters' efforts remain focused on discrediting their accusers. Rather, ethical hunters must undertake the uncomfortable and sometimes painful processes of moral deliberation and personal and collective soul-searching that these questions call for.

❦

The first difficulty we encounter in addressing the morality of hunting is identifying and understanding the relevant questions and answers. To me, the most striking feature of the current debate is the two sides' vastly different understanding of the meaning of the question, Is hunting a morally acceptable activity?

Those who support hunting usually respond by citing data. They enumerate the acres of habitat protected by hunting-generated funds; how many game species have experienced population increases due to modern game management; how much the economy is stimulated by hunting-related expenditures; how effectively modern game laws satisfy the consumptive and recreational interests of the hunting community today while assuring continued surpluses of game for future hunters; and how hunters, more than most citizens, care deeply about ecosystem integrity and balance and the global environment.

While these statements may be perfectly true, they're almost totally irrelevant to the question. Antihunters are not asking whether hunting is an effective management tool, whether it's economically advisable, or whether hunters love and appreciate nature. Rather, they're asking, Is it ethical to kill animals for sport? Are any forms of hunting morally right?

The hunter says yes; the antihunter says no, yet they are answering entirely different questions. The hunter answers, with data, what he or she perceives as a question about utility and prudence; the antihunter, though, has intended to ask a question about morality, about human responsibilities and values. It's as if one asked what day it is and the other responded by giving the time. While the answer may be correct, it's meaningless in the context of the question asked.

The point is that moral debates, including this one, are not about facts but about values. Moral controversy cannot be resolved by examination of data or by appeal to scientific studies.

An obsession with "sound, objective science" in addressing their opponents has led many hunters not only to avoid the crucial issues but to actually fuel the fires of the antihunting movement. Animal welfare proponents and the general public are primarily concerned about the pain, suffering, and loss of life inflicted on hunted animals, and the motives and attitudes of those who hunt. They're offended by references to wild animals as "resources." They're angered by the sterile language and, by implication, the emotionally sterile attitudes of those who speak of "culling," "controlling," "harvesting," and "managing" animals for "maximum sustained yield." And they're outraged by those who cite habitat protection and human satisfaction data while totally disregarding the interests of the sentient beings who occupy that habitat and who, primarily through their deaths, serve to satisfy human interests.

Antihunters insist that nontrivial reasons be given for intentional human-inflicted injuries and deaths—or that these injuries and deaths be stopped. An eminently reasonable request.

Even when hunters acknowledge the significance of the pain and suffering inflicted through hunting, they too often offer in defense that they feel an obligation to give back more than they take, and that hunters and wildlife professionals successfully have met this obligation. Granted, it may be that the overall benefits to humans and other species that accrue from hunting outweigh the costs to the hunted. Nevertheless, this utilitarian calculation fails to provide moral justification for hunting. Is it just, hunting's detractors ask, that wild animals should die to feed us? To clothe us? To decorate our bodies and den walls? To provide us with entertainment and sport?

These are the questions hunters are being asked. *These* are the questions they must carefully consider and thoughtfully address. It will not suffice to charge their opponents with biological naïveté, as theirs are not questions of science. Nor will charges of emotionalism quiet their accusers, since emotion plays an integral and valid part in value judgments and moral development. Both sides have members who are guided by their hearts, their minds, or both. Neither side has a monopoly on hypocrisy, zealotry, narrow-mindedness, or irrationalism. Opposition to hunting is based in largest part on legitimate philosophical differences.

❧

It has been said that hunting is the most uncivilized and primitive activity in which a modern person can legally engage. Therein lies ammunition for the biggest guns in the antihunters' arsenal; paradoxically, therein also lies its appeal to hunters and the source of its approval by many sympathetic nonhunters.

Hunting is one of few activities that allows an individual to participate directly in the life and death cycles on which all natural systems depend. The skilled hunter's ecological knowledge is holistic and realistic; his or her awareness involves all the senses. Whereas ecologists study systems from without, examining and analyzing from a perspective necessarily distanced from their subjects, dedicated hunters live and learn from within, knowing parts of nature as only a parent or child can know his or her own family. One thing necessary for a truly ethical relationship with wildlife is an appreciation of ecosystems, of natural processes. Such an appreciation may best be gained through familiarity, through investment of time and effort, through curiosity, and through an attitude of humility and respect. These are the lessons that hunting teaches its best students.

Not only have ethical hunters resisted the creeping alienation between humans and the natural out-of-doors, they have fought to resist the growing alienation between humans and the "nature" each person carries within. Hunters celebrate their evolutionary heritage and stubbornly refuse to be stripped of their atavistic urges—they refuse to be sterilized by modern culture and thus finally separated from nature. The ethical hunter transcends the mundane, the ordinary, the predictable, the structured, the artificial. As Aldo Leopold argues in his seminal work *A Sand County Almanac*, hunting in most forms maintains a valuable element in the cultural heritage of all peoples.

Notice, though, that Leopold does not give a blanket stamp of moral approval to hunting; nor should we. In fact, Leopold recognized that some forms of hunting may be morally depleting. If we offer an ecological and evolutionary defense for hunting, as Leopold did and as many of hunting's supporters do today, we must still ask ourselves, For which forms of hunting is our defense valid?

The open-minded hunter should carefully consider the following questions: To what extent is shooting an animal over bait or out of a tree at close range after it was chased up there by a dog a morally enriching act? Can shooting an actually or functionally captive animal enhance one's understanding of natural processes? Does a safari to foreign lands to step out of a Land Rover and shoot exotic animals located for you by a guide honor your cultural heritage? Does killing an animal you profess to honor and respect, primarily in order to obtain a trophy, demonstrate reverence for the animal as a sentient creature? Is it morally enriching to use animals as mere objects, as game pieces in macho contests where the only goal is to outcompete other hunters? Is an animal properly honored in death by being reduced to points, inches, and pounds, or to a decoration on a wall? Which forms of hunting can consistently and coherently be defended as nontrivial, meaningful, ecologically sound, and morally enriching?

Likewise, we who hunt or support hunting must ask ourselves: Does ignoring, downplaying, and in some cases denying the wounding rate in hunting, rather than taking all available effective measures to lower it, demonstrate reverence for life? Does lobbying for continued hunting of species whose populations are threatened or of uncertain status exemplify ecological awareness and concern? Is the continued hunting of some declining waterfowl populations, the aerial killing of wolves in Alaska, or the setting of hunting seasons that in some areas may sentence to slow death the orphaned offspring of their legally killed lactating mothers, consistent with management *by* hunters—or do these things verify the antihunters' charges of management primarily *for* hunters?

These questions and others have aroused hunters' fears, indignation, defensive responses, and collective denial. Yet no proponent of ethical hunting has anything to fear from such questions. These are questions we should have been asking ourselves, and defensibly answering, all along. The real threat comes not from outside criticism but from our own complacency and uncritical acceptance of hunting's status quo, and from our mistaken belief that to protect *any* form of hunting, we must defend and protect *all* forms. In fact, to protect the privilege of morally responsible hunting, we must attack and abolish the unacceptable acts, policies, and attitudes within our ranks that threaten all hunting, as a gangrenous limb threatens the entire body.

✻

The battle cry "Reverence for Life" has been used by both sides, at times with disturbing irony. Cleveland Amory, founder of The Fund For Animals, described in the June 1992 issue of *Sierra* magazine the perfect world he would create if he were appointed its ruler: "All animals will not only be not shot, they will be protected—not only from people but as much as possible from each other. Prey will be separated from predator, and there will be no overpopulation or starvation because all will be controlled by sterilization or implant."

A reverence for life? Only if you accept the atomistic and utterly unecological concept of life as a characteristic of individuals rather than systems.

But neither can all who hunt legitimately claim to hold a reverence for life. In a hunting video titled "Down to Earth," a contemporary rock star and self-proclaimed "whack master" and "gutpile addict" exhorts his protégés to "whack 'em, stack 'em, and pack 'em." After showing a rapid sequence of various animals being hit by his arrows, the "master whacker" kneels and sarcastically asks for "a moment of silence" while the viewer is treated to close-up, slow-motion replays of the hits, including sickening footage of some animals that clearly are gut shot or otherwise sloppily wounded. A reverence for life? Such behavior would seem to demonstrate shocking *irreverence*, arrogance, and hubris. As hunters, we toe a fine line between profundity and profanity and must accept the responsibility of condemning those practices and attitudes that trivialize, shame, and desecrate all hunting. To inflict death without meaningful and significant purpose, to kill carelessly or casually, or to take a life without solemn gratitude is inconsistent with genuine reverence for life.

To be ethical, we must do two things: we must *act* ethically, and we must *think* ethically. The hunting community has responded to its critics by trying to clean up its visible act: we don't hear many public proclamations of gutpile addictions anymore; we less frequently see dead animals used as hood ornaments while the meat, not to be utilized anyway, rapidly spoils; those who wound more animals than they kill are less likely nowadays to brag about it; and, since studies show that the public opposes sport hunting as trivial, hunters are coached to avoid the term "sport" when they address the public or their critics.

What's needed, though, for truly ethical hunting to flourish is not just a change of appearance or vocabulary but a change of mind-set, a deepening of values. Hunters may be able to "beat" antihunters through a change of tactics, but to win the wrong war is no victory at all. Some morally repugnant forms of hunting are *rightfully* under attack, and we can defend them only by sacrificing our intellectual and moral integrity. We should do all we can to avoid such "victories." Hunters must reexamine and, when appropriate, give up some of what they now hold dear—not just because doing so is expedient but because it's *right*. As T. S. Eliot, quoted by Martin Luther King, Jr., in his "Letter from Birmingham Jail," reminds us, "The last temptation is the greatest treason: To do the right deed for the wrong reason."

❧

Can anyone give us a final answer to the question, Is hunting ethical? No.

For one thing, the question and its answer depend heavily on how one defines "hunting." There are innumerable activities that go by this term, yet many are so different from one another that they scarcely qualify for the same appellation. Moreover, there is no one factor that motivates all hunters to hunt or even that motivates one hunter on each hunt; nor is there such a thing as the hunter's mind-set.

Second, and even more important, is the recognition that in most cases one cannot answer moral questions for others. Two morally mature people may ponder the same ethical dilemma and come to opposite, and equally valid, conclusions. The concept of ethical hunting is pluralistic, as hard to pin down as the definition of a virtuous person. Unlike our opponents, we who are hunting proponents do not seek to impose a particular lifestyle, morality, or spirituality on all citizens; we merely wish to preserve a variety of options and individualities in all our choices concerning responsible human recreation, engagement with nature, and our place in the food web. It's doubtful that any one system, whether it be "boutique" hunting, vegetarianism, or modern factory farming, is an adequate way to meet the ethical challenges of food procurement and human/nonhuman relationships in our diverse culture and burgeoning population.

Like education of any sort, moral learning cannot be passively acquired. In fact, the importance of answering the question of whether hunting is ethical is often exaggerated, for the value of ethics lies not so much in the product, the answers, as in the process of deep and serious deliberation of moral issues. To ponder the value of an animal's life versus a hunter's material and spiritual needs and to consider an animal's pain, suffering, and dignity in death is to acknowledge deeper values and to demonstrate more moral maturity than one who casually, defensively dismisses such ideas.

No matter the result, the process of moral deliberation is necessarily enriching. Neither side can offer one answer for all; we can only answer this question each for ourself, and even then we must be prepared to offer valid, consistent moral arguments in support of our conclusions. This calls for a level of soul-searching and critical thinking largely lacking on both sides of the current debate.

Today's ethical hunter must abandon the concept of hunting as fact and replace it with the more appropriate concept of hunting as challenge—the challenge of identifying and promoting those attitudes toward wildlife that exemplify the values on which morally responsible hunting behavior is based. Heel-digging and saber-rattling must give way to cooperation, to increased awareness and sensitivity, to reason and critical analysis, and to honest self-evaluation and assessment.

The Chinese have a wonderful term, *wei chi*, that combines two concepts: crisis . . . and opportunity. The term conveys the belief that every crisis presents an opportunity. I submit that the hunting community today faces its greatest crisis ever and, therein, its greatest opportunity—the opportunity for change, for moral growth, for progress.

I Like to Talk About Animals

✿

C. L. RAWLINS

I hunt, but I don't talk about it much—those late-night, throaty recitations make me nervous. I keep my rifle in a case, out of sight. And though I was born in Wyoming—where taxidermy is considered a fine art like painting or sculpture—those ranks of trophy heads on walls stare down at me like the jury in a capital case.

But I like to talk about animals. Having lived in the mountains of Utah and Wyoming as a ranger, grazing cop, and hydrologist, I've lived among wild animals. I see them when I'm not hunting, which is most of the year, and they see me walking in the woods or skiing. And over the years I've come to regard them not as strange or symbolic but as familiar.

Of those I've hunted, antelope are the most curious. In summer, with no thought of hunting in my head, I can sit in the willows with one finger raised and then crooked, just one motion. A young buck will approach. He'll come within a hundred feet, stomp a front hoof, snort, and flee. If I don't move, he'll come closer, trailed by more timid bucks. He'll stomp and huff again, and they'll dash as one—a pretty sight.

If I can sit still in the heat with flies and gnats inspecting my nose, in time the young buck will come very close. He'll wish to examine, freckle by hair, the creature performing this strange, one-fingered act. Can he sense that I don't intend to kill him?

I think he can, not being foolish. But he's inquisitive to a fault. He comes so close I can see the moist linings of his nostrils, and the dust shining in his coat where he rolled, and the mild shock in his dark eye as it meets mine.

I end the game by standing up. The buck spins, hind feet kicking grit. He almost collides with his followers, who wheel a quarter-second late, and this time they *fly*. Zero to forty-five, in a snap, and for the first half mile they barely touch the ground. Thus I praise antelope.

I can hunt them on foot from my house, which makes them sensible prey, but I haven't drawn a tag for three years. So mostly I hunt deer, which are fairly easy to find and can be packed home without major fuss.

But more than hunting deer, I like to watch them. And some deer like to watch me and enjoy hearing me talk or sing. Some does will relax and waggle their ears and gaze at me with such soft, dimensionless being that I fall in love. How can I say this, and say that I kill them?

Because we have to eat.

Why don't we just eat vegetables?

We do. This year there were frosts in June, July, and August, so we harvested potatoes, turnips, and beets, but the peas froze, and forget corn and squash. We grow onions and garlic, to braid and hang in the cellar. I built a greenhouse for tomatoes and peppers, and we make jam from berries and syrup from wild rosehips.

But otherwise our food is grown elsewhere and trucked in: rice, beans, wheat, fruit. The damage wrought by industrial agriculture is well documented, so I won't repeat the numbers here. In specific, quantitative terms I can do a fair amount of harm by eating cornflakes and a banana each morning.

And I agree: it's foolish to graze a steer in Wyoming, fatten it on grain in Iowa, slaughter it in Omaha, warehouse it in Salt Lake City, and then truck it to Wyoming again. So we buy pasture lamb and grass-fed beef from our neighbors and save all that fossil fuel.

Eat low on the food chain, you say. Good idea. But there isn't one big universal food chain. On this chilly steppe, *low* means grass and tough forbs, or sage and bitterbrush. I can't eat them, but cattle and sheep can, with a lot of support: irrigated hay, fencing, vaccine, and predator control. Or antelope, deer, and elk can, with less trouble and expense. Or bison, if we let them.

My principle here is that where you live should mean something. And the rules of life are not the same in every place.

But of course we want them to be. Our national consciousness drives us to it, and our restless mobility, and the written word, and our electronic net. We love what is uniform: the french fries at Mc-Donald's, universal ethics, and global markets. We shy from the messy specifics of place and from the conflicts that come from living too near the natural world.

If I lived in a money-haunted place, a city where a deer can't live; if I lived in rooms and on wheels; if hunting seemed to me nasty, atavistic, and contrived, I wouldn't hunt. I'd eat pasta salads with balsamic vinaigrette, perhaps, and things rolled in grape leaves. And I'd pay with my credit card.

🌿

While I can make a localized case for hunting, the custom of killing for sport makes me sick. In childhood I tormented cats and dogs for the feeling of power it gave me. With my first gun I shot a lizard, a crayfish, a robin, and a baby jackrabbit, and it changed me. I can still see the diminishing flail of the sparrow's wing and hear the rabbit's breath as it kicked a circle in the sand.

I could see myself in those animals. What had been a game to me was suddenly not one. That's the worst part of hunting—to pull the trigger knowing what will result: pain, shock, blood, death. To die of wounds, whether by tooth or bullet, hurts.

But it doesn't last forever. And there is no branding or castration; no being herded by electric prod into a crowded, heaving truck; no frantic struggle over a concrete floor awash in blood. It doesn't have to be ugly. The whole point of a rifle and scope, of knowledge and practice, is that the animal goes quickly from wildness into death.

To see one's power to inflict death as the point of hunting, or to boast of it, is ugly indeed. When I stand in a cluster of men at a party and they start raising imaginary rifles and jerking invisible triggers, I head for the other end of the room.

But I like to talk about animals. It doesn't seem to me that deer are afraid of death in the way that we are. For six winters I lived in a canyon in Utah where I could watch mule deer on their winter range, or at least what was left, above a valley consumed by streets and houses. There were coyotes, but the deer didn't seem to hate them or even to mind them much. Freelancing, the coyotes would eat cottontails, yap dogs, and stray cats: fast food. You get tired of it.

To eat deer, the coyotes had to organize. I watched them in twos and threes in the blue dawns, testing. Both coyotes and deer moved with a kind of respect for one another. The deer were not passive victims: I saw bucks lower their heads and drive coyotes away.

I noticed a young buck who limped, so the coyotes had noticed long before. I watched from the opposite ridge as two coyotes slowly separated him from his band. Alone, the buck moved with deliberation since to run would draw a charge from his gray attendants. A third coyote was waiting under a roll of willows along a deep coulee. I could see him, and the buck could not. When the buck passed, the coyote charged.

The buck plunged into the snow-filled gulley and floundered. The kill was quick. The coyotes feasted and basked, and then circled, tails a-flag, and then feasted again. The other deer shied a hundred yards up the hill and relaxed, some dozing in the sun, as if knowing that the day's death had come and passed them by.

I was a vegetarian that winter, but it made me hungry to watch. Back at the cabin, I devoured a pint of peanut butter with my bare hands.

❧

I like to read about animals, too. I'm a fan of biologists like E. O. Wilson and of thinkers like Paul Shepard. But I avoid hook-and-bullet magazines, which put me off with their photos of bows that look like missile launchers and weird-shaped rifles with ever larger scopes and ever more deadly loads. They promote technological prowess far above knowledge of animals or skill in the outdoors. And they focus on killing. They show animals with crosshairs superimposed, or sprawled with unshaven men hunched over them—a friend calls this *Horn Porn*. And it is. What it urges is that the act of possession is supreme.

❧

Hunting season, 1995. Before opening day small aircraft buzz the uplands to locate elk. Then bowhunters, dressed like commandos, form the advance guard. Later comes a wave of grunts in their chugging pickups, trailing horses and ATVs. Then the executives, in bush suits with matched leather gun cases, fly in their corporate 'copters to lodges and camps to pore over maps with glasses of single-malt, nodding like generals.

This doesn't make sense as a way of getting something to eat. Instead, it seems like a drama in which men troubled with frustrating, airless lives dress up as soldiers and cowboys. They marshal their weapons and movable goods to invade a primal landscape, one in which they are licensed to kill. And in this postfrontier passion play, animals are not food or wild companions, but the enemy.

I dread hunting season for its resemblance to war, which reveals something about us—American men—I'd rather not have to confront: our hunger for money and possessions, and our taste for killing, apart from legitimate hunger or need.

There's a kind of contempt in the way we hunt, for animals and the natural world. How many so-called hunters go out before the season to look for tracks? How many, on the ground they hunt, could name ten native plants? How many of them even know what a deer eats?

Richard Nelson wrote about the Koyukon, an Alaska tribe of hunters and fishers who studied animals and their habitats carefully. They hunted with a regard not just for the physical vitality of animals but for the spirit we have in common: *Every animal knows way more than you do. We always heard that from the old people. And they told us never to bother anything unless we really need it.*

I've been given game meat by friends who were tired of it, or didn't like it in the first place but still wanted to hunt, or were cleaning out their freezers before hunting season. One young doctor bragged that he'd filled all his tags—moose, elk, deer, and antelope—more than the freezer would hold: "So we took the antelope to the dump."

Against that, I remember helping a one-legged man load a little buck into his camper shell. He didn't flag me down. I just happened to notice (who wouldn't?) a man with a crutch trying to drag a deer through thick sage. His pickup wasn't as old as mine, but it was old.

His rifle was a relic—a 1903 Springfield in a plain walnut stock with a 4× Redfield scope. He kept saying how much his family loved that ol' deer meat, which seemed a kind of blessing. And we shared a drink of cheap bourbon that morning, a kind of *amen*, before he drove away.

❧

While I've been writing this, deer season has gone by. Brief storms have come and passed. The hills are dry. I went to my favorite spots and didn't see much sign. There was a little band of does in the thick brush on Boulder Creek, where I tracked a buck that I never saw. The last morning of the season, Linda and I rowed across Boulder Lake to try a patch of aspen and conifer isolated on the long, sage-covered moraine. Where we landed I saw a track, but it was tiny: an orphaned fawn or yearling doe. There were no deer in the little wood. And I don't mind.

I have no fear about lasting the winter, and can't pretend the disappointment of one who depends on hunting, but I can sense it. When we got home, I had a sandwich and fell asleep on the floor with the cat, in a patch of sun. And I dreamed of deer.

For the last week I've tried to see my home terrain as a deer sees. That imaginary leap focused my presence here in a way that idle or self-absorbed wandering never can. I hunted for a certain glossy, fat buck, and he eluded me, and so I praise him. With luck, I'll try again. Living where the animals live, this may come with the territory. I can't judge otherwise.

I don't know how a deer feels, looking at a coyote, or listening to me sing, but I can imagine. It's not enough to be a man, alone. The animals give me a whole other way to know this country, where I live, and a deeper way to share it. And so I praise their beauty and uncluttered lives.

If Elk Would Scream

❧

GEORGE N. WALLACE

I shot him badly.

Most people would have considered it a good shot—branches opening only one or two feet in front of me and elk crashing single-file through the edge of the timber a hundred yards away. You couldn't tell if there was a bull or cow or calf coming . . . it was like being in a shooting gallery abandoned to nature for a hundred years and overgrown, but with the targets still moving. Then I saw him, a royal bull elk, and shot reflexively with half a second of visibility. He seemed to go down or out of sight immediately.

As I ran across the clearing, never taking my eyes off that spot, cows and calves came crashing back across in front of me, startled by something up ahead. I wanted badly to watch them, but obeyed my grandfather's and now my own rule: "Don't lift your eyes from that spot." Suddenly he was there.

He tried to stand but fell, his back broken, his teeth bared in silent pain. If elk would scream, the woods would have fewer hunters. I thought, "I've never shot an elk this big; what a trophy. If I shoot him in the head, I'll ruin that mount. My God, man, he's suffering, shoot him. No! To hell with the trophy, you're just like the hunters you despise."

I shot him at the base of the brain. He quivered, looking ahead wide-eyed, straining, then slowly all the life force slid from those eyes and his muscles lost their tension. He took one last, long, slow breath and died. I cried inside and out.

❦

It began early, that beautiful day on Bull Mountain, close to the Wyoming-Colorado border. It was clear blue and gold-green, with the aroma of spruce-fir needles and rotting aspen leaves interrupted now and again by gusts of upslope breeze bringing the smell of wet sage.

The bull and I had started our relationship about an hour before and a thousand feet higher. I had been scouting, moving quickly all morning. There were several places with elk-on-the-move signs: deep, fresh prints four and five yards apart at times, with newly exposed dirt and pine needles lying loosely ahead of each track. Occasionally, these tracks would slow to a walk and be interspersed with round dung from elk too pressed to pause. You could follow tracks like these for hours and never get close. What I was looking for were those nice fresh coils of dung leisurely deposited amid oval patches of bent grass and salt-and-pepper tracks. After five hours, I had dropped into the edge of such a yard.

Elk under pressure feel secure only in unapproachable places. Flanked on two uphill sides by steep, dry ridges covered with dog-hair lodgepole pines, the terrain leveled out into a moist pocket fed by several seeps. Shade and moisture produced a dense stand of young fir with a visibility of five or ten feet. Openings near the seeps were luxurious with yellow grass.

A whole different metabolism kicks in when you come to a place like that. I crouched periodically to look through thinner lower branches. There were light tracks and sign everywhere. I moved one step at a time, placing each foot in between forest litter, eyes shifting from ground to foreground, straining. I have good eyes, bad ears, and a compensatory nose. It smelled different there in that patch. When the wind came I quietly removed my jacket to expose my wool shirt. I moved individual branches to one side and weaved slowly forward so as to avoid the sound of needle or twig on fabric. After twenty minutes and two hundred feet like that, I froze. The odor was strong. The hair on my neck stood up.

I held my breath, waiting, and then twenty yards in front of me elk exploded down the hill, not slipping and weaving through the timber but crashing over young trees before escaping onto narrow trails below. In seconds I was alone with only an occasional twig pop sounding far below. The air was filled with the essence of fir and the sweet heavy musk still rising from grass beds where it had been collected and pressed by seven thousand pounds of warm elk over several hours.

I hadn't moved. Having no view, let alone a shot, I knew these elk would run five miles if pursued, but perhaps slow to a walk in half a mile if they heard nothing in pursuit and hadn't smelled me.

Repeated encounters like this had given me a sense about how elk move in different kinds of terrain. After a moment or two I swung widely upslope and moved as fast as possible toward Trollop Creek. They would, I hoped, turn and move across the slope and then up the drainage about a hundred yards into the timber away from the stream—but on which side? I ran to a point where the forest above the stream opened up with larger trees, and I could see about two or three hundred feet.

I waited five minutes, and they didn't come. I remembered another pocket that lay along the stream below at the bottom of a steep cliff and rockslide. I went down the trail I had expected the elk on, a bad idea, and as soon as I reached the pocket I heard them move and distinctly saw one large elk dropping from sight.

This was my first notion that this was a big bull herding his harem. They headed down toward aspen and visibility. This time I went more directly after them but still stayed upslope since I knew they wanted dark timber.

Running and leaping, making no pretense of being quiet, trying to sound like another stampeding elk—which sometimes works—I dropped a thousand feet in elevation with the elk until we came to a mix of fir, aspen, and clearing on broken terrain.

To stay in the timber they had to turn now, and I headed, breathing hard, up a little open promontory that would give me a commanding view. I had nearly reached the opening, when there they were. They had turned and were headed back up, charging single file through the timber on the other side of the clearing—cow, calf, cow, calf, calf, cow . . . bull.

✣

I want to sit here for another half hour with the elk, as if at the bedside of an old friend. Just sit as I have done before and try to figure out why it is I do this.

Kill and then mourn. Maybe it's my only chance, as Thoreau said, to get this close to some "hard matter in its home," so large and warm, smelling grand. A more developed rendering of whatever primitive reverence we feel when looking at a majestic head mounted in a museum or bar. But I can't sit. It is almost dark. Nancy is in school, I'm in school, Dave and Tom are eating more. This year we really need the meat. I would never waste an ounce of him. I want him to know that.

The sun is down, and I feel a chill on my sweaty back. My hands are deep inside him now in steaming blood and viscera. I feel the smooth, warm lobes of liver and remove them. I strain my thirty-six-inch reach all the way up to his diaphragm to cut the peritoneum that will release this mountain of viscera. The jays are already here. Half inside, I find the heart, cut it free, and cradle it in my hands. Grandpa Gallegos, more Indian than Spanish, used to cut off the tip of the heart and eat it at once. "This gives you the strength of the animal," he had said. Lungs free, I put my head and arms in his heart space and remove his esophagus.

Should I be sad? He lived better than most. He had the whole country to himself, had his own harem of eight cows—had lived five or six glorious years up here. He was certainly better off than the steers in my pasture. Here there are no sharp or electrified wire boundaries.

He wore no constricting band slowly cutting off the flow of blood to his testicles. He didn't stand corralled and knee-deep in snow and his own dung waiting to be fed, earmarked, dehorned, and injected, only to be herded, prodded, trucked, and knocked on the head at the end of two years.

Using all my strength I raise his head and shoulders slightly, draining most of the blood to where I can scoop it out. I wipe out the body cavity with my bandanna and case the exposed meat with a coat of blood.

It is near dark, and the dew, which soon will freeze, is forming.

Steam is still rising from his great muscles. The last life heat he gives up to heaven—to the crescent moon and evening star. Moving quickly now, spurred by the chill, I cut sturdy branches to spread the body cavity to the cool air and then cover the opening with boughs to keep out leaves and jays. Finally, I tie my bandanna to a branch above him to serve as a dubious coyote repellent.

Taking the folding saw, knife, heart, and liver, I descend to Trollop Creek. There I lay organs and tools in a cold pool to soak. Taking the heart, I gently knead out the remaining clotted blood, then the liver. I place them on a rock where they glisten in the moonlight. His heart rests; his blood begins its journey to the sea.

Climbing back up to the kill site, I pack the twenty-six pounds of heart and liver, gather other equipment, shoulder my rifle, and turn for a last look. A change has taken place. I see him as meat for the first time. Component parts—meat, hide, antlers, cape, divisible into quarters, loins, ribs, in turn divisible into steaks, chops, roasts, stew meat, sausage, and hamburger. About seven hundred pounds, less hocks and viscera, which we will pack out on our backs. Seven hundred divided by eight trips—eighty-seven pounds per trip, all uphill. It'll be ten o'clock by the time I make camp.

❧

Postscript, 1995: The heart of the (this) hunter looks for a piece of Eden. It feels right to hunt in a place where the land is healthy. When the buck is sneaking from his daybed, he should not at once have to jump a fence, cross a road, and be exposed by our activities on the land. He should be able to slip unseen, if he can, into wild tissue. The covey of quail that explodes from beneath the thicket of wild plum should have several other thickets to choose from in the remotely sensed seconds that follow. If arroyos or wetlands should lie between to confound the hunter's route, so much the better.

It is in the wild and healthy places that nature can both protect and occasionally spare us one of her wild creatures. Entering a healthy landscape we can allow the predator within us to stretch its legs and claim rightful membership as part of that ecosystem. The more we eliminate the wet and wild places from our farms and ranches, the more we dice and cut, spreading our homes and business deals over first the farms, then the hills above them, along all the lake shores and streams and into the forest, the less we will be able, in good faith, to pick up the shotgun or rifle and take to the fields that are left. Even if we do find a few relict patches that look healthy, we must know that the game we seek is cut off and more vulnerable to our presence now. We must wonder, at some point, if we still have the right.

The hunt described above took place in 1981. Since then, I find myself leaving the gun in the rack more and more, choosing instead the shovel and a bundle of seedlings to carry afield. Still hunting, I cradle the spade across my arm and quickly bring it to my shoulder when the rooster flushes. Still stalking, in the commissioners' hearing room, I listen to the sprawl-boosters talk about yet another proposed development in the wrong place and feel the predator in me stir, looking for a way to defend its territory of ten thousand years.

Dealing with Death

✿

M. R. James

My first shot breaks the great buck's back. He collapses heavily among the stunted pines beneath my tree stand, front legs flailing the brittle November grass and patches of old snow where he sprawls.

Biting at the shooting glove on my right hand, I free cold, wait-numbed fingers and fumble with the stiff haul line, lowering my weapon. Then I unsnap the buckle to my safety belt. Standing and drop-sliding down the white pine's trunk, I can hear only the harsh scraping of my heavy boots, the frantic thrashing of the stricken buck, and the wild pounding of my hunter's heart.

The deer has managed somehow to get his forelegs under him. He is dragging his ruined hindquarters behind him as I approach. The snow creaks tightly with each step, and I see the buck's ears acknowledge my presence although he doesn't turn to look at me. I am thankful for that.

Easily overtaking the struggling deer, I move beside him, hold for the lungs, and shoot him again through the chest. He paws briefly at the frozen ground and tries to rise, twin streams of vapor trailing from the wounds in his side. The buck's final breaths cloud the cold evening air. Feeling more sadness than elation, I step aside and watch him die.

When his struggling ceases, I move to him and grasp a heavy, bone-white antler beam, turning his head to rest it in a more natural position. Kneeling, I stroke his rut-swollen neck and thick shoulder, my fingers feeling the fading warmth while smoothing the ruffled pelage. An empty, spreading sorrow tempers any satisfaction. But I know he has had his chance.

I first saw this buck a week or more ago at the onset of rut. He was halfheartedly trailing a slender doe through a light rain that would turn to snow before nightfall. I drew on him twice, perhaps three times in all, but I did not shoot. The range was long, beyond my self-imposed limit for consistent accuracy. So I simply watched admiringly from my stand in the pine, hoping for another chance.

It came two days ago. The great buck, this time in the company of four does, passed beneath me at less than forty yards—but purposefully on the move. Again I drew, swung briefly with him, hesitated, and merely watched him trot out of sight. Afterward, the memory of his wide rack haunted me. Yet I knew I was right again to let him go.

Then, only short minutes ago, I heard a deer walk out of the woodlot to my right. A tall pine, a twin to the one containing my stand, hid the animal until it was nearly under me. A flash of antler shouted "Buck!" seconds before he stepped into the opening beneath me. I recognized him in an instant. At less than twenty yards there was no mistaking this buck. And as he stopped to look back, I shot quickly—hitting high, nearly missing him after all but breaking his back instead—ending it forever for both of us.

It is nearly dark by the time I wrestle the buck into position at the head of a nearby ravine and field dress him. My arms, bathed to the elbows in hot blood, steam in the faint light as I retrieve his heart and liver, slippery warm and heavier than you might think, stand, and begin the uphill hike from the pine grove toward the buttery rectangle of my kitchen window glowing in the near distance.

I haven't taken a half-dozen steps when I see them and stop. Two—no, at least three—shadowy does stand silhouetted along the fence line, staring downslope toward me. They are posed as rigidly as concrete deer on a suburban lawn. I can feel their eyes on me. I can sense their acknowledgment of the buck's death. And, standing there, I share their loss. But I know the seed of the great buck is in them. Somehow for me that makes his death more acceptable.

Then, ignoring the silent Cervidae trio, I continue purposefully uphill through the cold, late-fall darkness, gripping the deer's cooling organs like some Stone Age savage returning to his cave, wondering if I can ever kill again but knowing full well I can . . . and will.

❧

I first watched an animal die when I was six, maybe seven. And I remember it still.

There was a crisp crack from the .22. I jumped. The steer staggered but retained its footing. Wide-eyed, I stared at the small, black hole centered in the beast's forehead near a swirl of white hair. Then the steer rolled its own widening eyes and took a single step before dropping to its knees in the dusty barnyard.

A man in overalls stepped near and laid his knife's thick blade along the steer's throat beneath the jaw. His hand jerked and blood geysered, darkening the bright steel and staining the thin denim of wash-whitened pants.

"Gotta cut the throat while his heart's still pumping," the farmer explained. "Little rifle don't kill right off. The animal's dead but don't know it. He'll go down for good when he runs outta blood. Meat tastes better if a critter is bled 'fore he dies."

That steer fed us through the fall and into the winter. I ate its flesh eagerly, yet I remembered the pools of dark blood slowly soaking into fine barnyard dust and how a heavy, metallic smell lingered even after the red turned to black.

Catching a chicken for Sunday dinner was part of farm life, too. A straightened wire coat hanger with a hook twisted in one end was a surefire chicken catcher. You simply walked into the pen, into the scattering flock flowing before you like a wave of water kicking in some pond's shallows on a summer day, reached out with the hanger, hooked a fryer by a leg, and drew the squawking bird close enough to grab by the feet. Then you carried it to the stained chopping block, positioned the bird just so, raised the hatchet, let it fall, and released the headless bird for its final, wing-flapping dash. I can still see the severed head lying in the grass by my scuffed boot, its yellow beak opening and closing in soundless protest, its lemony eye dulling, blinking slowly while the bird's mind somehow registers the finality of my actions.

But I also remember the smell of fried chicken above plates heavy with mounds of mashed potatoes hidden beneath rivulets of ladled brown gravy, a warm slab of buttered bread drooping in one hand, a fork clutched in my other.

There on the farm, death was a part of life. Watching, causing death, to me, became as natural as life itself.

I shot my first rabbit when I was eleven. I carried a twelve-gauge pump through a picked soybean field and kicked the cottontail from the stubble where a combine had dropped a clump of brown stalks. The cottontail zigzagged away. The shotgun rose and bucked against my shoulder. An unseen scythe of lead pellets cut the rabbit down. We ate the rabbit that same day, spitting occasional shot onto the plate as we chewed the tender, pink meat.

Whirring bobwhite quail—handsome, white-faced cocks and yellow-cheeked hens—dropped amid puffs of feathers beyond my shotgun's moving barrel. Rusty orange fox squirrels, their mouths and forepaws stained brown from walnut husks, fell among cuttings in the dead leaves beneath nut trees where they had come to feed. Greenheads, jumped from ice-rimmed drainage ditches, cartwheeled into the cattails while my gloved hands jacked spent shells from the chamber and I sucked in sharp winter air with a tang of cordite. And I forever remember slogging from the pit in a muddy field of picked corn, a brace of giant Canadas tolling silently against my back with each step.

No whitetails lived nearby in those days. I was a college student before I hunted and killed my first deer. But I had learned my deadly business well. And those early dealings with animals and death prepared me for the cyclical business of life. Few people today are similarly blessed.

How can any man or woman, city born and bred, expect to know firsthand—to *understand*—that killing is a daily part of life for all of us? They know, of course. But a lack of thoughtful interest, even outright denial, is easier without any personal involvement. Such people are safely distanced from the death of the meat they eat, the leather they wear. Unlike me, they have never watched a steer or chicken die. Unlike us, they have never killed for themselves. There is no blood on their soft, white hands.

They pay someone else to do their killing. The veal cutlet on the platter is simply meat, not a brown-eyed, milk-fed, living and breathing calf born and raised for the sole purpose of slaughter somewhere out of sight behind concrete-block walls. There is no blood, urine, and fecal matter mingling on the polished aisles of grocery stores. There are no steaming piles of intestines, no sounds of hide being ripped away from muscle, no odor of death in the conditioned air. No, the veal they eat appears miraculously among other choice cuts of meat, wrapped in sanitary cellophane, weighed and priced by the pound, waiting in stainless-steel coolers behind whispering glass doors. Not dead animals. Meat.

And today's fried chicken comes similarly prepackaged or in candy-striped cardboard boxes. There are no headless bodies doing their death dances. No hands reaching into the warm abdominal cavity, fingers pulling entrails and organs free. No scalding water loosening feathers while filling the air with that cloying wet-chicken smell. Not dead birds. Meat.

Again, how can anyone who hasn't seen and touched death know or understand? I know, in fact, that they cannot. And I realize that each successive sheltered generation in turn widens the growing chasm between man and the land. Between those of us who kill and those who are mere consumers. Users.

Righteous modern man says, "Let us call ourselves 'civilized' and pick and choose which animals live and which die and by what means. Let us pay others to kill the animals we need for food and clothing; however, let us look with disdain upon those who still kill for themselves as did their ancestors and their ancestors' ancestors."

Sadly, I note, we live in an increasingly hypocritical world. If the emotional issue is one of life itself, I ask, does not the calf waiting in the feedlot surely value its existence as much as the deer standing in the forest shadows? Yet what choice or chance does the fatted calf have when human wisdom determines it should die? And how many calves ever escape their prescribed fate? Compare the calf with a fawn, born free yet fated by nature to almost certainly die a violent death. Such is the way of wild things. So what is it, I muse, that somehow makes veal acceptable table fare while venison is not? If it is not a matter of life, it surely must be the means of death.

Walt Disney lied to all of us. Brutal death is a daily part of life in wild places. Bambi is an anthropomorphic children's story. Deer do communicate, but they do not talk to one another in human voices. Any animal sound it is possible to name or imitate—the snort, howl, grunt, bleat, bark, roar, cough, or mew—is a poor substitute for human speech, just as the stamping of a hoof, the flick of an ear or tail, and the flashing of erectile rump hair are inadequate substitutes for human gesturing or posturing.

And though wild animals recognize death, they neither anticipate its coming nor cognitively reason ways to avoid it. Maternal instruction, innate instinct, and firsthand experience based on trial and error may be excellent tools of survival; however, too many predators feed daily on the weak and unwary, and too many roadways are dotted with the unrecognizable pulp of careless wildlife to credit wild things with self-preserving logic or thought.

Few wild animals die of old age. And their fate, their early death, is not cruel; it is simply the way of the wild. While some may call Mother Nature harsh, uncaring, savage, merciless, implacable, unrelenting—and worse—she defies all these humanistic accusations. Her world was around long before modern man, with his troubled conscience, stepped in. Quite likely it will be around after the last human animal joins the dodo and the dinosaur in the oblivion of extinction.

Despite our ever-changing, ever-indignant world with its growing ignorance of and indifference to the ways of the wild, I remain a predator, pitying those who revel in artificiality and synthetic success while regarding me and my kind as relics of a time and place no longer valued or understood. I stalk a real world of dark wood and tall grass stirred by a restless wind blowing across sunlit water and beneath star-strewn sky. And on those occasions when I choose to kill, to claim some small part of nature's bounty for my own, I do so by choice, quickly, with the learned efficiency of a skilled hunter. Further, in my heart and mind, I *know* the truth and make no apology for my actions or my place in time.

Others around me may opt to eat only plants, nuts, and fruits. Still others may employ faceless strangers to procure their meats, their leathers, their feathers, and all those niceties and necessities of life. Such is their right, of course, and I wish them well. All I ask in return is that no one begrudge me—and all of us who may answer the primordial stirrings within our hunter's souls—my right to do some of these things for myself.

In the Snow Queen's Palace

❧

MARY ZEISS STANGE

The ancient Norsemen called her Skadi, "the Dark One," Goddess of Winter and Mother of the North. Only she could love the tundra expanse where, in her element, she danced snowstorms into being. Huge furry white hounds pulling her ice-crystal sled across the drifted plains and through snow-canopied forests, Skadi aimed her icicle arrows with skill and precision. Huntswoman extraordinaire, she chose her quarry carefully, with an eye to the tender young ones. One chilling shot to the heart was all it took to make them hers, forever.

Yet the Norse did not regard Skadi with fear or loathing, awesome as her power was in its glacial finality. No doubt they recognized that some darkness is the inevitable cost of human existence—as inevitable, indeed, as the blizzards of northern winters, as certain as death itself.

It takes a southern imagination, one trained in the seasonless sameness of the Mediterranean, to concoct a heaven of sweetness and light, an unnatural realm where death has no dominion. And so, early Christian missionaries turned Skadi, the benevolent rescuer of those too young or too weak to suffer the rigors of winter, into the malevolent Snow Queen. It was she, they said, who tempted children away from home, captivated them, turned their tender little hearts to ice.

The stuff of fairy tales, you say? Twentieth-century rationality would have it so. Yet a primal imagination still flickers in the heart of the modern-day hunter. There is wisdom in the ancient legend of the winter goddess. It is a wisdom born of hunting in northern climes, where extremities shape experience, where nothing comes easily except, perhaps, the drawing of a last breath.

❧

The winter of 1985–86 brought record-breaking cold to the northern Great Plains. Beginning early in November, an unremitting flow of arctic air swept down from Alberta into the Dakotas and eastern Montana, bringing early snow cover and daily high temperatures around ten below zero, when the sun was shining. At night, the thermometer regularly plunged to thirty, forty, fifty below. On still days, the air itself felt frozen. When the wind blew, the congealed air shattered into myriad invisible particles, minuscule projectiles that pierced through layers of clothing and found their way through the tiniest cracks . . . Skadi's arrows, a settler from an earlier time might have mused.

The first Europeans who tried to make a living off this land were, after all, well acquainted with the ways of the Snow Queen. Winters are typically harsh in this country. Today, long-abandoned homesteads dot the countryside, bearing mute testimony to the cold, dark, and open despairing winters their inhabitants must have endured.

This landscape is scarcely more forgiving now than a century ago. Driving the gravel highway in the southeastern corner of Montana, one passes a reminder of the tenuousness of living in these parts. Before a cluster of now-vacant buildings that once formed a settlement with town hall, school, and post office, hangs a large and carefully crafted wooden sign. It reads simply, "Albion: 1914–1964." Did Albion's demise have something to do with the winters here?

So I would have believed in November 1985, though the extreme chill of that season seemed oddly appropriate to me. My mother had died horribly the preceding spring, after a long struggle with cancer. In the fall, my thirteen-year-old cat also developed cancer; I'd had him put to sleep in October. I was overworked and underpaid, doing a one-year stint teaching English at a state college in western South Dakota. My husband, Doug, meanwhile, was between teaching jobs and frustrated about it. We were as near a subsistence economy as we had ever been, or hope to be again, living close to the bone. Hunting had never been mere sport to me, but in these circumstances it took on a special urgency, not only because we needed the meat (we hunted for that every year) but because it lent some degree of normalcy, or sanity, to a world otherwise gone askew.

So the weather, brutal as it was, could not keep us indoors as the end of deer season drew near. It may have been a matter of not giving in, when the conventional wisdom would have been to settle down by a cozy fire with a brandy and a good book. But the wisdom of hunters is in any case unconventional. Better to risk frostbite and endure what could only promise to be, in physical terms, an utterly miserable experience, than to let deer season slip by for another year. With subzero temperatures the day-to-day norm, it seemed more reasonable to be out braving the same elements as the deer than to be shut up, unnaturally, indoors. There has to be, between hunter and hunted, more than a fair-weather kinship.

On the day before Thanksgiving, Doug and I set out for a place not far from Albion, public land along the Little Missouri River where we had frequently seen mule deer in the trees hugging the shallow riverbank. We drove, mostly in silence, in the predawn darkness, our breaths frosting the windshield. As we neared our destination, the day gradually came on, sunrise in the form of a soft shimmering of light through the crystalline air. It would be an overcast day, and bitingly cold.

We were hunting antlerless deer, having both filled our "A-tags" earlier in the season. Since this was a hunt for meat, and since safety dictated limiting our outdoor exposure, this outing had a no-nonsense feel about it. Doug brought the pickup to a stop and cut the engine. Staring ahead through the windshield, on which lay a fresh veneer of frost from our suffused exhalations, he sighed after a moment or two, "Come on, let's get this over with."

Roused from the fairly comfortable reverie into which I'd slipped in the relative warmth of the cab, I reluctantly opened my door and, though I had known it was coming, was stunned by the assault of numbing cold on my face.

As the daylight increased, so did the wind. We would need to walk a broad arc across wide-open pastureland in order to get downwind of the deer we felt reasonably sure would be lingering along the creek that feeds the river there. Even with the wind at our backs, the cold was excruciating. Doug remarked that he thought the tears in his eyes must be freezing; my eyelids, too, scraped when I blinked. Breathing was difficult, virtually impossible when facing into the wind. The sun, a translucent disk, was retreating into the frigid sky. Snow would be falling before long.

After several hundred yards of crunching through ice-encrusted grass, we sprinted along a fence line toward the creek bed. Skidding down an embankment where the fence dipped toward the creek bottom, we were suddenly brought up short by what lay ahead: a little fawn, curled as if asleep, snugly nestled in the snow drifted against a fence post. The tiny deer was frozen solid. It might have died days, or mere hours ago. Doug knelt and stroked the fawn as one might a cat or dog found napping by the woodstove. We kept a few moments' quiet vigil; a little death like this could not go unmarked, unmourned. Then we continued down toward the creek.

It was a relief to descend into a prairie cut, between the sheltering walls of the creek. Ordinarily, one of us would have walked the meandering creek bottom while the other walked the rim on the alert for deer jumping ahead. But today was a day to err on the side of prudence, so we stayed together, the wind whirling overhead.

With miles of uninterrupted rangeland extending east and west of the Little Missouri, this waterway is a major deer run, providing not only shelter but an escape route from danger. Yet there were surprisingly few tracks or other deer sign here. We worked our way slowly, quietly along. I became aware that aside from the dead fawn, a couple of shivering magpies were the only wildlife we had seen.

At one point, where the creek doubles back on itself, there is a small grove of ash and poplar. Rounding a curve in the creek, we came within sight of a stand of thicker cover, and there we spotted four deer—a small buck, a rather large doe, and two fawns. They knew we were there, scarcely a hundred yards off, but they remained motionless, looking in our direction. We continued to weave cautiously through the creek bed toward them. When we were within fifty yards, we eased up the bank and into the open. Still, the deer stood as if frozen in space and time.

Stressed to the limits of endurance by so much cold so early in winter, the animals were conserving every bit of energy they could.

This helped account for the absence of deer sign in the creek; this little group probably never strayed from these trees if they could possibly avoid it.

We stopped perhaps twenty-five yards from the deer. They began edging away, clearly reluctant to expend the precious energy they would need to flee. They were, in effect, trapped by their instinct to survive. In such a situation, shooting was unthinkable. We stood as motionless as the deer. Then, exchanging a quick glance and a wordless nod, Doug and I turned away and tracked across the snowswept pasture in full view of the unmoving deer, without looking back.

Circling back to the creek, we followed a different branch now. It was midmorning, and our own energy reserves were ebbing. Taking a shortcut back to our pickup, we started across a stubble field toward the fence line we had walked along earlier. Almost immediately, we spotted some deer at the far end of the field, several hundred yards off. No more than indistinct shapes, they appeared and disappeared, phantoms in the now thinly falling snow. With the wind in our favor and the snow as much camouflage for us as for them, we proceeded along the fence until we were perhaps two hundred yards away. Steadying my 30/06 on a fence post, I focused the scope and saw a doe, another doe, a fawn, another fawn.

Teeth chattering and my right hand burning with cold (I had to remove my deerskin mitten in order to shoot), I thought about the fawn we had seen curled peacefully in the snow, about those deer paralyzed for sheer survival in the trees. "I'm taking the one farthest to the left," I whispered to Doug, who was also aiming his rifle. I placed the crosshairs for a heart shot and fired. Doug's shot came an instant later.

We killed the two fawns.

The Hunting Problem

✿

BRUCE WOODS

The killing bothers me.

Even so, I haven't stopped hunting. Killing is, after all, the only way to make meat, and I enjoy meat. Raising grain kills, too. Every additional acre in cultivation is an acre not available as wildlife habitat, an acre lost to indigenous flora, an acre that loads another chamber in humanity's slow game of pesticide roulette.

But that's the stuff of rationalization, of apologia; I'm after more elusive game here. If the killing bothers me, what exactly is there about hunting that I like (or need) enough to cause me to tolerate the resulting deaths? What return do I get for my discomfort?

How, too, am I reimbursed for the hundreds of hours I spend each year on rifle practice and on preparing, component by component, the most accurate ammunition I'm capable of; on working out with bow and arrow, computing and extending the maximum distance at which I can invariably put an arrow into a circle the size of a deer's heart/lung area; on the constant exercising of my ability to estimate ranges, something that I practice almost subconsciously whenever I walk anywhere; or on scouting the woods before and after hunting season, attempting to reconstruct the activity of animals from the tiny clues left behind by creatures that owe their lives to their elusiveness?

There are a few relatively easy answers. I hunt, despite the killing, because it puts me in the outdoors during its most beautiful seasons and in its most lovely environments. I hunt for the chance to observe truly wild animals without contaminating their activities by making them aware that they're being observed. And I see many, many animals while hunting that I don't, for one reason or another, attempt to kill. (In the past year of bowhunting, for example, I've released one arrow; the results are in my freezer, which is emptying week by week, an hourglass to the upcoming deer season.)

I hunt, and force myself through the training that I feel any hunter must have, because hunting reminds me that I do have a home in this world. One of my favorite of Gary Snyder's poems, "By Frazier Creek Falls," includes the lines, "We can live on this earth / Without clothes or tools!" Gary reminds me that we were designed, by God, evolution, whatever, to survive and thrive upon the wilds of this planet. And hunting allows me to make use of those aspects of my design. Because I hunt, I know what my local whitetails are likely to be feeding on with each change in season; I know how to read tracks and picture each footstep of the animal at the end of them, to learn something of its size and condition through telltale strands of hair or fur rubbed into rough bark, to decipher the daily diary of feces, and—yes—to translate the bright dribbles and spews of a blood trail.

Because, you see, the real answers to the hunting problem aren't easy.

It has been said that we don't hunt to kill, but kill to have hunted. That's true, as far as it goes. The philosopher Ortega y Gasset speculated that "the only adequate response to a being that lives obsessed with avoiding capture is to try to catch it." There's some truth in that, too.

But perhaps not truth enough to justify the killing. To do that, I have to follow the trail into the swamp, to the place where Hemingway said things become tragic.

Because beyond the quest for healthful meat or curiously fulfilling sport, and culminating the pursuit and the always sudden and magical appearance of the animal, I think the core of my love of, my need for, hunting is found in the primitive, by which I mean ancestral, ecstasy felt at two moments.

I mentioned before that many animals are passed up by hunters. The reasons for this are varied. The shot might be too difficult to bring off with confidence; the hunter could decide to wait for a larger, older animal; or the hunter might simply not be emotionally ready, at the time that the animal shows, to take the irreversible step of deciding to attempt a killing.

But when I am ready, when the range and position of the animal presenting itself are correct, when I'm sufficiently confident of my equipment and abilities, when all of this is as it should be, that moment of decision, marked by the sudden knowledge that I am going to attempt to kill, is overwhelming and even addicting.

We often say, in the grip of great emotion, that we "forget everything." From the decision to shoot until the collapse of the trigger, until the freeing of the arrow, I am truly not aware of the frustrations of my daily job, my hopes and fears for my family, or even the familiar aches and awkwardness of my body. Consciousness becomes concentrated into a laser-focused bond between the eye and the animal. At such moments I am as pure a creature as I'll ever be, involved in an act of monumental seriousness. It really has little to do with sport as the term is used today, and it sure as hell isn't a game. It combines the delicious, fearful anticipation of shouldering a great responsibility with the euphoria of discovering that you can, for however brief a moment, bear its weight.

And then I also hunt for the moment after the shot. Because, and I must face this, too, there is a primitive sort of triumph in having killed; the hand reaches out beyond the body to touch with terrible magic, to make food. The war of celebration and regret that defines such moments leaves me awash with emotion, hyperaware of colors and scents and feeling physically lighter, as after extraordinary sex or a purging cry.

So now we must turn our attention to the event in between these defining moments. The success of the hunt demands that it, the killing, be gotten over with as quickly as possible. That's the reason for the scouting and study of natural history, the regular, disciplined physical and mental training. Because killing is always ugly, and if poorly done it can forever poison the moment of anticipation with doubt, replacing triumph with self-disgust.

Killing to eat is too ugly, in fact, to leave to others all of the time. That would be a shirking of responsibility akin to, in my mind, forcing a subordinate to tackle a firing that's your responsibility, or using the telephone to tell a lover you have a venereal disease.

You might say that the ugliness of the killing, and the dipping of my hands into the hot, reeking, slippery-organed soup of it, is the price I pay to remain, as I choose to be and as my body's design directs me to be, an omnivore.

Sure, the killing bothers me. It's supposed to. And if it ever stops bothering me, I pray I'll be big enough to let go of hunting forever. Because to hunt and not despise the killing would be to become not an animal but a form of human that is already far too common in the festering cities of this world.

Taking a Life

❦

MIKE GADDIS

A venerable friend closed a recent letter with a troubled thought: "We're off to Mattamuskeet tomorrow. We have to shoot steel shot. I can't find any particular fault with that, considering. But I couldn't find any steel shells for my old sixteen, and I'm not willing to shoot steel in any of my good doubles. So, I think I'll take the middle seat in the blind, just watch, and drink coffee. Not a bad idea. I couldn't shoot a swan anyhow, don't want to shoot another goose, and don't care a whole lot about shootin' a duck! Wonder what's happening to me—I must hold the boyhood beanshooter record for songbirds and vermin."

I understood perfectly. He wasn't saying he wouldn't shoot, just that it wasn't the first consideration any longer. Such feelings increasingly pervade my own thoughts. By the time I make my friend's vantage, I'm sure my feelings will be as intense as his. I'm not sure, though, that this is cause for worry.

❦

On a bitingly cold morning last fall, I shot a good white-tailed buck. Approaching to where he had fallen, I felt swelling inside me the mix of accomplishment and remorse I have almost come to dread. There are no apologies for this. I met him fairly on his own terrain, and the kill was clean. Such an experience is gratifying to a hunter, though it involves death.

Yet the day that will return most vividly to mind will be another from the same season, when I didn't raise a gun but merely accepted the privilege that made me an observer. That day I was working a field-trial dog from horseback. It was unseasonably balmy, with great gusts that roared and bullied their way through the trees in the barren December woods. To gain shelter, I followed a deep-woods property line en route to a promising bean field. The wind continued to howl, and hearing was impossible above the gale.

Halfway there, a tremendous blast nudged my horse forward, and lingering oak leaves undaunted by fall were ripped from their death hold and hurled by in a disorienting swirl. In the same instant, I became conscious of a deer. Not just a deer, but an antlered buck. He rose from his bed a scant thirty feet away, took a few bounding leaps, and stopped behind a bit of cover. I could imagine his mind racing, fighting for a signal from his bewildered senses. I rode a few yards farther for a better line of sight. The buck moved, too, but not to bound away as I had anticipated. Instead, he lay down at the base of a huge oak, melting himself into the mute tones of bark, stretching to full length, and dropping his antlers to his neck.

Intrigued, I rode closer, thinking that he was injured and weak. This was not the case. As I neared the tree, he started to get up. The movement was quick and coordinated. The eyes were bright. But once again, he changed his mind and eased slowly back.

I sat spellbound within six feet of a legal buck with a handsome spread of heavy, eight-point antlers, he looking at me and I at him, each in disbelief of the other. I had never been so close to a live buck of this caliber. His russet coat gleamed with the bloom of peak condition. I admired each polished tine of his antlers as I might a wall mount. I thought of my gun. It rested in the saddle scabbard at my leg. As quickly, I dismissed the thought. I would not have shot him under the circumstances had he broken every record in Boone and Crockett's book.

The buck made no further move to rise, and I sat watching until my dog doubled back to call me on, and I turned to go with her. He remained as I left him until lost from view.

I rode in distraction for several minutes, thinking about what had happened. The wind had robbed the buck of his normal faculties; he took the best alternative at hand. Had I not been watching him, I would have ridden by unawares. The ability of a whitetail to evaporate in sparse cover is uncanny. When the buck changed his mind about leaving the second time, it must have been a submissive reaction to the horse.

I would never have believed it could happen. I never expect it to happen again.

Over the years, hunters who truly love the woods and wild things come to revere such moments of privilege. As often as not, no shot is fired.

❧

Alvin Conner is the closest thing to a mountain man this century can muster. In body or spirit, he spends every conscious hour somewhere in the Uwharrie backwoods of Randolph County, North Carolina. He's pushing eighty now and has hunted doggedly all those years. In his territory, his exploits have become fireside tales. A wealth of game has fallen to his gun. Yet he spends more time hunting and less shooting these days. He's bringing along some grandsons. His pleasure is in watching them attempt the things he's done—in teaching them how. When we talk, it's different now. Rather than dwell on shooting conquests, he tells of the duel between a red-tailed hawk and a gray squirrel on a pristine morning last spring, of watching a doe give a fawn its first lessons in stealth. This relentless man of the quest has mellowed.

Not only that, but the last time I saw Jeff, the eldest grandson, he began the conversation by marveling at the seven-point buck that had spent the morning polishing the velvet off his antlers within a few feet of the stand. The buck he didn't shoot. He could have started with the one he had taken, because it was among the best that season. He did get around to that, as should be. The point is, his priorities were in the right order. Somewhere between Jeff and his grandpa, something's working.

It takes time and character to come to Al Conner's perspective. It's born of respect, respect for life and living. Not the least of this is self-respect. If that seems a paradox in one who has chosen to hunt and kill, it's no less true. Hunting, fundamentally, is a life-and-death proposition. While the urge is almost involuntary, the action is not. There's a conscious decision behind the trigger. Handling it responsibly demands maturity.

I've grown to accept maturity as a product of age, for the years are revealing. It is a point I would not have had time for in the rush of my boyhood days, when I too wreaked havoc with a slingshot or BB gun; one I never would have conceded in the cockiness of my teens or even fully appreciated in the growing awareness of my thirties. But it was there, waiting for me.

Things come back now, across the years: my Grandpa Betts, on the close of a day at quail, telling me, "I know more than a man probably ought to know about the *how* of things. What I need to know more of is the *why*."

Inescapably, our middle years become introspective. The edge is off; the fever of youth has become manageable. We can enjoy a few achievements but can't bask there, for there are miles left in the journey. The questions become larger, the answers more elusive.

Most sobering of all, perhaps, is that for maybe the first time we can look down the road and sense that it has an end. Death becomes a growing presence. We contemplate our own. Suddenly, it dawns that life is extremely fragile. Suddenly, it is evident that no one ever has clear title to life. It's simply an open-ended loan, to be called without notice at fate's whim. But there are places yet to go, things left to do. Life grows dearer, is guarded more closely, savored more fully. For many who hunt, these revelations bring a deep quandary. There is a growing reluctance to take a life, faced with the enlightened appreciation of our own.

Feeling so, I ask myself if there will come a time when I quit hunting. The answer must be no. I love the frost on a promising November landscape, the slavering excitement of a brace of pointing dogs, the tightness in my throat as I walk to their first point, the unnerving rise of the birds, the tender retrieve of feathers to hand.

I love the baying of hounds under a hunter's moon, the rustle of fallen autumn leaves under my feet, running with wild abandon through the half-light toward the lure of the tree bark, the riotous din of the dogs, the heft and feel of the burlap sack against my back.

I love the careening whine of shearing ice in the predawn of a hard freeze as I clear the way for a waterfowl set, the poetic harmony of a barking skein of geese in the pastels of daybreak, cupped wings over decoys, the shivering retriever against my leg, the loyalty and power of his response at my bidding toward a fallen bird. I love the quest and conquest and all the traditions and trappings of the sporting life. Nothing else has so completely captured my soul.

Yet, like my friend, I remain troubled. To hunt is to take a life. Where is the rationale that puts that right with the conscience of my middle years?

The antihunting faction has frequently attributed human traits and emotions to game birds and animals in its appeal for support. It is an effective political strategy, but forty years afield tell me it falls short of fact. The behavior of wild creatures is driven largely by instinct, and there is neither the time, need, or inclination for the deep reasoning and contemplation through which human emotion is defined and classified. But neither can I accept the premise that much of the hunting establishment seems to expound—that life other than human is devoid of feeling and is, individually, of small consequence. I abhor the surging tide of crass commercialism that has neutered sporting ethics and, worse, uses game and fish as mere pawns in a scheme of mercenary advantage.

What I do believe is that the life of wild creatures has both dimension and sensual fulfillment. I believe the bond between a pair of Canada geese, though not love by human standards, has similar elements and that each finds pleasure, confidence, and security in the presence of the other. Are those words too emotionally suggestive? Then perhaps the problem is the limits of our own language in defining behavior that seems so similar to behavior we describe with emotional words. Suddenly, we border on a challenge to our self-appointed superiority.

The mourning dove softly moaning in the greening of spring is sensuously happy. The whitetail basking in a mountainside "hot spot" on the first clear day after a winter storm is at peace with its world. A black bear with an arrow deep in its chest senses pain. What are the human emotions of love, hate, avarice, and greed but sensual experiences that have been labeled?

We stand alone, though, in our ability to contemplate the loss of life, to understand its finality, to comprehend what's forever gone. Out of respect and self-respect, those of us who hunt must apply this greater wisdom on behalf of the wild things we pursue. This is the responsibility decency calls us to acknowledge and practice rather than push aside. For it is inescapable. The life we will take is not all that different from our own.

The necessity for a kill is never easily explained by one who hunts, as the explanation must be understood by another who doesn't. Surely the urge and emotion spring from instinct as honestly and purely as do the wiles of the chosen quarry. That those instincts should burn more strongly in some is likely a genetic property. Therein is grounds for neither persecution nor apology. In the absence of a kill, there is a void. As the relationship between a man and a woman rarely finds complete expression short of a physical sharing, the hunt is incomplete less possession of the prey. When you boil away the social pretext in either case, the respective behaviors are basic to man's bent for survival and conquest.

The philosophy I hold as truth. The reality of the kill comes harder. What becomes important ultimately is the bridge between.

I'll give you a case in point. Tommy Mock is a comfortable man with whom to share a day. Being outdoors with him is almost spiritual. He's from rural south Georgia, where a man's religion is important to folks. Tommy's is turkey hunting.

We spent several days after spring gobblers this past April. Most of it was invested in a dominant tom on his strutting zone in a broad expanse of open pasture. He roosted in or around the inundated timber standing in the beaver pond on the eastern edge, and a good bird he was. There were two other mature gobblers in the area, but his authority on this piece of ground had been settled. In the dawning minutes of a new day, he proclaimed it so, his heavy gobbling overpowering the undercurrent of songbird chatter like percussion notes in a woodwind arrangement. Come flydown time, he simply pitched out and glided into the pasture to his strutting post. To the south was leased land, beyond our means. West sprawled the barren pasture. The challenge was to call the old gentleman across the pasture to a dark and foreboding edge. We'd have to toll a few hens along to get him started because he was doing pretty well with the ladies where he was.

To me he seemed invincible, and I said as much. Tommy didn't answer, but he didn't have to. His wry grin, almost apologetic, was reply enough. The stage was set exactly as he would have it. That's why we were there.

Our commitment was total. Mornings we parked the truck a

quarter of a mile away and stole to the pasture edge well in advance of day. We took every pain and precaution. First we played it straight. Then we added the hen decoy. Tommy's a better than fair hand on a turkey call. He offered the old gobbler every seductive pleading he could muster. The old man came back with a gobble at every beckon. Haughty, swollen, and spread under the stage lights of sunrise in the natal swell of spring, he was magnificent. But he wasn't buying. We watched and waited for hours while he put the jakes in their place and bred the hens, then we tried again. He turned us down cold.

My last morning there, Tommy gave me an option on another bird. But by then, I was vested too. Predawn found us at the pasture. This morning something was different. We didn't hear his deep gobble, just the baritones of his rivals. Shortly they flew out and cautiously advanced into the field. We called, and they responded. At least they *were* on the way, until a trio of hens arrived with a better offer.

"We might as well try something drastic," Tommy said. "We're not doin' anything like this! I'm goin' way round the beaver pond and come in on those birds from the back side. If we get lucky, one of them may come your way. I don't know where the main man is."

I was left with orders to create a diversion of yelps every fifteen minutes or so. I'd been through about two runs of yelps when the big man opened up, not forty yards to my left. The first roll of gobbles left me breathing raggedly and trying to get my heart back down out of my throat. He gobbled steadily for the next half hour, still hung up in his roost tree. Apparently the old boy was so close he saw us put the decoy over the fence before day and elected to sit tight. I think the rival birds with his hens finally got his goat.

Tommy had to be somewhere near the gobbling bird. I knew what he would do, but it was a full hour before he was back and I got the story.

"I wasn't fifty yards from him when he gobbled the first time. It made my neck crawl! Took forty-five minutes for me to cover the difference, but I made it to the tree. He was in a big oak right on the edge of the pond. It took five minutes more to make him out. I had the gun on him."

"I didn't hear you shoot."

"I probably should have."

"I know why you didn't."

Even after all the work and frustration, Tommy didn't want the big tom on those terms. What he wanted was to call him fair and square across that open pasture. Unless and until that happened, the shooting could wait. He was a wise and grand old bird, and if he was brought to bag, it would have to be on a proper field of honor.

I had a long ride back from Georgia. I was traveling alone and had plenty of time to think. I spent hours listening to the dialogue in my restless mind. The experience with Tommy and the gobbler had brought me face to face with a man I'm beginning to recognize again and feel better about. The man is me, and maybe I'm not wandering lost after all.

It's just that I'm becoming more demanding about the conditions of a hunt, about the companions with whom I choose to share it and the dignity afforded whatever we're hunting. It is ever more crucial to me that the moment in which I take a life, while my own continues, be one I can approach and walk away from with self-respect. In the end, I answer to me, no one else.

❧

I'm out about as much as ever these days, but I don't push quite as hard, and I take less game. I never set out to keep score anyhow. It was never in me.

I'm no longer driven to prove myself endlessly. Hell, I've been there. Some of the things that make for a fine day outdoors I'm finding I never even noticed before.

"A vineyard is not judged by the strength of its harvest," my grandpa said, "but by the quality of its wine."

Now, I understand.

It Wouldn't Be the Same

✤

ROBERT F. JONES

My friend Edward Hoagland called one day with an intriguing suggestion. Though he's one of the finest nature writers in any language (*The Courage of Turtles*, *African Calliope*, *Balancing Acts*, and others), Hoagland doesn't hunt or fish. He'd been asked to review Howell Raines's new memoir, *Flyfishing Through the Midlife Crisis*, and wanted to check his understanding of certain angling terms.

Our discussion had gotten around to the subject of catch-and-release.

"A fisherman is basically a predator," Ted said, "and I'm wondering, can a predator's instincts really be satisfied just by hooking a fish and then letting it go?"

"Certainly," I said. "Nowadays I release nearly all the fish I catch. Sometimes I'll spend five or ten minutes reviving them after I've caught them, to make sure they're OK. There's no reason in the world—except ego—to kill, say, a tarpon or a bonefish. They aren't worth eating. Trout are delicious, of course, but they're still more valuable alive than dead. It's more fun to catch them than to eat them, and when you've reduced a trout to a pile of bones neither you nor any other angler can ever catch it again."

"Wouldn't the same be true in hunting?"

"I suppose so," I said, taken somewhat aback. "But there's no way you could do it."

"Why not?" he persisted. "You could use one of those laser guns like they have in carnival shooting galleries—you know, the kind that tells you instantly when you've hit the target. You've often said that the climax of the whole bird-hunting experience comes at the moment you actually hit the bird when it's in midflight."

Beep—you're dead?

"Trust me," I muttered lamely. "It wouldn't be the same."

Hoagland later included the notion of electronic bird shooting in his *New York Times* review of the Raines book: "Hunters have not yet had the chance to learn a hunting counterpart to 'catch-and-release,' but I suspect that by the turn of the century some entrepreneur will be earning millions with a radar or heat-seeking technology that tells a hunter when he has 'killed' a bird."

I've been pondering Ted's proposal ever since.

Why *wouldn't* zap-and-release bird hunting be as rewarding as the real thing?

Certainly, game birds are at least as valuable, both aesthetically and from a culinary standpoint, as "trophy" trout or even salmon. Some birds—ducks and woodcock in particular—are mighty thin in the air along their flyways of late, as scanty in numbers as trout in many eastern streams where bait fishermen have equal access with fly fishermen. By the same token, though for different reasons, wild quail are getting harder and harder to find, and a pen-raised bobwhite is to its wild namesake as a hatchery rainbow is to a stream-bred one: pale, puny, and stupid.

So too, for the most part, are the pheasants, chukars, Hungarian partridges, and other pen-bred game birds released by shooting preserves (at outrageous prices) for hunters to bang away at these days.

And for all the talk of "game cycles," most experts admit that the "highs" of each succeeding ruffed grouse cycle produce fewer birds than the previous high—a fact verified by the historical record. Frank Woolner, in his excellent book *Grouse and Grouse Hunting*, talked with an old Massachusetts market gunner of the late 1800s who told him that "350 birds a man was a fine season's bag." Nowadays even a fanatical grouse hunter—afield every day with a savvy dog and a crack shooting eye—would be hard-pressed to kill a quarter that many a season anywhere in New England or the Upper Midwest.

Though studies show that hunters kill only a small percentage of the wild birds that die each year—perhaps 5 or maybe as high as 10 percent—those few birds, if left alive, would undoubtedly breed more birds for the next season. And on and on and on . . .

Ergo: If no-kill angling can be rationalized by the greater aesthetic value and ever-lessening numbers of the truly wild fish available to breed, then so too could no-kill bird hunting.

Another consideration is public opinion, which as we all know is swinging ever more stridently against blood sports of every kind.

Twenty years ago I was hunting near my home, which was then in the northernmost reaches of New York's Westchester County. The area was still "country" in those days. It was late afternoon, and as I neared the two-lane road across from my house, the dog flushed a grouse which I killed in heavy cover. I went out on the road as the dog made the retrieve, and called him to me. I was just taking the bird from him when a school bus came around the corner and stopped to let off my children. The rest of the kids on the bus just gaped at me through the windows.

My God, what an appalling sight: a man with a smoking gun, his hands all dripping with blood, and a great hairy slavering brute of a dog dropping a dead, harmless little tweety-bird into those murderous meathooks! As the bus drove on past us, the kids pushed up their windows and booed us all.

The boos would be even louder today.

None of these schoolchildren, of course, had ever hunted—none but my own. Those kids didn't realize that the blood on my hands was from brier cuts, they didn't know what it took to knock down a bird in close, heavy cover, nor could they realize the amount of hard work it had taken to make the Labrador retriever a good gun dog. They didn't have an inkling of what our hearts felt—mine and the dog's—at the moment when the gun bucked against my shoulder and that bird puffed and tumbled and the burnt incense of gunpowder wafted back to us. And they never will, no matter how much we talk or write about it. The schools and the newspapers and television and the movies will see to that.

But just as no-kill fishing has altered the public image of the angler—from that of a leering, beer-guzzling, knock-'em-on-the-head trout killer to a gentle, Waltonesque, nature-loving yuppie wearing lots of neat gear—I have no doubt that the sort of zap-and-release bird hunting suggested by my friend Ted Hoagland would at least to some degree alleviate the venomous societal prejudice against us.

❧

Maybe I'm just an old stick-in-the-mud, but I say to hell with it.

The hunt is more than a gallery game. At its best (and at the risk of sounding absurdly uncool), let me say that I feel it can be a sacrament, combining in its ancient sequences—oddly ritualistic but never exactly the same—the basic mysteries of baptism, confirmation, absolution, transubstantiation, marriage, and extreme unction.

Think about it.

Each time we go afield, we're baptized anew in the fellowship of the natural world. I defy any bird hunter to tell me he doesn't feel blessed by the subtle changes that occur, day by day, almost hour by hour, in even the most familiar of his coverts. Shifting light, falling leaves, winds boxing the compass and changing the angles of a hunter's approach; rain, mud, snow, scorching sunlight—then the always astounding flush, a fresh revelation each time it occurs, though we've seen it a thousand times before. The bird wings out more swiftly than thought . . .

Each time we go afield, we're confirmed in our belief that this is where we rightly belong, pounding these hills or wading that swamp, shivering in the cold rustling confines of the blind, pushing through the thorns or pausing to catch our breath on the windswept hilltop, watching the indefatigable dog seek out the truths or falsities of the next thick covert . . .

Each time we go afield, we're absolved of the petty sins of our daily nonhunting round: of sloth, surely, for we work at the hunt if we're doing it right; of falsity, for there is only truth in the field (the lies may come later, of course, when we talk to our friends about it—but never forget, your dog knows); of greed, if we only shoot them on the wing; of hubris, if we make no excuses for missing; of cruelty, if we shoot straight and kill clean; of lust, if we love and respect the birds we kill; of despair, if we enjoy the bad days along with the good. We pay the penance for our sins in sweat and thorn slashes.

Each time we kill a bird, we die a little ourselves, and in that death renew our love for what we've killed. Each time we kill a bird, we pledge our eternal troth to it, as at a wedding altar. Each time we kill a bird, we anoint it with the oil of our compassion and pray for its soul on the Spirit Road.

And each time we partake of the flesh of the birds we've killed, we become one with their essence.

Hunting, like religion, is incomplete without death. Indeed it *is* a religion, older, deeper, and more visceral than Judaism or Christianity or even Islam, as old at least as the Pleistocene cave paintings of the Dordogne or Altamira. It has its own prayers, of thanks coupled with a plea for forgiveness each time we kill what we seek; its own dark sacraments and rituals and symbols: its own distinctive art.

That's why it's not a gallery game.

Why Men Hunt

❧

John Madson

Fifteen years ago, when my friend John Mitchell was writing *Bitter Harvest*, he solicited my views on hunting.

We spent most of a day in a johnboat on a Mississippi River backwater while he asked penetrating questions and I provided fuzzy answers. He finally observed that my perceptions of hunting were metaphysical—and he was right, supporting Voltaire's contention that "when the speaker and he to whom he speaks do not understand, that is metaphysics."

I once spoke at a seminar of biologists and offered some general, rather superficial reasons for why men hunt deer. They do so for many reasons, any one of which may be enough.

A common one, of course, is the meat reason. The woods are full of people who claim to be hunting for prime meat, although I've a hunch that this is a standard alibi for busting the first deer that comes along. Yet there are some real meat hunters—men who are pretty good at judging wild meat on the hoof, who have the patience and experience to carefully pick and choose, and who take pride in the quality of their venison. There are still a few old hands who will pass up a trophy buck for a plump little forkhorn—although they are often experienced hunters who have already taken their share of trophy bucks.

Then, of course, there's the trophy reason. In its shallowest context, it is simply an exhibitionist effort to display prowess and status. In a deeper context, it goes beyond that.

Aldo Leopold once observed that "poets sing and hunters scale the mountains primarily for one and the same reason—the thrill to beauty. Critics write and hunters outwit their game for one and the same reason—to reduce that beauty to possession."

Those trophy antlers on the wall may represent a hunter's effort not only to possess beauty, but also to keep something important to him from slipping away and being forgotten. And if the trophy testifies that here is a strong and skillful hunter—well, what's the use of denying it?

And so the great stag has been stalked and taken.

Ten thousand years ago the hunter might have stood by a fire and recounted the great deed to his clan brothers, while the old men nodded their approval and stripling boys back in the shadows listened in wonder. It hasn't changed much. The trophy hunter, the ethical killer of the great stag, or bear, or ram, still commands attention by the fire as he recites his deeds. His peers still salute him, the old men still nod and remember, and boys still dream of tomorrow's hunts.

Most of us will never kill the great stag. Yet we have all taken deer that held special trophy value for us, and such value is not always a measure of tine and beam. It may be just a measure of hard, solid hunting in which both man and deer conducted themselves well, so that neither was shamed.

Trophy hunting has been bitterly condemned for an alleged deterioration of a game stock by killing off the best males. Yet neither the mathematics of genetics nor the observed facts of breeding within wildlife populations add support to that contention. A five-by-five mule deer buck is nearing the end of his days and has already done his share of genetical work. Still, that is empty sophistry if the taking of that trophy is unethical—in which case it is not a trophy at all.

Companionship can be a strong element in hunting. For as long as men have hunted, they have banded into special hunting packs with their own taboos, traditions, and rituals. And sometimes the companionship and the rituals become more important than the hunt itself, and sometimes the greatest pleasure is in anticipation and recollection, with the hunt only serving to bond the two.

A considerable part of modern sport hunting (as with much of our daily living) is the exercise of technology. That is, the employment of gadgetry for its own sake. I plead guilty to that in part, for a fine rifle or shotgun plays a significant part in my enjoyment of hunting. I admire the skill and artistry that go into the making of such guns—but I am uninterested in any gun, however beautifully wrought, if I cannot shoot it well. I count myself as a good shot. When the day comes that my eyes and reflexes impair that ability, I will not hunt again.

Critics of hunting are fond of pointing out that wildlife has scarcely a chance against our highly efficient technology. But the fact is, wildlife has an edge of its own—and it is likely to be enhanced by our increasing dependence on gadgets and decreasing reliance on our legs, eyes, ears, patience, and the savvy that accrues from years of experience. A good working definition of a game species is one that is fitted with survival equipment enabling it to take advantage, while a genuine sport hunter is one constrained by ethics and respect to give advantage.

But as much as anything else, one of the greatest urges impelling such a hunter is his search for freedom, and for the genuine personal adventure inherent in such freedom. Just as game species may be the truest indicators of quality natural environments, so hunting can be an indicator of quality natural freedom.

Dr. Murdock Head told of a noted physician who was visiting an Adirondack deer camp for the first time. He was not a hunter; it was all new to him. As he stood by the cabin door one evening, watching hunters dress deer while their companions offered unsolicited advice, listening to the good laughter and easy talk, the doctor turned to his host with a look of sudden comprehension and said, "Why, these men are free!"

Pascal once observed that the virtue of hunting is not in possessing game but in pursuing it. By being absorbed in looking outward for game, "the hunter is absolved of the really insupportable task of looking inward upon himself." And so the hunter's eyes are directed outward instead of inward, and myriad nagging, worrisome concerns are overlain with the illusion of being part of an older, freer world.

I once asked an old river rat of long acquaintance why he was such a deeply committed hunter. He thought for a moment and replied, "Why—to git away from the house and git out amongst 'em mainly."

Homer once said much the same thing: "The hunter goes his way 'neath frigid skies unmindful of his tender spouse."

Theodore Roosevelt was far more diplomatic about it: "Sweetest little wife, I think all the time of my little laughing, teasing beauty . . . and I could almost cry I love you so. But I think the hunting will do me good."

(I know wives who would agree; hunting gets their husbands out from underfoot during a time of year when they're not much good around the house anyway.)

The genuine hunter is probably as free as it's possible to be in this technocracy of ours. Free not because he sheds civilized codes and restraints when he goes into the woods, but because he can project himself out of and beyond himself, out of and beyond the ordinary, to be wholly absorbed in a quieter, deeper, and older world.

You know how it is. When you go into the woods, your presence makes a splash and the ripples of your arrival spread like circles in water. Long after you have stopped moving, your presence widens in rings through the woods. But after a while this fades, and the pool of silence is tranquil again, and you are either forgotten or accepted— you are never sure which. Your presence has been absorbed into the pattern of things, you have begun to be part of it, and this is when the hunting really begins.

You can always feel it when those circles stop widening; you can feel it on the back of your neck and in your gut, and in the awareness of other presences. This is the real start of the hunt, and you'll always know when it happens and when you are beginning to hunt well.

There were those times when I was a kid, hunting and trapping and sometimes spending several days and nights alone in the woods, when I'd have a flash of insight that was often gone as swiftly as it came—a vague sense of what aboriginal hunters must feel, what real hunting, pure-quill honest-to-God real hunting is all about. One strong flash of this to a boy—one swift heady taste of an utter wild freedom and perception—is enough to keep him hunting all his days. Not just for meat or horns but for that flash of insight again, trying to close the magic circle of man, wildness, and animal.

Is bloodlust a prime motivation of hunting, as some of our critics contend?

The late Dr. C. H. D. Clarke pointed out that perverted and inadequate people may indeed hunt, but contended that this is not the story of hunting. The human investment of hunting with magic, he felt, was a logical development of being able to think about nature and wonder where the next feast was coming from. When the magic is truly embedded, it is part of our inheritance. Hunting still has (for some of us) its prehuman excitement and prestige, and its human magic, and when we hunt there is a deep satisfaction that comes from a contact with nature that is healthy and traditional. Bloodlust it is not.

The deepest fear of the primitive hunter is of offending the spirit of the game. Clarke once saw an old Eskimo who, when young, had been deliberately blinded by his fellow hunters. They were afraid because the man had been disrespectful to a caribou he had killed. For such a sin there had to be a terrible expiation. We do not do that anymore, nor do Eskimos, but the unethical hunter is at least uneasy—and if he is an Eskimo he may be afraid.

Sport hunting, Clarke went on, can surely put us inside the world of nature. The real hunter goes into that world of nature not as a casual onlooker, but as an active participant.

There are many uses of outdoor October, and I savor them all. I could drink that ale-golden month to its dregs and never touch a gun. But without hunting, some of the savor would be missing. Lovely and rich as autumn would still be, a certain condiment would be gone, and I think I know what that is. It is seeing grouse and pheasants and quail and mallards at close hand, as any predator might, and seeing how fine-tuned, ingenious, and intricate their responses to predation can be. I might watch game birds and animals at all seasons under a full range of conditions and yet never know them as I do when I am hunting them well and they are doing their usual fine job of parrying my thrusts.

Hunters may try to reduce their motives to such tangibles as trophies, meat, good dog-work, companionship, exercise, freedom in quality environments, or simply "adventure." Underlying all that, however, are deeply embedded reasons that neither hunter nor psychologist is really equipped to fathom.

Hunting's severest critics are much surer of themselves. The kindest thing they say about hunters is that we are cruel and dangerous children; at our worst, we are barbarians that revel in the joy of inflicting pain and death. And there is some truth in all of that. We cannot deny that such hunters do exist; to do so is to delude ourselves. On the other hand, the shrill antihunting critics seem unable to understand the motives that impel what I choose to call the "genuine hunter." That is, the person with a deep personal bond to the game he hunts and the habitats in which he hunts it. Such emotion can result only from the respect that grows from experience and reflection.

Our critics deplore hunting on an emotional basis, just as we hunters defend it. Each extreme would do well to share a more objective position. Both hunter and antihunter should be governed by sound biological principle. Hunting cannot be condoned if it is not based on biological management and does not demonstrate respect for game and the habitats in which it is hunted. On the other hand, hunting is best defended by adherence to sound biological principles and demonstration of a genuine respect for nature.

Why do men hunt? It goes far beyond anything I've said here. How can one explain the inexplicable? But after more than fifty years of hunting, I'm pretty sure of two things: that hunting is too deeply rooted in the metaphysical to allow clinical examination, and that it's a happy man who keeps his youthful appetite for that sort of metaphysics.

The Hunter's Spirit

❧

JIM POSEWITZ

It was only an image, the shadow of a big man moving through blowing snow at the edge of dark timber; an image crossing over from expectation to reality. At first the emerging shape would vanish with each gust of swirling snow only to reappear as the wind chased itself on up the narrow valley. He'd gone out in blackness before dawn to hunt the high ridges and timber-tangled slopes that formed the east side of a wild piece of Montana's Gallatin Range known as Cinnabar Basin. Now, several hours past lunch, we watched the deep edges of the storm, anxious for his return.

We didn't realize it then, but now in retrospect, the hunter carried the symbol of our tradition; he had become our icon carrying the hunting heritage from our generation to the next. All we knew on this day, however, was that we were anxious for his return. There was a Cinnabar Foundation board meeting scheduled for the afternoon; the morning hunt was part of the operating rhythm of the organization.

The Cinnabar Foundation was created ten years earlier by one of Montana's most dedicated environmentalists, and each year the board gathered at the founder's ranch to consider requests for funds and award grants. The grants were dedicated to the preservation of wildlife, wilderness, and environmental quality and were awarded to a broad spectrum of conservation organizations in Montana and the Greater Yellowstone Ecosystem.

The ranch itself was one of those "end of the road" places planted at the foot of a deep, timbered canyon containing thick cover that securely sheltered elk. The foundation's board was handpicked on the basis of their commitment to environmental quality; they were active hunters, and the fall board meeting was plotted to include November storms. The half day of board business normally spanned three days, and now and then members, or their offspring, would be granted the gift of a fine elk or mule deer from this rich and wild place.

As the emerging hunter trudged across the final meadow, we awaited the account of a morning spent crossing rocky, windswept ridges and probing deep, silent, timbered pockets where, even in a minor blizzard, the snow settled softly. He was a competent hunter, completely at home in wild places, and we never really worried about his safety—only wondered and talked about packing elk off the mountain and such. This day he had not taken an elk but simply enjoyed the hunt and himself.

On the porch he secured his rifle, shed a snowy coat, then paused to pull off his boots. In the frigid November air, the heat of his exertion formed a frozen vapor that engulfed him. Ice caked his scraggly red beard and the thick tangle of hair spilling from a hat that simply couldn't hold it. An exhausted smile warmed his face. His broad white suspenders, lettered in red, said "Budweiser." His girth hinted the same.

We were always glad to see the big guy, not because we doubted he would come down from those windy ridges or emerge from the timbered canyons, but because within ourselves we knew how much there was to this man. We knew our hunters' passion to sustain the world's "last best place" was carried on his heavy shoulders as more than a Montana boosters' slogan. We knew how deeply he was invested in the dream of a life filled with wild places, free rivers, and opportunities to hunt and fish, and so we trusted our dream to Phil Tawney's dedication. It seemed like such a secure investment in a man who was so strong, young, full of life, and so totally committed to wildlife, wilderness, and environmental quality. It never occurred to us that there would be a day when this hunter would not emerge from the storm.

In the modern world, the land and its dimensions often become generated abstractions—the result of images created by writers, photographers, filmmakers, promoters, teachers, and even poets. They become images to be mass-produced, media-multiplied, and fed to the people. Montana was no abstraction for Phil Tawney. His land was real; its truth came to him molded by three generations of his own people, then tempered with his own experience as a hunter, timber cutter, angler, packer, ranch hand, wilderness wanderer, and conservation activist.

Phil's year was a full circle. He knew when the early stone fly hatch came to the Bitterroot River and how a similar big bug would later feed hungry trout on the Blackfoot River, Rock Creek, and the Big Hole. Phil's circle included the midsummer caddis flies on the upper Clark Fork and the late mayfly emergence on the Missouri. The first hint of autumn would send him out onto the sage and grasslands of the pronghorn, or into the Bob Marshall Wilderness where the aspen turned gold and the elk turned to the passion of the season.

Later, it would be time for "Huns" and pheasants whenever an opportunity could be squeezed into a frantic schedule of business and an overload of public service. The short days of December would find Phil waiting for fat mallards to settle into the spring creeks of Bitterroot Valley, and later, calculating the days until the stone flies would come again. The hunter and angler in Phil Tawney knew this rhythm of the land. He understood it, his life was part of it, and, more than anything else, he appreciated it.

❧

In 1971, University of Montana students Phil and his wife, Robin, came to the Montana legislature to show their appreciation for the land that nurtured them and would in good time do the same for their children: Land, Mikal, and Whitney. They came at first as students and legislative interns, then returned in 1973 to help Montana Wildlife Federation lobbyist Don Aldrich. At that time, these three were the entire and only environmental presence at the state capitol. After the 1973 session, they formed the Montana Environmental Information Center, and from this nexus the preservation of the good earth found a permanent and growing advocacy.

From 1971 through 1975, Montana resource law went through a

transition unprecedented in the state's history. Practically every major law that had to do with protecting land and water was either initiated or reformed. Frances Bardanouve, who served in the legislature for three and a half decades, called 1973 through 1975 the period of "Renaissance in Montana." For fish, wildlife, and the environment, the revival was real. It was a time in our social evolution when progress was possible, and the Tawneys lived at the core of that possibility. Toward the latter part of this renewal, Robin gave birth to their first born, a son, and they christened him Land.

Life for Phil was a progression with purpose. After creating several public-interest organizations, he left Montana to study natural resource policy at the University of Michigan. When the Tawneys returned, Phil served as the executive secretary of the Montana Democratic Party and then went on to study law at the University of Montana. By the time he began practicing, he was experienced, comprehensively educated, and battle hardened. He understood the environment, he understood politics, he understood the law, and he knew more about human nature than any dozen people twice his age. And his direction never strayed; Phil Tawney had his feet firmly embedded in the forest duff and his eye fixed on a star. Through it all, he never lost his passion for hunting and angling, and his experiences afield remained an unerring navigational compass.

As an attorney, Phil continued to supply drive and energy to the conservation movement, both personally and professionally. He helped create and served on the boards of the Cinnabar Foundation, the Teller Wildlife Refuge, and the Forever Wild Endowment, a wilderness preservation foundation. The nature of his participation was intense, and his leadership powered every group he associated with. When the Rocky Mountain Elk Foundation brought itself to life, Phil was there when they needed him most as an adviser, fundraiser, chief legal counsel, and friend. Within a decade, RMEF erupted from a concept to a ninety-thousand-member international conservation organization of enormous energy and accomplishment.

Phil never saw the world as a place laden with impossible obstacles. His world was merely loaded with insurmountable opportunity. The man could never see the perils, only the possibilities. Complex projects that intimidated most mortals attracted Phil. They were simply dragons in need of slaying.

Nowhere was this more evident than in campaigns to preserve

land for elk and other wildlife. When we gathered in Missoula to pay our respects to Phil's memory on January 14, 1995, elk were also on the move. The storms of January moved them from the easy pastures of summer to winter ranges that held survival. Elk came from the battered ranges of Yellowstone north to the rich grasslands of Dome Mountain, from the snowy Gallatin Range to the open slopes of Crystal Cross Mountain, from the Gravelly Range to the open hills of Robb Creek, and from Arizona's high Escudilla to the fertile pastures of the Sipe White Mountain Ranch. These are some of the real places where Phil invested his genius and energy. They are places where the world of wildlife was made whole again. And they are places that now make the hunter's dream an undeniable truth. In the spring, cow elk will bless the earth with strong calves that will run and leap and dance . . . on the open palms of Phil Tawney's work. My memory hears the big guy laugh, and my heart sees his smile.

&

In September of 1993, Phil and I drove to the Teller Wildlife Refuge in Montana's Bitterroot Valley for a board meeting, and as always we talked about all there was to do. For the first time, Phil fell asleep en route, and we made light of it, dismissing his nap as a peril of the pace and the possibility that my lecturing was indeed dull.

In October he called to share the news: his battle with cancer had begun. I was with him when they took him for his first chemo treatment. He talked of all there was yet to do, and as they wheeled him down the corridor he looked back and I saw in his eyes a fear now burned into my brain without reprieve.

In June of 1994, my son and I were on our way to the Blackfoot River to fish the stone fly hatch and stopped over to keep Phil company during another treatment. The conversation was still on what was left to do and the hope of remission. In October, we planned an elk hunt up Fish Creek, where a few years earlier he'd been thrilled to see three wolves cross a high basin. The horrible word "relapse" trashed our plans, but still there was hope.

I saw Phil for the last time in late December of that year. In a Missoula hospital, I held his hands and whispered that we would carry on and there would be some wonderful wild place restored in his memory and that we would find the star he navigated by, and that we would be true to it and to his dream. I wept, and still I weep.

I now feel Phil's hands pressed softly in mine and realize that when the time came to say good-bye, with every emotion within me swelling beyond my capacity to contain, the words I found were the words of hunters . . . emotions bursting forth in a promise from one hunter to another.

Now, in contemplation, I realize that this promise, this commitment, was not unique between us. We simply were taking our turn in a process as old as our American commitment to the preservation of nature—a process beginning at Walden Pond, later empowered by Theodore Roosevelt the hunter, and then carried to us by the likes of Iowa's "Ding" Darling, Wisconsin's Aldo Leopold, and millions of other hunters . . . North Americans, rich and poor alike, who over the generations quelled the market killers, restored our wildlife, and along the way preserved the democracy of hunting—for Phil, for me, and for you.

❧

A few years before all this began, a companion and I had camped on the open plain north of Winnett, Montana, in anticipation of the opening of pronghorn season. Phil and Land were on their way to join us. Night settled over us, and a moonless sparkling celestial dome wrapped itself around us as we waited, anticipating the arrival of the big guy and all the excitement that traveled with him.

When we finally settled down for the night, we set a lantern out on that vast dark plain so Phil could find his way to our camp. It was a simple light, put up on a boulder to hold it above the sage—a tiny beacon set out among the burning and exploding stars of the cosmos.

It was after midnight when Phil and Land pulled in, and at that moment all was right and happy again. We talked, traded news, and bedded down in anticipation of hunting among the sage and prairie grass in what promised to be a frosty dawn.

I look at the photos now and remember the man whose captured image smiles at me. The power of the man, his dreams, his vision, his irrepressible optimism, and in retrospect his remarkable achievement cannot die. These things live. They live in the wilderness he fought for, the elk he provided for, the fat mallards he saved a spring creek for, and the stone flies still awash in clean water. They live in the pronghorns that floated across the grassland in the photo's background and the one lying there at our feet. These things, like the spirit of Phil Tawney, all are born again. These things live in the land and they live in all of us. That is simply how it all must work.

Phil is gone, but his gifts pass to the hunters of still another generation. It will be good to go back to the prairie north of Winnett, to let the night return to that high plain and embrace me . . . and to set the lantern out again.

The Hunter's Eucharist

❧

CHAS S. CLIFTON

Although hunting is one of humanity's oldest activities, it is condemned by many modern people. And I speak here not of subsistence hunting (although some extremists condemn even that), but of hunting by people who have other sources of food as well.

As I see it, in a world struggling to find a new attitude toward nature, nothing separates the players as much as their attitudes toward wildlife, attitudes fostered by religion and spiritual perspectives.

Much of the modern world's attitude begins with Genesis, in which God tells the first people, "Be fruitful and increase, fill the earth and subdue it, rule over the fish in the sea, the birds of heaven, and every living thing that moves upon the earth."

Other Old Testament passages serve to reinforce the message: the animals were put here for us.

But more recently, a moral perspective has developed that sees killing animals as entirely vicious and hunters as essentially ignorant victims of circumstance—or at least that's how they see hunters who belong to hunting cultures like those of precontact North America. The rest of us who hunt are simply regarded as depraved and perverted. Under pressure from decades of such moral disapproval, a number of contemporary thinkers and writers have brought forth a view of hunting's value based on spiritual values and aligned with modern environmentalism.

Historically, Christian moralists approved of hunting—but with certain reservations. The "Hunting" entry in the *New Catholic Encyclopedia*, for example, declares that hunting is morally permissible: "Catholic theology classifies the capture of a wild animal as title of ownership. . . . However, unnecessary cruelty must be avoided, such as making captured animals suffer a long time." Priests, however, were forbidden to hunt frequently or clamorously (for example, riding to hounds) because such conduct did not conform to clerical decorum.

Protestantism scarcely modified that view. When it did, the modification more frequently came as a condemnation of hunting for being an insufficiently sober and industrious activity.

In 1885, the editor of a pioneering American conservation journal, *Forest and Stream*, looked back a decade or so and recalled how "a man who went 'gunnin' or 'fishin' lost caste among respectable people just about in the same way that one did who got drunk." Frivolity was the sin, not killing.

And, of course, Enlightenment science and philosophy continued on the same course—less the divine sanction.

But today, many Christian thinkers are too busy coping with repeated assertions that the "Judeo-Christian ethic" is responsible for environmental destruction to worry about hunting specifically. As *Christianity Today* noted in its report on the 1992 Earth Summit in Rio de Janeiro, "The Christian presence at the forum was swamped by a plethora of feminist, universality, and monist groups who argued that a new religious paradigm must replace the old one, which was shaped by patriarchy, capitalism, theism, and Christianity. Many blamed the 'old paradigm' for the environment's destruction."

Opposition to hunting is gaining ground these days even though some opponents embrace incongruous logic. As a writer and acquaintance of mine recently put it, "It must be part of our New Age to pretend to admire 'primitive' cultures—their artwork and dances—but to be appalled by the act of killing and eating a deer or elk."

Through the ages, ambivalence has permeated Christian attitudes toward hunting. But no such ambivalence marks what is now called the animal-rights movement. As Peter Singer, one of its most influential thinkers, has written, "We didn't 'love' animals. We simply wanted them treated as the independent sentient beings that they are, and not as a means to human ends."

But if all species should be treated equally, and some of them are carnivorous, what is wrong with humans also being carnivorous? Where is the separation? Singer responds:

> It is odd how humans, who normally consider themselves so far above other animals, will, if it seems to support their dietary preferences, use an argument that implies we ought to look to other animals for moral inspiration and guidance! The point is, of course, that nonhuman animals are not capable of considering the alternatives, or of reflecting morally on the rights and wrongs of killing for food: they just do it. We may regret that this is the way the world is, but it makes no sense to hold nonhuman animals morally responsible or culpable for what they do.

The key phrase here is "We may regret that this is the way the world is." Underlying the animal rightists' objections to hunting—whether by two-legged, four-legged, flying, or swimming predators—is a fundamental disgust with nature that casts the predator as the bad guy.

This attitude pervades contemporary society. New Mexico writer Stephen Bodio, in his memoir *Querencia*, describes relaxing with some "very good, very civilized friends" and watching a PBS nature documentary:

> The usual cheetah began the usual slow-motion chase after the usual gazelle. The music swelled to a crescendo then stopped dead as the action blurred into real-life speed, dust, and stillness. Betsy and I raised our glasses and clinked them. Our hostess had left the room and her husband looked at us, puzzled. "You know," he said. "You're the only people I've ever seen who cheer the bad guys in the animal shows."

The attitude Bodio describes reflects an underlying belief that the material world is a botched job. But that idea did not begin with twentieth-century animal rightists. In Western thought, it can be traced back to the Pythagoreans, some early Gnostic Christians, and to the Manichaeans, another Middle Eastern religious group with Christian roots.

Among Gnostic Christians, material creation was commonly seen as the inferior production of a false god who used the enticements of the material world to lead humans astray. To lessen their ties with the world, therefore, both Manichaeans and Gnostics were frequently vegetarians who often avoided sexual intercourse and particularly the conception of children—because in their viewpoint, procreation served only to trap more divine souls in this evil, material world. At their most extreme, Manichaeans ate only fruit such as melons that separated naturally from the plant or vegetables that had been gathered by lower-ranking believers.

Today, a sort of neo-Manichaeism pervades the hunting debate. Advocates of the spiritual position that all killing is bad drift toward a dualism of absolute good and absolute evil, and their rhetoric strikes a sustained note of rage. Fundamental to the animal rightists' argument against hunting is the old Gnostic teaching that humans are not really part of nature but are trapped in it and owe it nothing.

Consider Ron Baker, author of *The Hunting Myth*, writing in *The Animals' Voice*:

> Obviously there is a great deal of difference between predation in nature and human self-gratification [on the one hand] and ecocide on the other! Natural predators evolved as meat-eaters and must kill in order to live. . . . Predators don't kill to be wantonly cruel. They kill because they must and there is no dishonor in that.

Let us merely consider his assumption about "evolution." Take the white-tailed deer, for example—a species found from the Atlantic Coast to the eastern edge of the Rocky Mountains. For tens of thousands of years, North Americans have enjoyed a predatory relationship with these animals. Thus, white-tailed deer evolved with humans as one of their "natural" predators. So how long, we might ask, must humans interact with the "natural world" before our actions are considered "natural"?

Or, as the Spanish philosopher José Ortega y Gasset asked, since humans' hunting is directly derived from our hominid ancestors' ways, at what time did humanity cross the line and step outside "nature"?

But the neo-Manichaean dualist is always troubled by the "wild" component in humanity. Hear the words of Edward P. Smith, commissioner of Indian Affairs, speaking in 1873 to a group of Oto chiefs who had traveled from Nebraska to Washington, D.C., to ask permission for a buffalo hunt. To their request Smith responded, "We must do one thing or the other, either let you continue wild as you are now, or make you like white men; and nothing keeps up this wild living like hunting."

Now compare the words of the well-known animal-rights spokesman Cleveland Amory: "Hunting is an antiquated expression of macho self-aggrandizement, with no place in a civilized society."

It is interesting to speculate what the Oto chiefs would have said to Cleveland Amory.

In my opinion, Amory, Commissioner Smith, Baker, and others who would separate humanity from the natural world and assign it to a different moral order are on slippery ground.

Although evolution may explain why our brains are larger and our ability to access information greater than our fellow creatures', scientists as yet cannot weigh and measure our morality. Men assume they are morally superior to all other animals and to their own human ancestors. But if such moral superiority really does exist, then why do modern societies teeter on the brink of nuclear and environmental destruction?

❧

Outdoor writers never tire of citing statistics about the growth in some animal populations since the bad days of the 1890s to 1920s, when market hunting began to be curbed. White-tailed deer and wild turkeys, for example, are far more prevalent than a century ago, whereas the numerical decline in waterfowl, for instance, can be laid at the feet of pollution and habitat destruction rather than hunting.

Regulated recreational hunting in the United States has not caused any wildlife species to become extinct, endangered, or threatened. But according to John Reiger, the former executive director of the Connecticut Audubon Society, antihunters "would prefer to condemn the hunter who shoots a dozen ducks every waterfowl season in a swamp that in many cases only sportsmen's money has preserved from the dragline and bulldozer, rather than [condemn] the developer who obliterates another swamp and takes it out of wildlife protection forever."

But a simple recital of success stories is not enough. A *spiritual* justification for hunting is necessary in modern times.

The notion that "wild" might also be "sacred" was supported by the nineteenth-century romantic movement. And long before that, in ancient pagan traditions, hunting was a sacrament, instilled with magical and mystic reverence. Today, revived pagans—modern people who uphold old pagan traditions—believe that man is an essential part of nature and not . . . above or apart from nature. As contemporary writers seek to express the value of hunting, many of them are integrating these old ideas—that the wild is sacred, and that man is an essential part of that wild. As a spiritual justification for hunting, this concept moves beyond the "old paradigm" viewpoint of man's dominion over the earth, yet flatly refutes the moral condemnation of humans-as-predators found among animal rightists.

When we look at hunting's place in the modern world, we see that for a large number of people—whether they hunt or not, whether they sanction the activity or not—the old "domination" rationale is no longer adequate to guide our relations with wild animals.

People opposing hunting are most likely to do so on the grounds that it causes pain and suffering. Animal liberationist Peter Singer applied this argument primarily to factory farming and medical experiments on animals. Although he does not acknowledge this fact, many hunters would go at least partway with him: my own father, who taught me to hunt, stopped eating veal years ago. But compromise and partial agreement are rarely good enough for absolutists.

There are dangers in this tendency to view the world in black and white. To show how alienation from nature can go too far, Stephen Bodio is fond of citing John Crowley's novel *Beasts*, about a society whose members withdraw into a huge building surrounded by a preserve, feeling that they, as humans, have damaged the earth enough. Such an action, Bodio writes, would be a crime, "a denial second in enormity only to an atomic war where we would take many other species with us."

Bodio argues that hunting encourages biophilia, a hands-on fascination with and participation in the natural world in all its aspects rather than a squeamish withdrawal from some of them, explaining that "hunting, done well, breeds involvement a lot better than looking at nature pictures does. My Audubon Society activities are more driven, my knowledge of threatened creatures and places is made more intimate by my hunting and fishing."

One can only hope that attempts to rewrite the cosmos to fit an old Manichaean moral scheme are doomed to fail before wild animals are replaced with shopping malls and monocultural fields of soybeans to feed the tofu market. To appreciate nature, we must be willing to enter wild animals' lives. Mysteries are always paradoxical, and this one is no exception. We enter the cosmic give-and-take; we admit our sometimes predatory nature and thus let the wild into ourselves, a true form of holy communion, a participation.

In a recent Reed College commencement address, poet Gary Snyder said, "I think the developed world can still find a way to be fully part of this planet—civilized, technological, hyperintellectual as it is—at the same time becoming 'nature literate,' knowing the details of nature well, and fully at home with the wild, both within and without."

Elsewhere, Snyder writes, "To acknowledge that each of us at the table will eventually be part of the meal is not just being 'realistic.' It is allowing the sacred to enter and accepting the sacramental aspect of our shaky temporary personal being."

Personally, I fear that to lose the attitude of humans and animals sitting at the same table and taking turns at the feast would be an abandonment of our participation in nature. We can no longer afford to think of nature as "out there" and separate from humanity—and, I would add, from divinity. Nor can we pretend that nature will always heal itself without us.

For some, an occasional sacred hunt immerses us in these connections. It is our pilgrimage to Eleusis, our sojourn in the desert, our journey to the mountain, our vision quest.

A Hunter's Heart

DAVID PETERSEN

September. The most august of months here in western Colorado. The flies and mosquitoes are gone, most of them, as are the buzzing swarms of motorized tourists. Autumn aspens illuminate the landscape with an ancient golden light. Days are sunny and T-shirt warm, nights crisp and star-spangled.

And best of all, September is rut; mating season for the lordly wapiti. The pungent incense of their fierce animal lust perfumes the mountain air, and the valleys ring with the brassy bugles of lovestruck bulls. It's an otherworldly music, the bull elk's bugle, like a calamitous crescendo of bluesy high notes blown on a reedy saxophone, proclaiming a wildness we can hardly imagine.

It's still dark when I wheel into a little-used trailhead at the end of a ragged dirt road bisecting a local parcel of land owned by the Colorado Division of Wildlife. As the sun also rises I buckle into my pack, lock my truck (oh yes, even here), and take the trail less traveled. My plan is to rendezvous with a young friend—a former student back when I was a former teacher at the local college—at his hideaway hunting camp . . . somewhere *out there*. The way from here to there is new to me and, Dan has forewarned, "real up." Once there, I'll have all the time in the world, so to speak, to enjoy the bugling elk, the gilded aspens, a seldom-seen friend's companionship, and as much mountain solitaire as I wish.

Onward.

Although this state-owned parcel is only a few miles from my frenetic, tourist-trampled hometown of Durango, the 6,900-acre foothill tract is home to peregrine falcons, eagles both golden and bald, wild turkeys, black bears, cougars, mule deer, elk, and more. Deer, elk, and their predators, especially, rely on this place and a dwindling few more refugia hereabouts to sustain them through the long and often brutal Colorado winters in these "progressive" times.

Until a handful of years ago, the Animas River valley, anchored dead center by Durango, remained blissfully undiscovered by exurban yupsters and the real estate hucksters that follow them like fleas, retaining its traditional agrarian nature and providing wildlife with abundant wintering areas in low-lying ranch pastures, especially along the cottonwood-sheltered riparian corridor of the river itself. (*Rio de las Animas Perdidas*, River of Lost Souls; an apropos name given the way things are going around here.) But discovered it eventually was, and every year more traditional wildlife habitat is transmogrified into obscene trophy houses for the conspicuous rich, redundant golf courses (three on the ground and a fourth on the drawing board), tacky commercial and industrial parks, noisy natural gas fields, and seas of suburban subdivisions to hold a floodtide of urban refugees that shows no sign of ebbing. The chamber of commerce calls it progress.

Wildlife call it hard times. Looking around me now as I hike through this severely stressed elk wintering ground, the signs of pending disaster are ubiquitous: the brushy little Gambel's oak, whose acorns and annual twig growth sustain a plethora of winter wildlife, have been cropped almost to their trunks. Not just here and there, but everywhere. Too many elk and not enough elk chow. Come the next killer winter (and come it will; it's overdue even now), this wildlife "refuge" will become a showplace of suffering, a cervid dying field. Progress.

But enough negativity; I'm on vacation.

Up and away, I eventually leave state land and cross some rancher's "bob-war" fence onto a cow-burned corner of adjoining private land. After an hour or so more of steady marching I cross another fence and enter the San Juan National Forest, where the faint cutoff path I've been following intersects a broad backwoods freeway known as the Colorado Trail. Were I to turn downtrail rather than up at this juncture, the CT would deliver me in due course to one of the most popular trailheads for mountain bikers this side of the Land of Moab.

And sure enough, within minutes here comes a pack of riders—three, four mesomorphic youths, skullcapped and body-painted in Lycra, their legs distended with straining muscle and pumping like piston rods on toys worth twice as much as my old truck. They give no indication of seeing me, though they must, and show no inclination to slow down, so that at the last possible moment I'm forced to leap off the trail or risk a head-on. As the pack speeds past, I wave them a single-digit farewell.

Shaken, I step back onto the trail and continue my uphill journey, breathing deeply, rhythmically, invoking a respiratory mantra intended to cool my boiling blood. Trailside encounters between bikers and hikers don't have to be this rude, and it disturbs me that they so often are. One potential source of friction, I suppose, is that mountain bikers tend to view themselves as competitive athletes and, consequently, are more focused on the performance of their equipment and themselves, and the relative positions of their competitor-companions, than on the surroundings through which they race in a sweat-slinging blur. Hikers, on the other hand, generally prefer contemplation to competition, scenery to speed. (The irony, I realize, is that a hiker one day may be a biker another. It's as if the activity dictates the personality.)

Time passes, as do the slow steep miles. The oak brush thickets and sunny ponderosa woods of the lower montane ecology gradually are supplanted by cool dark forests of spruce and fir bejeweled with flickering groves of quaking aspens. All around me now, millions of loose-jointed leaves answer to the midmorning breeze, whispering sibilant secrets in an ancient alien tongue.

And with the aspens come frequent sign and occasional sightings of the feral menagerie that thrives among the shady groves' fecund understory of ferns, giant cow parsnips, angelica, chokecherry, serviceberry, and a frenzy of wildflowers. Already this morning I've interrupted two conventions of big blue grouse as they pecked for brunch in the leafy duff; the grouse season is open and I'm carrying the proper license, but I'm not hunting just now, I'm hiking. A little farther along I'm treated to the pigeon-toed prints of an adult black bear. The heart-shaped tracks of deer and elk are everywhere, and the forest is alive with the happy chatter of birds and . . . I knew it was too good to last.

Fifty yards ahead, loping easily downtrail, talking and laughing, come three brethren backpackers—no, one brethren and two sistern. This time I am not forced, as I was with the speeding cyclists, but freely elect to step off the trail and make way. The hikers see me and—to my surprise, rather than offering their greetings—fall silent. When they come abreast I smile and say good morning and am doubly confused when they keep right on marching, their replies limited to a Hi and a Hello from the women, a silent nod from the man. A triple cold shoulder. Not that I care.

Or do I? Granted, I'm getting older and am no longer so pretty as I once never was, but even so, I can't imagine that I'm in any way *scary*.

The mystery is solved a few moments later when one of the women—they've rounded a bend and must think they're out of earshot—says, "A *hunter*!" hurling the word like a curse. After that I can hear no more, and just as well.

I should have known. Although I'm hiking in shorts and lugging a big brown backpack, I'm also wearing a camouflage shirt and cap and carrying a bow and quiver of arrows. Today I am not just a backpacker, I'm "a *hunter*!" Or I will be if I ever get where I'm going.

The more I reflect on this, the more it bugs me, notwithstanding I harbor judgmental generalizations of my own. Hikers, bikers, hunters, fishers, horse people—we're all out here for the same root reason—to enjoy *being out here*, albeit each in our own way. Further, we frequently play musical outdoor-activity chairs (with the exception of biker, I am at one time and another each of the above). It's just too damned bad that our gear, dress, and mind-set for a particular day's excursion so often seem to dictate not just the attitudes of others toward us, but our reactions to others as well. Protean role playing.

My map tells me I'm nearing the ten-thousand-foot contour, and my stomach tells me it's break time. Today's lunch menu (and tomorrow's and the next day's): dried fruit, a big slab of homemade elk jerky, a chocolate bar, and a quart of tepid water. I collapse in the

shade, jettison my sweaty pack, eat, drink, and shift into mental neu-
tral. A nap attack tries to ambush me, but there are unknown miles
left to hike and the sun is past its apogee, so after twenty minutes I
groan to my feet, saddle up, and stagger back out into the brilliant
heart of a perfect September day, rejoicing in my solitude.

For a little while, at least—ten minutes or so—when here comes
yet more traffic. (This unrelenting, unsolicited *society* is starting to
wear thin.) It's another mountain biker, apparently alone, catching a
free downtrail ride from gravity. I brace for the usual brusque encounter, but this day is made for surprises and the young man brakes
to a stop and awaits my approach. "Hi," he says as I draw near, smiling big and real. "You must be Dave. I'm Bill. Dan told me to watch
for you."

Now what the hell . . . ?

Though Bill is dressed in de rigueur biker black, I see now that he
too is a hunter, his short compound bow strapped across the bars and
bundles of camping gear appended everywhere. Bill tells me that he's
just come from two days of camping and hunting with Dan. Now it's
back to Denver and work for him while Dan ("the lucky SOB")
stays on for a full vacation week. Dan had advised me that a friend of
his I'd not met would be leaving camp the same day I'd be arriving,
but I hadn't expected a biker.

With no further ado, Bill offers to ride back up the trail with me—
"It's only a couple of miles"—to set me on the obscure elk path (just
one of hundreds bisecting the interminable Colorado Trail) that will
lead me, after a mile or so of bushwhacking, to Dan's cloistered
camp. I protest: "Too much trouble for you." Bill counters that I'll
never find it on my own, then dumps the bulk of his stuff alongside
the trail, wheels around, gears down, and pedals slowly, almost ef-
fortlessly back up the mountain. I follow at a fast, heart-pounding
shuffle, painfully aware that this blows hell out of my bikers-as-
buttheads stereotype.

When we arrive at the invisible cutoff, Bill wishes me good luck
and disappears. I leave the CT without remorse and follow the ser-
pentine, blowdown-clogged game trail until it peters out on a narrowing tongue of wooded ridge, where I find . . . nothing. No camp
in sight. As prearranged, I take a small plastic disc from my shirt
pocket, place it against the roof of my mouth, and blow, producing a
mew that sounds not unlike a lost kitten.

Silence.

I repeat the elk coalescence call and this time receive an in-kind reply from the shadowy forest below. I stumble down that way and right into Dan's little camp.

For what's left of the afternoon we catnap and talk. Come evening, we boil pure Rocky Mountain spring water to rehydrate our desiccated dinners. As dark approaches, the temperature drops in sync with the sun, prompting Dan to kindle a campfire I feel compelled to comment is "pretty damned thrifty."

"Well," Dan defends, "I usually camp cold when I'm hunting. Don't want to scare away the elk, you know. But it's going to be chilly tonight, so what the heck . . . we'll keep it small."

I'd have said "what the hell," but Dan is deeply religious and never swears. I too am religious, but in a radically different sense, which philosophical diversity leads to some fairly high-flown, high-tension dialogue. ("Nature," says Dan, "is God's grandest creation." "Nature," I counter, borrowing from Richard Nelson, "*is* God.")

Over tea (he) and whiskey (me), we cuss (me) and discuss (he) my day's perplexing trail encounters. The macho young bikers, we agree—well, boys will be bullies, especially in competitive gangs; to hell with them. More difficult to figure and far more bothersome is the behavior of that trio of hikers. I'm sure, I tell Dan, that my meeting with them would have been warmer had I not been carrying a bow and arrows. Why is that, young buddy?

"Well," says Dan, "maybe they've had some bad experiences with hunters in the past. Hunters are people, and a lot of people are slobs in everything they do, and it's human nature to draw negative generalizations from a few bad examples."

Right you are, professor. I consider my own biases—against mountain bikers, against public lands ranchers (a coagulation of scoundrels), against New Mexico drivers (the only requirement for an operator's license there, it would seem, is a prefrontal lobotomy), and other groups with whose members I've had repeated unpleasant run-ins. "But what," I abruptly offer, looking to justify my unjustifiable prejudices, "what of Sartre's *le pour-soi* and *l'en-soi*? What of *that* little distinction, eh Danny boy?"

"Nor," continues my wise young friend, cleverly ignoring my non sequitur and steering us back on track, "nor does the negative image of hunting that's put out by the popular media help any. In their view, only slob hunters, wildlife criminals, and animal-rights fanatics are newsworthy."

"Seems like it," I grant, recalling the devastatingly out-of-context TV documentary *The Guns of Autumn*; the joyfully bitchy print attacks (in *Esquire* and elsewhere) of a certain (to borrow Jim Harrison's description) "minor regional novelist" et al. And so on.

"But it's not only the news and popular media who distort hunting," I propose. "Just as bad are the hook-and-bullet rags who've sold their souls for advertising dollars and the Wildlife Legislative Fund of America and other industry-sponsored self-proclaimed 'hunters' rights' propaganda groups with their half-truths, entrenched denial, and paranoid right-wing ranting about 'the growing antihunting threat.' With a few sterling exceptions, outdoor magazines are so far right they make Limbaugh look left."

I have another slash of Dickel and creek water, torch a Swisher Sweet, and push on.

"The greatest threat to hunting isn't external, my friend; it's internal, arising from our collective failure to police our own ranks and morals. There's a lot wrong with hunting today, and I don't mean just illegal activities like poaching. The root problem is the hunting community's hardheaded refusal to admit that some things some hunters do, even when legal, are ethically indefensible: baiting, using hounds to tree bears and mountain lions then executing them like bass in buckets, rich man's globe-trotting trophy hunting, canned 'hunts' on fenced 'game ranches,' rampant littering and ATV abuse, road 'hunting,' contest killing, employing space-age technology to minimize challenge, dead animals conspicuously displayed on vehicles, alignment with the no-compromise anti-environment far-right radical militia mentality, and a general care-less-ness in our behavior afield."

Dan moans and nods agreement.

"Increasingly," I drone on, a little tipsy now, "these sins are dividing our ranks, forcing some ethical hunters to become nonhunters, converting nonhunters to antihunters, lowering the recruitment of young people into our ranks, and providing powerful ammunition to the rabid hunter haters. What was it Twain said? 'Ain't we got all the fools in town on our side, and ain't that majority enough anywhere?' Hunting today is fat with fools; it's a built-in flaw of democracy—any idiot can do any damn thing he wants. Modern hunting is badly in need of a good internal bullshit filter. We need . . ."

"Now just *wait* a darned minute," says Dan, feigning (I think) outrage. "You know danged well that there's an increasingly powerful political lobby of loony-tunes animal-rights nuts out there, urban innocents who fantasize a perfect world where *all* predation, human *and* animal, is eliminated, where lions lie down with fawns and wildlife populations are kept in balance with contraceptives. These turkeys have sworn to stop *all* hunting, not just the bad bits. And most of them are so blissfully ignorant of how the natural world works they couldn't tell a deer from a steer if it was standing on their Birkenstocks. More often than not, their arguments are biologically naive, unworkable, and ultimately immoral."

All right, Dan! My earnest opponent stops just long enough to fortify himself with the dregs of his tea, then bulls ahead.

"What the fanatical animal-rights types refuse to acknowledge is that humans evolved as predators, and nature *needs* predation, especially these days. Hunters didn't design the system, and now, with most of the big natural predators wiped out to make the world safe for our domesticated livestock, hunters, as ironic as it may sound to the uninformed, have become wildlife's closest allies."

No argument. I think of those state wildlife lands down the mountain. If it weren't for money extracted from hunters through license fees and special taxes on sporting goods, that land would be just another subdivision. Overcrowded and overgrazed it may be, but at least it's there, thanks entirely and exclusively to hunters. And yet, such pragmatic justifications of hunting fail to bear on the opposition's primary complaints, which are ethical and philosophical, not utilitarian.

Musing along these lines, I recall a story related to me by Dave Stalling, conservation writer for *Bugle*, the journal of the Rocky Mountain Elk Foundation. While backpack bowhunting in the Idaho wilderness recently, Stalling encountered a couple of hikers. The men identified themselves as attorneys for a major environmental group, out to enjoy some of the wilderness they worked daily (at West Coast lawyer wages) to protect. Across the next half hour, these gentlemen derided, berated, and verbally excoriated Stalling with a fierceness only barristers and ideologues can muster. For why? For being a hunter. Dave says he attempted to answer their charges calmly and reasonably, but they would hear none of it; their minds were made up and shut.

Finally, tiring of the game, Stalling wished his critics a good day and walked on. "Wait a minute!" one of the pair called after him. "Listen—we're kind of . . . well, *lost*; can you tell us how to get out of here?" Dave, a former Marine Corps recon ranger, pulled out his topographical maps and showed them the way. I wonder if I could have been so generous.

Dan's chintzy little fire flickers, flares, and fades to glowing embers. Likewise, our lively conversation has given way to silent introspection, and we never even got around to the real meat of the matter, the hardest question of all: the apparent hypocrisy of taking pleasure in an activity whose end goal is death, while claiming to care deeply (as many of us in fact do) about the very animals we work so earnestly to kill.

But such serious talk will have to wait for other evenings, other campfires. Dan and I rise sluggishly and stagger tentward. With no bugs or Bubbas buzzing about to annoy us, we decide to sleep with the tent flaps tied back and our heads poking out, the better to enjoy the sparkling firmament.

"I should probably warn you," says Dan as he zips into his sack (*Oh no*, I'm thinking, *the sonofabitch snores!*), "There's been something hanging around here the last couple of nights, making the weirdest noises. When it came last night Bill and I got up and shined our flashlights all around, but it went quiet and we never saw it. Sort of spooky."

I haven't a clue.

Sometime after midnight I'm awakened by a sharp jab to the shoulder. "It's back. Listen!" I listen, and sure enough, before long comes a loud, ethereal keening, like some demented demon's spawn in need of a diaper change. Real close.

"What the hell *is* it?" whispers Dan, forgetting for once to not cuss.

The banshee wails again, this time in stereo, and suddenly I know. "Porcupines," I say. "Making love."

"Well," says Dan, "I'll be hanged."

❦

Thanks to the amorous porkies we oversleep, waking only when the sun slaps our faces. In penance, we bolt jerky and unfiltered creek water for breakfast, grab our bows, and strike off for parts unknown. This entire huge basin is terra incognita to me, and Dan has generously volunteered to conduct an orienting tour.

During a laconic morning of quiet poking around, we find where elk have recently foraged and where their big cloven hooves have sunk deep in the mud of a spring seep. By examining their droppings—the older (hard and sun-bleached) turds are formless lumps, like dwarf cowpies, while the fresher (soft and shiny black) scats are acornlike pellets—we determine that the big herbivores are already shifting from their spring and summer fare of grasses and forbs to a fall and winter diet of woody browse.

And such other bits of natural history that only biologists and hunters bother to notice.

The high point of the morn comes when our noses lead us to a fresh wallow carved into a muddy spring seep, proving that at least one mature bull is lurking about, probably shaded up somewhere nearby even now, chewing contemplative cud and watching, listening, nostrils flared for danger. I drop to my knees for a closer reading of the spoor.

The story is clearly written: Some sex-crazed male has hooved the spring seep into a quagmire, urinated into the mess, stirred it all around, then rolled in it to cake himself with the funky brew . . . the wapiti way of dressing for a hot date. Nearby, a forlorn spruce sapling has been stripped of its bark and lower limbs by the hormone-enraged bull's aggressive horning.

I put my face down close to the reeking muck and inhale deep of its pungent, pheromone-laden aroma, prompting my wiseacre friend to quip, "Why'nt ya just roll in it and experience the *real* essence of elkness?"

I don't bother mentioning that I've already done that, back in my formative years as an elkoholic. An overwhelming error.

It's early afternoon when we sag back into camp for lunch and brief naps. Afterward, we fling a few practice arrows at a makeshift target, check the sharpness of our broadheads, and otherwise make ready for a serious evening hunt.

Dan plans to climb a nearby promontory and bugle. Any rutting bull within hearing (so the theory goes) will interpret the calls as a challenge to his territorial dominance and answer in kind, revealing his location. Might even come a-running, hot for a fight. More often, though, a vocally challenged harem master will simply herd up his cows and run away (to live and breed another day). But even a retreating bull will often bugle, granting the priceless gift of hearing him sing. Bottom line: you never know; sometimes the magic works, more often it doesn't.

Dan invites me to join him. I decline. For me, playing the silent, solitary predator is the quintessence of the hunting experience; companionship and conversation are best saved for the evening campfire. We exchange good lucks, and Dan strikes off uphill. I go low, headed back to a grassy little glen at the bottom of a nearby canyon where food, water, and wooded seclusion—the Big Three of quality wildlife habitat—are abundant, and where we cut fresh sign this morning. There, I'll lie in ambush; elk or no, it's a room with a view.

Time passes quickly, and less than an hour of light remains when I hear a high, clean, distant call that rises in steps through three octaves, sustains briefly, then comes crashing back to earth. Dan is nearly a mile away as the arrow flies, but sound carries well in this rarefied montane air.

No sooner has Dan's realistic fake bugle faded away than I hear, from much nearer, a low grunt and a brittle crashing of limbs. Adrenaline surges; my heart slams into overdrive. The sounds are coming from a wooded plateau directly across the little canyon from me, and I don't have to see the noisemaker to know who it is and what he's up to—a wapiti bull, infuriated by Dan's vocal challenge, is venting his outrage by stomping around and antler-thrashing some unfortunate tree.

When Danny boy pipes again, the bull answers immediately. The animal is close enough, a hundred yards or so, that I can hear not only the higher notes of his call but the deep, guttural, eerie underlying growls as well. Dan sings a third time, and the bull, by now hot as a first date, replies with a series of five rapid, braying grunts . . . *Yo mom-ma, suck-ah*!

And here I sit. I could enter the fray with a bugle or cow chirp of my own. That *might* bring the bull out of hiding and into the self-imposed twenty-yard range of my bow. Might also scare him off. My only other choice is to try stalking up the hill toward him. But only lovers, inexperienced hunters, and other fools rush in, and if I move as slowly and painstakingly as I should, I'll run out of daylight before I get there.

That's why we call it *hunting*.

Rather than take a chance on blowing this bull smack out of the neighborhood, I place my weapon on the ground beside me and lie back on the cool, leaf-cushioned earth to enjoy the sunset concert. Short of a miracle, there will be no killing this night—but the hunting could hardly be better.

❦

Why do I hunt? It's a lot to think about, and I think about it a lot. I hunt to acknowledge my evolutionary roots, millennia deep, as a predatory omnivore. To participate actively in the bedrock workings of nature. For the atavistic challenge of doing it well with an absolute minimum of technological assistance. To learn the lessons, about nature and myself, that only hunting can teach. To accept personal responsibility for at least some of the deaths that nourish my life. For the glimpse it offers into a wildness we can hardly imagine. Because it provides the closest thing I've known to a spiritual experience. I hunt because it enriches my life and because I can't help myself . . . because I have a hunter's heart.

The Heart of the Game

Thomas McGuane

Hunting in your own backyard becomes with time, if you love hunting, less and less expeditionary. This year, when Montana's eager frosts knocked my garden on its butt, the hoe seemed more like the rifle than it ever had been, the vegetables more like game.

My nine-year-old son and I went scouting before the season and saw some antelope in the high plains foothills of the Absaroka Range, wary, hanging on the skyline; a few bands and no great heads. We crept around, looking into basins, and at dusk met a tired cowboy on a tired horse followed by a tired blue-heeler dog. The plains seemed bigger than anything, bigger than the mountains that seemed to sit in the middle of them, bigger than the ocean. The clouds made huge shadows that traveled on the grass slowly through the day.

Hunting season trickles on forever; if you don't go in on a cow with anybody, there is the dark argument of the deep freeze against head-hunting ("You can't eat horns!"). But nevertheless, in my mind, I've laid out the months like playing cards, knowing some decent white-tails could be down in the river bottom and, fairly reliably, the long windy shots at an antelope. The big buck mule deer—the ridge runners—stay up in the scree and rock walls until the snow drives them out; but they stay high long after the elk have quit and broken down the hay corrals on the ranches and farmsteads, which, when you're hunting the rocks from a saddle horse, look pathetic and housebroken with their yellow lights against the coming of winter.

Where I live, the Yellowstone River runs straight north, then takes an eastward turn at Livingston, Montana. This flowing north is supposed to be remarkable, and the river doesn't do it long. It runs mostly over sand and stones once it comes out of the rock slots near the Wyoming line. But all along, there are deviations of one sort or another: canals, backwaters, sloughs; the red willows grow in the sometime-flooded bottom, and at the first elevation, the cottonwoods. I hunt here for white-tailed deer, which, in recent years, have moved up these rivers in numbers never seen before.

❧

The first morning, the sun came up hitting me in arbitrary panels as the light came through the jagged openings in the Absaroka Range. I was moving very slowly in the edge of the trees, the river invisible a few hundred yards to my right but sending a huge sigh through the willows. It was cold and the sloughs had crowns of ice thick enough to support me. As I crossed one great clear pane, trout raced around under my feet and a ten-foot bubble advanced slowly before my cautious steps. Then passing back into the trees, I found an active game trail, cut cross-lots to pick a better stand, sat in a good vantage place under a cottonwood with the ought-six across my knees. I thought, running my hands up into my sleeves, this is lovely but I'd rather be up in the hills; and I fell asleep.

❧

I woke a couple of hours later, the coffee and early morning drill having done not one thing for my alertness. I had drooled on my rifle and it was time for my chores back at the ranch. My chores of late had consisted primarily of working on screenplays so that the bank didn't take the ranch. These days the primary ranch skill is making the payment; it comes before irrigation, feeding out, and calving. Some rancher friends find this so discouraging they get up and roll a number or have a slash of tanglefoot before they even think of the glories of the West. This is the New Rugged.

❧

The next day, I reflected upon my lackadaisical hunting and left really too early in the morning. I drove around to Mission Creek in the dark and ended up sitting in the truck up some wash listening to a New Mexico radio station until my patience gave out and I started out cross-country in the dark, just able to make out the nose of the Absaroka Range as it faced across the river to the Crazy Mountains. It seemed maddeningly up and down slick banks, and a couple of times I had game clatter out in front of me in the dark. Then I turned up a long coulee that climbed endlessly south and started in that direction, knowing the plateau on top should hold some antelope. After half an hour or so, I heard the mad laughing of coyotes, throwing their voices all around the inside of the coulee, trying to panic rabbits and making my hair stand on end despite my affection for them. The stars tracked overhead into the first pale light, and it was nearly dawn before I came up on the bench. I could hear cattle below me and I moved along an edge of thorn trees to break my outline, then sat down at the point to wait for shooting light.

I could see antelope on the skyline before I had that light; and by the time I did, there was a good big buck angling across from me, looking at everything. I thought I could see well enough, and I got up into a sitting position and into the sling. I had made my moves quietly, but when I looked through the scope the antelope was two hundred yards out, using up the country in bounds. I tracked with him, let him bounce up into the reticle, and touched off a shot. He was down and still, but I sat watching until I was sure.

Nobody who loves to hunt feels absolutely hunky-dory when the quarry goes down. The remorse spins out almost before anything and the balancing act ends on one declination or another. I decided that unless I become a vegetarian, I'll get my meat by hunting for it. I feel absolutely unabashed by the arguments of other carnivores who get their meat in plastic with blue numbers on it. I've seen slaughterhouses, and anyway, as Sitting Bull said, when the buffalo are gone, we will hunt mice, for we are hunters and we want our freedom.

The antelope had piled up in the sage, dead before he hit the ground. He was an old enough buck that the tips of his pronged horns were angled in toward each other. I turned him downhill to bleed him out. The bullet had mushroomed in the front of the lungs, so the job was already halfway done. With antelope, proper field dressing is critical because they can end up sour if they've been run or haphazardly hog-dressed. And they sour from their own body heat more than external heat.

The sun was up and the big buteo hawks were lifting on the thermals. There was enough breeze that the grass began to have directional grain like the prairie, and the rim of the coulee wound up away from me toward the Absaroka. I felt peculiarly solitary, sitting on my heels next to the carcass in the sagebrush and greasewood, my rifle racked open on the ground. I made an incision around the metatarsal glands inside the back legs and carefully removed them and set them well aside; then I cleaned the blade of my hunting knife with handfuls of grass to keep from tainting the meat with those powerful glands. Next I detached the anus and testes from the outer walls and made a shallow puncture below the sternum, spread it with the thumb and forefinger of my left hand, and ran the knife upside down clear to the bone bridge between the hind legs. Inside, the diaphragm was like the taut lid of a drum and cut away cleanly so that I could reach clear up to the back of the mouth and detach the windpipe. Once that was done I could draw the whole visceral package out onto the grass and separate out the heart, liver, and tongue before propping the carcass open with two whittled-up sage scantlings.

You could tell how cold the morning was, despite the exertion, just by watching the steam roar from the abdominal cavity. I stuck the knife in the ground and sat back against the slope, looking clear across to Convict Grade and the Crazy Mountains. I was blood from the elbows down and the antelope's eyes had skinned over. I thought, This is goddamned serious and you had better always remember that.

❧

There was a big red enamel pot on the stove, and I ladled antelope chili into two bowls for my little boy and me. He said, "It better not be too hot."

"It isn't."

"What's your news?" he asked.

"Grandpa's dead."

"Which grandpa?" he asked. I told him it was Big Grandpa, my father. He kept on eating. "He died last night."

He said, "I know what I want for Christmas."

"What's that?"

"I want Big Grandpa back."

❧

It was 1950-something and I was small, under twelve say, and there were four of us: my father, two of his friends, and me. There was a good belton setter belonging to the one friend, a hearty bird hunter who taught dancing and fist-fought at any provocation. The other man was old and sick and had a green fatal look in his face. My father took me aside and said, "Jack and I are going to the head of this field"—and he pointed up a mile and a half of stalks to where it ended in the flat woods—"and we're going to take the dog and get what he can point. These are running birds. So you and Bill just block the field and you'll have some shooting."

"I'd like to hunt with the dog." I had a twenty-gauge Winchester my grandfather had given me, which got hocked and lost years later when another of my family got into the bottle; I could hit with it and wanted to hunt over the setter. With respect to blocking the field, I smelled a rat.

"You stay with Bill," said my father, "and try to cheer him up."

"What's the matter with Bill?"

"He's had one heart attack after another and he's going to die."

"When?"

"Pretty damn soon."

I blocked the field with Bill. My first thought was, I hope he doesn't die before they drive those birds onto us; but if he does, I'll have all the shooting.

There was that crazy cold autumn light on everything, magnified by the yellow silage all over the field. The dog found the birds right away, and they were shooting. Bill said he was sorry but he didn't feel so good. He had his hunting license safety-pinned to the back of his coat and fiddled with a handful of twelve-gauge shells. "I've shot a shitpile of game," said Bill, "but I don't feel so good anymore." He took a knife out of his coat pocket. "I got this in the Marines," he said, "and I carried it for four years in the Pacific. The handle's drilled out and weighted so you can throw it. I want you to have it." I took it and thanked him, looking into his green face, and wondered why he had given to to me. "That's for blocking this field with me," he said. "Your dad and that dance teacher are going to shoot them all. When you're not feeling so good, they put you at the end of the field to block when there isn't shit-all going to fly by you. They'll get them all. They and the dog will."

We had an indestructible tree in the yard we had chopped on, nailed steps to, and initialed; and when I pitched that throwing knife at it, the knife broke in two. I picked it up and thought, This thing is jinxed. So I took it out into the crab apple woods and put it in the can I had buried along with a Roosevelt dime and an atomic-bomb ring I had sent away for. This was a small collection of things I buried over a period of years. I was sending them to God. All He had to do was open the can, but they were never collected. In any case, I have long known that if I could understand why I wanted to send a broken knife I believed to be jinxed to God, then I would be a long way toward what they call a personal philosophy as opposed to these hand-to-mouth metaphysics of who said what to whom in some cornfield twenty-five years ago.

❦

We were in the bar at Chico Hot Springs near my home in Montana: me, a lout poet who had spent the day floating under the diving board while adolescent girls leapt overhead, and my brother John, who had glued himself to the pipe that poured warm water into the pool and announced over and over in a loud voice that every drop of water had been filtered through his bathing suit.

Now, covered with wrinkles, we were in the bar, talking to Alvin Close, an old government hunter. After half a century of predator control he called it "useless and half-assed."

Alvin Close killed the last major stock-killing wolf in Montana. He hunted the wolf so long he raised a litter of dogs to do it with. He hunted the wolf futilely with a pack that had fought the wolf a dozen times until one day he gave up and let the dogs run the wolf out the back of a shallow canyon. He heard them yip their way into silence while he leaned up against a tree, and presently the wolf came tiptoeing down the front of the canyon into Alvin's lap. The wolf simply stopped because the game was up. Alvin raised the Winchester and shot it.

"How did you feel about that?" I asked.

"How do you think I felt?"

"I don't know."

"I felt like hell."

Alvin's evening was ruined, and he went home. He was seventy-six years old and carried himself like an old-time army officer, setting his glass on the bar behind him without looking.

❧

You stare through the plastic at the red smear of meat in the supermarket. What's this it says there? *Mighty Good*? *Tastee*? *Quality*, *Premium*, and *Government Inspected*? Soon enough, the blood is on your hands. It's inescapable.

❧

It's New York City and the beef freaks are forgathering at Bruno's Pen and Pencil. In the kitchen the slabs quiver. In the dining room deals sear the air. Princess Lee Radziwill could be anywhere, fangs aloft to this meat that Bruno's Pen and Pencil's butcher's slaughterhouse killed for the princess. The cow's head and lightless eyes twirl in the rendering vat as linen soars to the princess's dripping lips.

❧

Aldo Leopold was a hunter who I am sure abjured freeze-dried vegetables and extrusion burgers. His conscience was clean because his hunting was part of a larger husbandry in which the life of the country was enhanced by his own work. He knew that game populations are not bothered by hunting until they are already too precarious and the precarious game populations should not be hunted. Grizzlies should not be hunted, for instance. The enemy of game is clean farming and sinful chemicals; as well as the useless alteration of watersheds by promoter cretins and the insidious dizzards of land development whose lobbyists teach us the venality of all governments.

A world in which a sacramental portion of food can be taken in an old way—hunting, fishing, farming, and gathering—has as much to do with societal sanity as a day's work for a day's pay.

❦

For a long time, there was no tracking snow. I hunted on horseback for a couple of days in a complicated earthquake fault in the Gallatins. The fault made a maze of narrow canyons with flat floors. The sagebrush grew on woody trunks higher than my head and left sandy paths and game trails where the horse and I could travel.

There were Hungarian partridge that roared out in front of my horse, putting his head suddenly in my lap. And hawks tobogganed on the low air currents, astonished to find me there. One finger-canyon ended in a vertical rock wall from which issued a spring of the kind elsewhere associated with the Virgin Mary, hung with ex-votos and orthopedic supplications of satisfied miracle customers. Here, instead, were nine identical piles of bear shit, neatly adorned with undigested berries.

One canyon planed up and topped out on an endless grassy rise. There were deer there, does and a young buck. A thousand yards away and staring at me with semaphore ears.

They assembled at a stiff trot from the haphazard array of feeding and strung out in a precise line against the far hill in a dogtrot. When I removed my hat, they went into their pogo-stick gait and that was that.

❦

"What did a deer ever do to you?"

"Nothing."

"I'm serious. What do you have to go and kill them for?"

"I can't explain it talking like this."

"Why should they die for you? Would you die for deer?"

"If it came to that."

❦

My boy and I went up to the north fork to look for grouse. We had my old pointer Molly, and Thomas's .22 pump. We flushed a number of birds climbing through the wild roses, but they roared away at knee level, leaving me little opportunity for my over-and-under, much less an opening for Thomas to ground-sluice one with his .22. We started out at the meteor hole above the last ranch and went all the way to the national forest. Thomas had his cap on the bridge of his nose and wobbled through the trees until we hit cross fences. We went out into the last open pasture before he got winded. So, we sat down and looked across the valley at the Gallatin Range, furiously white and serrated, making a bleak edge of the world. We sat in the sun and watched the chickadees make their way through the russet brush.

"Are you having a good time?"

"Sure," he said and curled a small hand around the octagonal barrel of the Winchester. I was not sure what I had meant by the question.

&

The rear quarters of the antelope came from the smoker so dense and finely grained it should have been sliced as prosciutto. My Canadian in-laws brought edgy, crumbling cheddar from British Columbia and everybody kept an eye on the food and tried to pace themselves. The snow whirled in the windowlight and puffed the smoke down the chimney around the cedar flames. I had a stretch of enumerating things: my family, hay fields, saddle horses, friends, thirty-ought-six, French and Russian novels. I had a baby girl, colts coming, and a new roof on the barn. I had finished a big corral made of railroad ties and two-by-sixes, I was within eighteen months of my father's death, my sister's death, and the collapse of my marriage. Still, the washouts were repairing; and when a few things had been set aside, not excluding paranoia, some features were left standing, not excluding lovers, children, friends, and saddle horses. In time, it would be clear as a bell. I did want venison again that winter and couldn't help but feel some old ridge runner had my number on him.

I didn't want to read, and I didn't want to write or acknowledge the phone with its tendrils into the zombie enclaves. I didn't want the New Rugged; I wanted the Old Rugged and a pot to piss in. Otherwise, it's deteriorata with mice undermining the wiring in my frame house, sparks jumping in the insulation, the dog turning queer, and a horned owl staring at the baby through the nursery window.

&

It was pitch black in the bedroom and the windows radiated cold across the blankets. The top of my head felt this side of frost and the stars hung like ice crystals over the chimney. I scrambled out of bed and slipped into my long johns, put on a heavy shirt and my wool logger pants with the police suspenders. I carried the boots down to the kitchen so as not to wake the house and turned the percolator on. I put some cheese and chocolate in my coat, and when the coffee was done I filled a chili bowl and quaffed it against the winter.

When I hit the front steps I heard the hard squeaking of new snow under my boots and the wind moved against my face like a machine for refinishing hardwood floors. I backed the truck up to the horse trailer, the lights wheeling against the ghostly trunks of the bare cottonwoods. I connected the trailer and pulled it forward to a flat spot for loading the horse.

I had figured that when I got to the corral, I could tell one horse from another by starlight; but the horses were in the shadow of the barn and I went in feeling my way among their shapes trying to find my hunting horse Rocky, and trying to get the front end of the big sorrel who kicks when surprised. Suddenly Rocky was looking in my face, and I reached around his neck with the halter. A twelve-hundred-pound bay quarter horse, his withers angled up like a fighting bull, he wondered where we were going but ambled after me on a slack lead rope as we headed out of the darkened corral.

I have an old trailer made by a Texas horse vet years ago. It has none of the amenities of newer trailers. I wish it had a dome light for loading in the dark, but it doesn't. You ought to check and see if the cat's sleeping in it before you load, and I didn't do that, either. Instead, I climbed inside the trailer and the horse followed me. I tied the horse down to a D-ring and started back out when he blew up. The two of us were confined in the small space and he was ripping and bucking between the walls with such noise and violence that I had a brief disassociated moment of suspension from fear. I jumped up on the manger with my arms around my head while the horse shattered the inside of the trailer and rocked it furiously on its axles. Then he blew the steel rings out of the halter and fell over backward in the snow. The cat darted out and was gone. I slipped down off the manger and looked for the horse; he had gotten up and was sidling down past the granary in the star shadows.

I put two blankets on him, saddled him, played with his feet, and calmed him. I loaded him without incident and headed out.

I went through the aspen line at daybreak, still climbing. The horse ascended steadily toward a high basin, creaking the saddle metronomically. It was getting colder as the sun came up, and the rifle scabbard held my left leg far enough from the horse that I was chilling on that side.

We touched the bottom of the basin and I could see the rock wall defined by a black stripe of evergreens on one side and the remains of an avalanche on the other. I thought how utterly desolate this country can look in winter and how one could hardly think of human travel in it at all, not white horsemen or Indians dragging travois, just aerial raptors with their rending talons and heads like cameras slicing across the geometry of winter.

Then we stepped into a deep hole and the horse went to his chest in the powder, splashing the snow out before him as he floundered toward the other side. I got my feet out of the stirrups in case we went over. Then we were on wind-scoured rock and I hunted some lee for the two of us. I thought of my son's words after our last cold ride: "Dad, you know in 4-H? Well, I want to switch from Horsemanship to Aviation."

❧

The spot was like this: a crest of snow crowned in a sculpted edge high enough to protect us. There was a tough little juniper to picket the horse to, and a good place to sit out of the cold and noise. Over my head, a long, curling plume of snow poured out, unchanging in shape against the pale blue sky. I ate some of the cheese and rewrapped it. I got the rifle down from the scabbard, loosened the cinch, and undid the flank cinch. I put the stirrup over the horn to remind me my saddle was loose, loaded two cartridges into the blind magazine and slipped one in the chamber. Then I started toward the rock wall, staring at the patterned discolorations: old seeps, lichen, cracks, and the madhouse calligraphy of immemorial weather.

There were a lot of tracks where the snow had crusted out of the wind; all deer except for one well-used bobcat trail winding along the edges of a long rocky slot. I moved as carefully as I could, stretching my eyes as far out in front of my detectable movement as I could. I tried to work into the wind, but it turned erratically in the basin as the temperature of the new day changed.

The buck was studying me as soon as I came out on the open slope; he was a long way away and I stopped motionless to wait for him to feed again. He stared straight at me from five hundred yards. I waited until I could no longer feel my feet nor finally my legs. It was nearly an hour before he suddenly ducked his head and began to feed. Every time he fed I moved a few feet, but he was working away from me and I wasn't getting anywhere. Over the next half hour he made his way to a little rim and, in the half hour after that, moved the twenty feet that dropped him over the rim.

I went as fast as I could move quietly. I now had the rim to cover me and the buck should be less than a hundred yards from me when I looked over. It was all browse for a half mile, wild roses, buckbrush, and young quakies where there was any runoff.

When I reached the rim, I took off my hat and set it in the snow with my gloves inside. I wanted to be looking in the right direction when I cleared the rim, rise a half step and be looking straight at the buck, not scanning for the buck with him running sixty, a degree or two out of my periphery. And I didn't want to gum it up with thinking or trajectory guessing. People are always trajectory guessing their way into gut shots and clean misses. So, before I took the last step, all there was to do was lower the rim with my feet, lower the buck into my vision, and isolate the path of the bullet.

As I took that step, I knew he was running. He wasn't in the browse at all, but angling into invisibility at the rock wall, racing straight into the elevation, bounding toward zero gravity, taking his longest arc into the bullet and the finality and terror of all you have made of the world, the finality you know that you share with the princess and your babies with their inherited and ambiguous dentition, the finality that any minute now you will meet as well.

He slid a hundred yards in a plume of snow. I dressed him and skidded him by one antler to the horse. I made a slit behind the last ribs, pulled him over the saddle and put the horn through the slit, lashed the feet to the cinch Ds, and led the horse downhill. The horse had bells of clear ice around his hooves, and when he slipped, I chipped them out from under his feet with the point of a bullet.

I hung the buck in the open woodshed with a lariat over a rafter. He turned slowly against the cooling air. I could see the intermittent blue light of the television against the bedroom ceiling from where I stood. I stopped the twirling buck, my hands deep in the sage-scented fur, and thought, This is either the beginning or the end of everything.

What the Hunter Knows

❧

THOMAS MCINTYRE

What an absurd time to be a hunter. Yet has there ever been a more vital one?

At no other point in history has the idea of the hunt and the hunter been under such intense assault, and for such disheartening reasons. Half a century ago, Ortega y Gasset could fault the stupidity of the time; but he was explaining, then, why hunting was not considered a serious matter, not why it was judged an abomination. Today one is tempted to view the assault as being not so much stupid as cynical—except that the true cynic ("cynic" = "doglike") is one, as animal-poet Vicki Hearne points out, who simply does not "believe in anything an animal cannot understand"; and what natural animal, whether predator or prey, cannot understand the hunt?

Something more than cynicism must be at work, then. Something to do with the rise of mass culture and our society's increasing estrangement from the wild and its native processes. Something that questions our very presence on the planet. Something that is more pathogenic than accidental, the symptoms all too widespread.

A basic tenet of popular culture, from film to television to most literature and even much music, is that hunters signify a malignancy of the human spirit that is bound to rage against nature. In the press, sublimely blockheaded editorial writers for behemoth metropolitan dailies huff about the supposed noxiousness of hunting while national-newsweekly columnists intone, apparently ex cathedra, "The fact is that hunters are pests." A highly regarded writer of fiction, whose fiction hardly anyone has ever read, knows enough about what the marketplace of ideas will bear these days to pen an astonishingly venomous and hate-speech-filled essay for a "major magazine" that in its lighter moments characterizes hunters as "piggy," "insatiable," "malevolent," "vain," "grossly inept," "avaricious," and "atavistic" "*persecutors of nature*" (italics, oh yes, mine).

If hunters are "persecutors of nature," then nature's saviors would have to be drawn from the ranks of nonhunters. And the exemplar of salvation we find there is none other than the "more environmentally aware public." This (certainly nonhunting) public is said to be, more than ever before, concerned about and frequently anguished by pollution, recycling, toxic wastes, global warming, and the "saving" of creatures both great and small. Unfortunately, while these are all extremely urgent matters to be concerned about, recognition of them, whether individually or in sum, fails to constitute any sort of awareness of the environment. "Concern" alone cannot be the *tao* that leads us to *awareness* of the environment or nature or the wild. Do we come to love something merely because we are concerned about it; or mustn't our concern arise from love, love from knowledge? Vladimir Nabokov, ardent hunter of butterflies (a northern blue bears the trinomial *Lycaeides sublivens* Nabokov in testament to his passion), scoffed at John James Audubon's clumsy renderings of butterflies: "Query: Can anyone draw something he knows nothing about?"

Ironically (though hardly laughably), the more-environmentally-aware-public is, on the whole, increasingly *unaware* of the actual environment. Nor is it likely to be otherwise, when the vast majority is now urbanite and suburbanite, less than half the population acknowledging so much as a single day in a year involving itself with wildlife, if only to watch it in flight. (If puling things like statistics are called for, then let it be noted that the average hunter spends seventeen days afield annually, while another class of hunter, as we shall see, never truly leaves the field.)

The political correctness of the moment, in fact, openly discourages contact with wildlife and the wild as the trend toward the restricting of access to national park, wilderness, and forest lands grows, and even the simple viewing of animals in zoos and aquariums is condemned. Added to this, as an article in the *Los Angeles Times* put it in 1994, "technology is rapidly separating us from the natural world, blurring the distinctions between what is real and what is not, substituting vicarious stimulation for actual experience, and giving us no leisure relief from the relentless acceleration of time." Today for most people the "wild" they are carpet-bombed with through the modern miracle of television appears more authentic than any they have ever found the time to encounter on their own, or are ever likely to.

One suspects that this pandemic isolation of people from the wild and wildlife (an essentially inhuman and recent plight to which our evolution has had absolutely no time to adapt) would produce enormous unspoken and probably unconscious resentments and frustrations that find some bitter relief, again to quote Hearne, in the "bizarre social and political assaults currently under way against everyone in this culture who has a genuine relationship with animals."

Although our attraction to wildlife predates the first time we ever held a gun and occupies our thoughts, and dreams, during the hours and days when we are not holding one, many of us have found hunting to be the most profound way for us to form a genuine relationship with wild animals and the nature they inhabit. So the virulent attack upon hunters should not puzzle us; we can and do affiliate with wildness in ways few others are privileged to. What we should find far more intriguing is the whole breed of hunters, fully conscious of all the reproach, mockery, denunciation, and finally, envy of their special intimacy with the wild—and yet equally (and genuinely) aware of their obligations to it—who do not merely persist in hunting, but who see it as a vigorous aspect of their environmental ethos, even as the badge of it. What is it in hunting that can create such defiance and determination? What can it be that this hunter, this *neohunter*, knows?

That the hunter has a special relationship, more nearly a kinship, not only with wildlife but with the wild itself has long been understood, however grudgingly. It is hardly news that the hunter-conservationist, and his tremendous record of success, is a tradition that dates well back into the previous century to the line of Gifford Pinchot, George Bird Grinnell, and Theodore Roosevelt. It was hunter-conservationists, as we all know (or should), who played some of the most crucial roles in the creating-preserving-maintaining of wildlife laws, parks, refuges, forests, rivers, species, and who were justly honored in their day for these accomplishments. There is something different about the new hunter-*environmentalist*, though, more than just the fatuous modern suspicion that "hunter-environmentalist" has to be some kind of oxymoron. For one thing, the hunter-environmentalist, the neohunter, finds himself (or herself) in an era when there is more science to weigh, more understanding, and not merely intuition, of nature's mechanisms, of how the loom operates. Simultaneously, society as a whole seems in the throes of a powerful antiscience, antireason revolt, with bathos and sensationalism fitting more neatly into nine-second sound bites than do logical explanation and rational discourse, and making fifteen-minute icons out of those who would rather see the looms smashed than repaired and maintained in some working order—if that repair means human involvement. (All this, one should add, much to the delight of the greed-merchants who merrily go along shaving away the wild under the cloud of dust that gets kicked up.) Consequently, the odds in favor of any real salvation seem much slimmer these days, while the stakes have never been higher.

The hunter-environmentalist lives today at a historical moment when new and creative tactics—not just new in light of the last hundred years, but of the last twenty-five—need to be looked at and tried if those parts of our environment that are most worth maintaining are going to be. There needs to be an entirely new way of seeing the wild. And who is most capable of doing that?

Returning at dark from Walden Pond, carrying his string of fish, Thoreau glimpsed a woodchuck crossing his path. He felt a "strange thrill of savage delight" and the temptation to seize the woodchuck and "devour him raw," hungry not at all for meat, but for "that wildness" the woodchuck represented.

"In wildness is the preservation of the world," and what wildness the more-environmentally-aware-public may never know, not having hunted, can never be the same. Of course, it would be politic to say that what they can know is not necessarily something lesser, only different. Except that is not true. Thoreau knew that he owed his "closest acquaintance with Nature" to his youthful hunting, and that we "cannot but pity the boy who has never fired a gun; he is no more humane, while his education has been sadly neglected"; and that hunters, "spending their lives in the fields and woods, in a peculiar sense a part of Nature themselves, are often in a more favorable mood for observing her . . . than philosophers and poets even, who approach her with expectations. She is not afraid to exhibit herself" to hunters. It was through no other way but hunting that Aldo Leopold learned to "think like a mountain," even when that hunting led him to the remorseful extreme of seeing the "fierce green fire" die out in the eye of a she-wolf.

And where does "hunting-environmentalism" lead?

Boone and Crockett Club. Ducks Unlimited. Foundation for North American Wild Sheep. Game Conservation International. The National Wild Turkey Federation. Pheasants Forever. Quail Unlimited. Rocky Mountain Elk Foundation. The Ruffed Grouse Society. Waterfowl U.S.A. Whitetails Unlimited. And on, "for perhaps the hunter is the greatest friend of the animals hunted, not excepting the Humane Society." Certainly not above criticism (even from hunter-environmentalists), certainly not always "correct," hunter-originated environmental organizations have, nonetheless, created enormous benefits for wild animals.

Yet the argument is heard that the only reason all these organizations exist is so they can sustain and increase the types of animals their members most desire to hunt. As if this somehow nullifies all the work they do, as if we can suddenly afford the enormous luxury of rejecting any genuine assistance given to any wild animal for any reason, even perceived selfishness; as if the world is somehow not a better place for there being more wild sheep, quail, or ducks in it. Not to mention that it is disingenuous to accuse an elk foundation of being solely about elk, a grouse society solely about grouse, or a wild turkey federation solely about wild turkeys. What every one of them is about is habitat, the environment, "the land" as Leopold defined it; no means exists to separate the wild from its wildlife and expect either to survive, and the benefits received by game animals by and large spill over onto nongame species as well. Simply because they have chosen to concentrate on those parts of the land that have the most direct impact on the animal whose clan they have decided to become cannot possibly discredit these organizations' efforts.

But perhaps the greatest impetus to depreciate the successes of these "totemic" societies stems from their being such successes. For a generation, many in the mainstream (i.e., nonhunting) environmental movement around the world have been promulgating a variety of now-questionable nostrums to protect the environment. Yet how, as one example, have severe command-and-control edicts from a distant capital, the removal of any legal economic value from their wildlife (both dead and alive), and other forms of "eco-colonialism" that have been imposed upon them in the name of environmental immaculacy possibly enhanced native peoples' relationship with the natural world into which they were born and have the most direct contact with and effect upon? How could this widely accepted approach to environmental preservation ever intensify native people's resolve to husband the wild? How has the entire doctrinaire, bureaucratized, abstract, and ultimately disembodied concept of "saving" brought all the people any closer to the land and increased their genuine knowledge of it?

And why do so few nonhunting totemic societies exist to work directly for the benefit of individual nonhunted species, endangered or otherwise, unless the passion hunters feel for the hunted is an especially powerful, valuable, and unique force in the realm of conservation? Hunters spend $500 million a year on licenses, have spent billions for wildlife restoration over the years through Pittman-Robertson and other taxes and fees, plus millions upon millions more in contributions to their totemic societies, almost all to the direct benefit of wildlife. (The Elk Foundation, as one example, places nearly eighty-five cents of every dollar it receives into its projects, while the very best of the mainstream environmental organizations do well to spend fifty cents.) Where, exactly, do all the monies raised by the nonhunting environmental movement go?

Today the purposes and practices of at least some mainstream environmental organizations have grown suspect. Some of these organizations seem more and more to have become primarily fundraising entities whose continued existence is based upon their expertise, in the words of photographer, writer, hunter, and environmental gadfly Peter Beard, at indulging their contributors' taste for "heroism through money." (Although hard times or simple "sympathy fatigue" has also led today to the shrinking of that once abundant eco-dollar, leaving much of the mainstream environmental movement in sorry financial straits.) And while the (increasingly fewer and smaller) checks are being written (and scrabbled after), the lawsuits filed, the publicity campaigns mounted, the press releases issued, the new headquarters buildings constructed, the gift shops stocked, the hyperthymic mailings posted, the pious public service announcements filmed, the perpetual conferences held, the outraged protests staged, the battles waged to turn the wild into just another in the long line of society's "victims"—while the dogs, in short, bark, the neohunter is out there, seeing what can be done, and doing it, seemingly, more effectively, driven by desires and faith stronger and more lasting than any that can be acquired by simply admiring or being moved to pity by glossy pictures of faraway wild things. And perhaps that makes some environmentalists, particularly the professionals in the so-called mainstream movement, rather nervous about the fate of their fiefdoms.

As the neohunter has a look around, he does so in a way perhaps unique in environmentalism. Claims of his blunderheadedness and hamhandedness—his "Bubba-hood"—to the contrary, the neohunter (no, not all hunters are neo, but more become so, perhaps out of nothing more than the instinct to survive, on a daily basis) has learned to differentiate an ecosystem from an ought-six. He has come to understand that an encounter with wildlife is not the discovery of a target of opportunity, but a meeting with a different beating heart and living spirit. Refusing to accept the wild as a victim, he is willing to be alert to all of it, to be able to recognize its sorrows while acknowledging the very tangible joys it is unafraid to exhibit to him. He is someone, even in this age of unbelief, who actually believes he still has a genuine place in the, yes, grand scheme of things. The neohunter takes his own dollars and his own energies and does not wait around for somebody else to do it for him, realizing, as Clemenceau said about war being much too important to be left to the generals, that the wild is far, far too precious to be left to the bureaucrats, public or private.

While it has been suggested that hunters should go out and join mainstream environmental organizations (and they should) to help preserve hunting, members of those organizations would do well to be joining the totemic societies founded by hunters to help preserve the environmental movement, not to mention the environment itself. Far from being a persecutor of nature, the neohunter may in fact be the last best hope the wild has.

Knowledge and alertness, then, are what inform the neohunter's activism. The true neohunter is constitutionally incapable of rejecting out of hand any reasonable means of sustaining or improving the environment simply because that means is judged, by either end of the ideological spectrum, to be "incorrect." The neohunter understands that the natural world, the *real* world, the realest world we can have in this life, is chock-full of conflicts and conundrums and that between the moment of our birth and that of death there are no absolute truths out there, at least none that we can claim full comprehension of, because this system we call the wild is forever changing, as all vital systems do. And so we are obliged always to be on our toes.

This living on the qui vive, which is after all the primeval and essential human *and* hunting state, may be the most important gift that comes from being a neohunter. Two sentences sprang out at me from a novel once. The main character, half Inuit, half European, thinks to herself, "I am not a hunter. And I'm asleep inside." And I thought, I am a hunter. And I'm wide awake. And I mean to stay that way.

There may, indeed, be ways other than that of the neohunter to be awake, but there are assuredly none that are the same (and for me, none I have found to be more sustaining). In the end it may be this unique state of wakefulness, this being alert to all that is around us to the fullest capacity of our senses, that is what matters most about being a neohunter. Matters most to us and to what there is of the wild that remains for us to be alert in, interacting with it so we can know, love, and care for it; knowing, loving, and caring so that we can continue to interact. After all, who can say what sound a falling tree makes if no one ever goes into the forest?

Query: Can anyone save something he knows nothing about?

Space Age Technology, Stone Age Pursuit

✤

DAVID STALLING

The wind was erratic near the top of the ridge; I hoped my chemical scent shield would conceal my odor from the bull elk below. I heard him before I saw him, the heavy crunching of hooves on leaves distinct through my sound amplifier. A serenade from my latex cow call stopped him, then excited him. He let out a high-pitched scream followed by several guttural grunts that, through my headphones, nearly burst my eardrums. Then silence. I turned the amplifier level down on my hearing enhancer and checked my infrared game scanner. It detected a large heat source 150 meters due north. I had him located. But my best cow-calling efforts couldn't coax the bull closer, so I whispered into my throat microphone to my partner, waiting in a spruce thicket below.

"Can you hear him?"

"Yeah."

"I'll keep him talking. You move in."

The plan worked. While I got the bull riled up enough to rip a small fir out of the ground, my friend stalked within forty yards of the massive monarch. Placing the red dot from his laser sight on the bull's vitals, he shot. At nearly three hundred feet per second, released from a Galactic Eliminator compound bow with overdraw, it didn't

182

take long for the graphite shaft to find its mark. The razor-sharp car-bon blades opened on impact. The bull ran fifty yards and dropped. According to my pocket global positioning system, we were only a quarter of a mile from the trail where our ATVs were parked. A perfect beginning and end to the September primitive weapons elk season.

❧

The hunt is fictitious. The equipment and methods aren't. A look through most any hunting equipment catalog shows a plethora of technology available to the modern hunter, including trail-monitoring devices to photograph, record, and store animal movements, game scanners, hearing enhancers, night-vision goggles, range finders, variable-power rifle scopes, latex calls, animal scents, how-to books and videos, state-by-state hunting unit statistics, ATVs with gun mounts, and thousands of other gadgets designed to increase our chances of finding and killing wildlife. Technology has saturated the world of hunting—come opening day, D-day, the assault begins.

I once spent fourteen numbing days on a mountain in northern Norway, wearing Gore-Tex over wool to fend off the wind and sixty-below cold, covered by white camouflage to hide from British troops below—"the enemy"—in a giant NATO war game intended to warn Russia there'd be hell to pay if it dared cross the nearby border in an attempt to gain control of the North Sea. The cold war at its coldest.

I was a Marine sergeant in a Force Recon unit, traveling to every clime and place to detect and report enemy movements and activities. We had state-of-the-art technology to help us get the job done: PVS5 night-vision goggles, satellite communications gear, remote sensors to detect movement around our perimeter, global positioning systems to determine precise locations, high-powered variable scopes on our M40 7.62mm sniper rifles. Swift, silent, and deadly. We used our skills and technology against the Gadhafis of the world . . . and in Norway I joked with my buddy from Mississippi, "What if we could use this stuff for hunting?"

I was kidding. Yet today you can find this stuff in outdoor cata-logs. "Let cold war technology help you find and kill game." At least we're not calling in air strikes on elk—though maybe we would if we could. Several years ago, hunters in northern Idaho were shooting elk from a half mile away using .50-caliber rifles mounted on off-road vehicles. A game warden from Wyoming tells me that every year, more and more hunters are using airplanes to locate elk, radioing their sightings to friends on the ground.

"Elk are the enemy, kill them at all costs. They win or you win."

A few years ago, I read an antihunting brochure printed by the Humane Society of the United States that referred to hunting as "the war on wildlife." At the time I was angry, defensive. But they might be onto something.

In our defense, we hunters claim that the "antis" are detached from the natural world—they've drifted too far from the death-begets-life reality of Mother Nature—while we hunters retain a special relationship with Earth. Yet last year I saw a group of hunters heading for the mountains of Montana in a mega motorhome with a satellite dish on top (can't miss those football games) and *two* trailers in tow—one carrying four ATVs, the other a freezer to store game meat. A week later, I ran into some hunters in the backcountry who were using portable radios to let each other know if and where they found elk. Back to nature?

Physical fitness and woodsmanship skills decline in direct proportion to technological advancements. What good is a laser sight if a hunter won't—or can't—walk more than a mile from the trailhead? Elk are probably more vulnerable to tenacity than to technology. I once met a frustrated hunter who sat on a ridge all day, bugling to elk in a steep canyon below. "How do you get them to come to you?" he asked. I guess he believed the elk-call ad that claims the call "forces bulls to bugle and come in . . . even if they don't want to!" and the warning on a bottle of cow elk urine: "Use too much, and bulls may try to breed you."

✻

Technology takes its toll. Particularly when too many hunters armed with gadgetry invade the ever-shrinking habitat of wildlife. After all, do I have a better chance of killing an elk with a longbow or a laser-guided missile?

Between longbows and missiles lies a staggering array of equipment. And of choices. Hunters must decide which technologies uphold their notion of fair chase. The problem is not new. Gunpowder and matchlock rifles made it easier to bring down animals in the fifteenth century. Long-range guns and railroads helped to nearly wipe out bison and elk four centuries later. Some people predicted that the advent of the repeating rifle would destroy most, if not all, large game animals in North America. Concerned hunters and other conservationists initiated laws to control hunting seasons and bag limits, and outlawed methods of killing that gave unfair advantage to people. Elk, deer, and other wildlife flourished as a result.

But technology advanced. Better rifles, more efficient muzzle-loaders, faster bows, variable scopes, and four-wheel-drive vehicles ushered in regulations such as limited-entry hunting, road closures, and restricted hunting seasons. Each time technology surges forward, killing wildlife becomes a little easier, more people join in, wildlife become more vulnerable, and more regulations are needed.

During the late 1970s, Idaho elk herds crashed after too many people with high-powered rifles and scopes took advantage of virtually unlimited hunting opportunities. The Idaho Fish and Game Department reacted by instituting bulls-only hunting. The state's elk herds prospered. Then came diaphragm elk calls. Hunters became good at imitating the whistles, grunts, and squeals of bulls in rut. Entrepreneurs marketed calls, writers wrote about them, how-to videos became ever more popular—everybody got in on the act. In hunting units where the peak of the rut coincided with early rifle seasons, bull numbers dropped drastically. Then came more regulations, limiting the effects of technology by allowing only primitive weapons during the rut. And technology raced onward.

Primitive weapons evolved. Compound bows with overdraw, dramatic draw-weight let-offs, and increased arrow speeds largely supplanted longbows and recurves. Muzzle-loading rifles with synthetic stocks and scopes can now shoot accurately at distances once considered the exclusive province of modern center-fire rifles. Success rates have increased. So have the number of "primitive weapons" hunters. High-tech gear makes hunting easier, attracting more people to the sport. A compound bow doesn't require the time and patience of a recurve to master.

Good, say some hunters. If hunting is to survive, new hunters must be recruited. The hunting industry warns us that the *percentage* of Americans who hunt has declined steadily over the past twenty years. True. What it *doesn't* tell us is that the actual numbers of hunters, particularly elk and deer hunters, have climbed just as steadily. About 4.5 million people hunted big game in 1955, compared to 10.7 million in 1985. In Colorado, the number of people hunting elk each year has rocketed from 102,000 two decades ago to more than a quarter million today.

In a state-produced hunting video, a Colorado wildlife biologist advises hunters to choose a strategic spot where they think other hunters might push elk to them; a common tactic in today's crowded woods. Hunting magazines tout similar techniques. In the meantime, big-racked bulls are growing more scarce in elk herds not protected by limited-entry, branch-antlered regulations, adversely affecting breeding behavior, calf survival, and the long-term health of herds. Regulations to restrict the killing of big bulls are slow in the making—lots of hunters buying licenses translates to more money for fiscally strapped fish and game agencies.

But what about biological and ethical concerns? In a talk delivered to fellow wildlife managers, biologist (and now U.S. Forest Service chief) Jack Ward Thomas explained it well:

> When we allow, even encourage, hunting situations that essentially remove mature bulls as a functioning part of elk ecology, we need to carefully examine our motivation and rationale. When we allow the elk's highly evolved breeding ritual to essentially disappear in more and more places . . . we need to look closely at what we are doing. When we allow hunter densities so high that . . . in more and more places groups of elk run from hunter to hunter until they stop, tongues lolled out, too exhausted to run any more, we need to examine why we allow such to occur. . . . Elk deserve better from us. Hunters deserve better from us. Our culture demands better of us. It seems to me essential that hunting shame neither the hunter nor the hunted.

Do we really need *more* hunters . . . or *better* hunters, more conscientious hunters? Quality versus quantity. A fish and game commissioner from Idaho recently observed that his state is approaching levels of hunting pressure unacceptable for continued successful management of elk, and that hunter density and overcrowding are reaching levels unacceptable to many hunters. There are more than 250 million people in this country. Do we really want a majority heading for the hills each fall with rifle and bow? With motorhomes and ATVs? With night-vision goggles and infrared heat sensors?

No doubt the hunting industry does. Hunting technology is big business—a business that, granted, has contributed immensely to wildlife conservation through special excise taxes on hunting and fishing equipment and contributions to nonprofit conservation groups. Technology also creates jobs. And, of course, the technology wouldn't exist if there weren't plenty of hunters willing to spend lots of money to improve their chances of filling a tag. This intimate relationship between industry and hunters makes it difficult to question the effects of technology on hunting, hunters, and the hunted—especially in a time of growing paranoia over the antihunting movement.

"You're either with us or against us."

Don't question the ATVs whining through the mountains, often illegally. Don't question bear baiting or executing hound-treed cougars. Challenging the sanctity of hunting—any part of hunting—can get you labeled "one of *them*," an "anti," with McCarthy-like vengeance.

Half a century ago, hunter-environmentalist Aldo Leopold contemplated the relationship between technology, industry, hunters, and the hunt. From his 1949 essay collection, A *Sand County Almanac*:

> I have the impression that the American sportsman is puzzled; he doesn't understand what is happening to him. Bigger and better gadgets are good for industry, so why not for outdoor recreation? It has not dawned on him that outdoor recreations are essentially primitive, atavistic; that their value is a contrast-value; that excessive mechanization destroys contrasts by moving the factory to the woods or to the marsh. The sportsman has no leaders to tell him what is wrong. The sporting press no longer represents sport; it has turned billboard for the gadgeteer. Wildlife administrators are too busy producing something to shoot at to worry much about the cultural value of the shooting. . . . I do not pretend to know what is moderation, or where the line is between legitimate and illegitimate gadgets. Yet there must be some limit beyond which money-bought aids to sport destroy the cultural value of sport. . . . Our tools for the pursuit of wildlife improve faster than we do, and sportsmanship is the voluntary limita-

tion in the use of these armaments. It is aimed to augment the role of skill and shrink the role of gadgets in the pursuit of wild things.

Proponents of technologically advanced gear say it allows quicker, cleaner kills and helps hunters find and recover wounded animals. But what of shooting, hunting, and tracking skills? What of ethics?

A survey of Missouri bowhunters revealed that hunters using compound bows with release aids and lighted sight pins killed 28 percent more deer—but wounded 75 percent more deer—than hunters using traditional recurves and longbows. The hunters who didn't wound game were generally more experienced, knew the limitations of their weapons better, and were more conscientious about shot selection. Wounding, the survey showed, is based on hunter skill and ethics, not equipment. Many of the hunters using high-tech gear thought their equipment would make them more proficient at killing deer. Maybe it did—but far too many of those deer died in thickets where only crows and coyotes ever found them. Technology creates an illusion of proficiency.

But even when high-tech gear does help a hunter make quicker, cleaner kills, how far should the technology go? In the right hands, a 7mm magnum with a three-by-nine variable scope can be deadly at three hundred yards. How about a tripod-mounted .50 caliber at a thousand yards? How about a heat-seeking, laser-guided projectile? How much technology is too much technology? And who is to decide? Are sound amplifiers acceptable? What about regular hearing aids? How about devices that enhance vision, such as binoculars and scopes? At what point does the search for quicker, cleaner kills exceed the concept of fair chase?

The Boone and Crockett Club defines fair chase, in part, as the skill to use your five senses with the stealth of a predator hunting food. The late John Madson described it this way: "A good working definition of a game species is one that is fitted with survival equipment enabling it to take advantage, while a genuine sport hunter is one constrained by ethics and respect to give advantage."

In *Beyond Fair Chase*, Jim Posewitz charts the evolution of fair chase from the days of loincloths and obsidian spear points to Gore-Tex and 3,500-feet-per-second chunks of metal:

When the hunter with a spear in hand stalked wildlife in the primal forest, the pursuit was well within the bounds of fair chase. That situation is past. Technological advancement, the human population explosion, and the loss of wildlands require a new balancing act between the hunter and the hunted ... there is a constant flow of products developed to provide advantages to hunters. Sights, scents, calls, baits, decoys, devices and techniques of infinite variety fill the marketplace. In each case, an individual choice must be made as to what sustains fair chase and what violates that concept.

In some cases, state governments decide. Recently, Idaho outlawed electronic or enhanced-illumination sights, radio transmitters, electronic range finders, and telescopic sights during bow and muzzleloader seasons. Bows that can shoot more than one arrow at a time, bows with more than 65 percent let-off, and explosive, barbed, and expanding broadheads are also illegal.

But the final solution must lie with individual hunters choosing to simplify the gear we carry into the woods—deciding we don't mind pursuing a slightly more *in*vulnerable quarry.

✻

Each fall since leaving the Marine Corps, I've chased elk through the mountains of western Montana. There's no doubt that technology contributes to my efforts and success. I drive a four-wheel-drive pickup to the trailhead, then carry a Gore-Tex-lined goose down sleeping bag and Kevlar-framed camouflage fleece pack far into the backcountry. And I kill elk with a compound bow, aluminum arrow shafts with plastic vanes and razor-sharp, carbon-steel broadheads after bugling them in with latex diaphragm calls. To get the meat home, I recruit the help of a friend, who hauls horses and mules to the trailhead with a large truck and horse trailer.

Sure, elk are vulnerable during the rut. But they're also vulnerable when snow piles high in November; bugling elk into sure bow range is every bit as tough as tracking wary, solitary bulls in snow to within rifle range. I chased and bugled in seven bulls during my most recent bow hunt. All came within a hundred yards. One passed only twenty yards away, but I couldn't get a clear shot. The bull I finally killed came in silently to eight yards after I tracked him through rough country for five hours.

I've killed several elk with my compound bow, and several using my 7mm magnum with variable scope. Technology helps—but it doesn't replace hard work and persistence. I hunt alone, on public land, hiking long distances into steep, rugged mountains—country I hike, snowshoe, and ski into year-round, studying and admiring elk and elk country every chance I get. When I hunt, I chase elk until dark, sleep wherever I am, and continue the pursuit at dawn. "Travel light, freeze at night." I won't shoot more than thirty yards with a bow, and in the thick timber I hunt, I've never taken a shot longer than a hundred yards at elk with a rifle. I've spent many warm September days chasing rutting bulls, and many cold November days following their tracks in snow, without seeing an elk. On days like those, it's tough to believe elk can be vulnerable to any kind of technology.

But they are. And I don't want them any *more* vulnerable. Hunting is *supposed* to be tough, the meat *earned*. Real hunting is stalking, tracking, and penetrating an animal's natural defenses. Certainly, we all buy equipment designed to make elk hunting easier. But today more than ever, we need to question just *how* easy we want it to be. We need to see ourselves as *hunters*, to think a lot more about *why* we hunt.

And we need to remember that fair chase is rooted in a deep respect for the hunted.

An Appeal to Hunters

❧

RICK BASS

My friend's two oldest daughters and I were walking through the tall grass, midsummer. We were hiking to a lake to go fishing. A lone alder tree graced the meadow. The grass was chest-high to me, chin-high to the girls—almost teenagers. They're in love with the woods already.

"Look," I said, "there's a deer resting under that tree, watching us. Look at how its face looks like a lion." I lifted them onto my shoulders so they could get a better view. The tree under which the deer-lion rested was about forty yards away.

"It *is* a lion," said Amanda.

"No," I said, "it just looks like one. Sometimes does' faces can be really round. It's just looking straight at us, with its ears pinned back. When it turns its head, you'll see." I chuckled, set Amanda down, and picked up Stephanie.

"Oh, it's definitely a lion," Stephanie said. "It just turned its head. It doesn't have a muzzle like a deer. It's a lion."

I set Stephanie down and squinted. I'd meant it as just a joke. It *did* look like a lion—but how could it be, just sitting out there in the open like that, under that lone tree? Like some old hound taking a nap.

I'd heard that lions can be easily intimidated, and, in the uncom-

191

mon cases of attacks on humans, that they can be turned back relatively easy. There had been an incident over in Glacier National Park
where a lion had attacked a small boy taking a pee. The boy's father
had chased the lion away with a flashlight. It's true he had to strike
the lion with the light—he didn't just turn it on—but he repelled the
attack. (It's thought that in national parks, lions become accustomed
to humans and lose their natural fear.)

Conventional wisdom (sometimes an oxymoron, in studies of the
natural world) holds that even one small dog can tree a lion; the lions
just haven't evolved to fight. They're hunters—killers—not fighters.

And just the night before, strangely enough, I had been watching
a documentary in which a lion in an enclosure had rushed up behind
the cinematographer and leapt on him. The man almost stumbled,
but turned and swatted at the lion once, and the lion dropped off and
ran away.

So it was with these images in mind that I told the girls to stay on
the trail, and to keep the canoe paddles for security, while I strode
out across the meadow—breaststroking through the high grass—to
make that lion get up and run away.

I have the good fortune to live in a wild place—not a national
park, just deep woods. Where I live is a predator's showcase; there's
no other place like it in the lower forty-eight. The Yaak—my valley—has not just lions, wolves, and grizzlies, but also lynx, coyotes,
martens, fishers, badgers, wolverines, owls, both eagles, hawks, bob-
cats, and black bears. If it hunts for a living, it's still found in the
Yaak. You may only see some of these predators a few times in your
life, with luck, but with lesser luck you can still find their spoor, or
their tracks—which is my point. The animals are wild up here, and if
you do see one, it is almost certainly going to be the back end of it,
running quickly away.

And so, in the spirit of Yaak, I wanted to see this lion run away; I
wanted to see that graceful flow.

This lion did not seem the least interested in running, however,
and as I strode out to meet it, there occurred some vague point where
hesitation entered my mind, and when I was close enough to see the
lion's eyes, and the creamy facial markings, and the black eye shadow,
like mascara—was it my imagination, or was the lion licking its
lips?—my stride became less resolute.

I still had it strongly in my mind that a full-grown man could just shoo a lion away; but now I held that conviction, that confidence, less strongly. Perhaps this lion had not seen that documentary.

I came on anyway, as if hypnotized. An eerie compression began to build, in that dwindling space between me and the lion. How close would it let me come? Where did I cross over from being predator to prey?

It came down to one last step. I paused. The zone of my encroachment had pressured up, to a point where something had to snap; when I stepped across that line, the lion would either lunge at me or jump up and run away.

I didn't want to take that step, but it was beyond my control: something ancient demanded that I push it.

I took another half step and felt the bubble break.

The lion leapt and whirled back toward the woods, its long tail floating behind it. It was not a juvenile cat, as are sometimes involved in incidents with humans—displaced adolescents pushed into new areas with less prey. This was a mature adult—big as Dallas, it looked. I was real glad it was going the other way.

Curious creatures, wild animals, I thought. It occurred to me that they like a little mystery, a little unpredictability, in their lives too.

The girls and I went on down to the lake. We were getting in the canoe when Amanda said, "Look, there he is again!"

The lion had come back out into the tall grass. It was closer. When it saw us looking, it ducked its head down into the grass, and up went its tail, like a periscope. The tail twisted and writhed like a question mark, trying to entice me to come back.

This time I didn't jack around. We left calmly but quickly. We walked back down the trail, through that tunnel of tall grass like gunfighters, revolving all the while to be sure nothing was behind us, and trying to hear rustlings of grass over the thumpings of our hearts.

❧

I want to tell you, those of you who may be lacking predators in the systems where you hunt, what a joy it is, the other eleven months of the year—or even that twelfth month, especially that twelfth month, the hunting month—to find the carcass of a lion-killed doe freshly cached beneath a spruce tree, with the entrails pulled clear but not eaten. I want to tell you how rich that feeling of wildness is, and how full the senses are, the engagement of the senses that we seek, as hunters, to see ravens circling a kill that is not our own, and to see the prints of coyotes, or wolves, coming in and leaving the lion's kill. And of the thrill of walking a game trail and finding a thing as simple as a bear's scat in the middle of it.

It all makes me feel less alone in the world—and it makes me feel richer. I think many of us are feeling increasingly a certain cultural ostracism, a misunderstanding from a society that is frightened by our passion for hunting—and our passion for being in the woods. But the good thing about this alienation is that it makes the bond between those of us who do hunt that much stronger. We don't feel the need to explain or defend ourselves when in each other's company.

And that is the feeling I get, too, walking through the woods and finding the faintest remains of a kill—a fragment of hoof and half a skull; a bit of hide—or a giant bear shit, full of leaves and berries and glittering ants.

All the arguments we've heard and made about hunting, all the unnecessary defenses—*It's in my blood*, or, *I like gathering my own food*, or, *It allows a full engagement of the senses that make us human* (especially that one)—come together so gracefully and completely, when hunting in one of the few systems (perhaps the only system) in the lower forty-eight that still has all of its predators (as well as its full complement of prey, rest assured). You tend not to "stumble along," hunting a stretch of woods—or a valley, or a mountain—that still has its predators. You hunt better; and you're hunting real prey, not a lesser, unraveling species.

When I come upon a skeleton, a ship of bones in the woods—and no matter whether of a trophy buck or a yearling doe—I remember the poet Robinson Jeffers's line, "What but the wolf's tooth / whittled so fine / the fleet limbs of the antelope?"

❧

I think that one of hunting's dirty little secrets—or rather, not so much a secret as simply an unswept corner of the closet—concerns our ambiguous relationship to fellow predators: not so much the feelings we do or do not have for them, but the way we let others, who are not in the woods, speak against these species' survival. I'm talking about the politics of wilderness: of the cores, the security areas critical to big predators' survival.

Because of year-round fertility, high reproductive capabilities, relatively small home ranges, and high deer populations, lions are thriving in many places; but bears and wolves are getting shin-kicked, clubbed, beaten back toward extinction. (A hundred wolves in a state the size of Montana does not, in my mind, constitute a "recovery.") And—with few exceptions—hunters' organizations are not sticking up for these largest predators, the megafauna, and just as important, neither are we using our full power to stick up for the wildlands in which these last great predators are holed up. It might surprise hunters to find out how many of the congresspeople who defend with such force the rights of gun owners seem not so interested in the rights of the ecosystem of which we are a part: that country which is sometimes referred to (where it can still be found) as "the big wild." It's well established that most trophy deer and elk are found, or are living, in the backcountry—where, strangely enough, the lions, bears, and wolves are living too, and they've been there for the last million years.

The reason the big wild is not defended for hunters as earnestly as are the ownership and purchasing requirements of guns has to do with big timber, and big timber's contributions to political campaigns; and with our inaction, I fear (for we do have the power to change this). Meanwhile, our last roadless areas dwindle each year. There are already four hundred thousand miles of roads in the national forests—over eight times the length of the U.S. interstate system.

The wolf's song, never more muted, is almost gone in the West. But it seems to be especially the great bear, the grizzly, that is in perhaps the direst of straits; and ironically, this fiercest of predators is about 90 percent vegetarian. It hunts only about 10 percent of the time—about like us, it occurs to me. In Yellowstone, the wildest protected area in the lower forty-eight, there are only 200 to 250 grizzlies, in a country that was once swimming in them; and in all of the West, less than 1,000. The number of breeding-age females is the most alarming statistic; in the Yellowstone system, of those 200 to 250 bears, only about 30 to 35 are reproductive females. Take that and the fact that a sow keeps her cub or cubs (two, sometimes three are born, but mortality can be high) for three years or longer before breeding again—and the fact that females don't breed until around the age of six—and you can see that if we want a wild country with grizzlies in it, for our children and grandchildren to be awed by, we need to act fast; and that the only thing that can help a grizzly is big country, and lots of it.

But it seems to me that as hunters we're kind of sitting back and letting the roadbuilding happen—letting all these tax-subsidized roads get built into the last federal wildlands. Lest anyone be sold the bill of goods offered by the U.S. Forest Service about the so-called new and revolutionary, system-friendly concept of "Ecosystem Management" (EM), I refer you to the following memo regarding EM, written by the chief of the Forest Service, to all regional foresters:

> There may be situations where you are unable to conduct timber sales in roadless areas. . . . If this situation occurs, I do not expect you to substitute timber sales in roaded areas to compensate for any short-fall in the timber yields expected to derive from entry into roadless areas. However . . . you should proceed in an orderly fashion to enter more such areas.

"Orderly fashion," my ass. Out of the way, grizz; out of the way, bull trout and cutthroats, wolves and caribou. Get along now. Go somewhere else. Or go to hell.

Food is one requirement for the survival of any species, but too much of land management uses the ruse of "increasing food supply" (i.e., clearcutting and roadbuilding with its early successional characteristics) as justification for washing the last of the big wild away. What about the requirement that's in scarcest supply these days—the requirement of security? To me as a hunter it's as important to have that out there as it is to hunt itself. Managing simply for an ever-increasing "food" requirement, besides becoming quickly counterproductive, would be like putting up my rifle and going only to the grocery store for my food—and for the same food every day. I need the shelter of the woods, too, to be a hunter; I need the idea of the big wild, as well as the thing itself. I need to know it's out there, and that I can go into it. Wallace Stegner wrote in *The Sound of Mountain Water*:

> What I want to speak for is not so much the wilderness uses, valuable as those are, but the wilderness *idea*, which is a resource in itself. Being an intangible and spiritual resource, it will seem mystical to the

practical-minded—but then anything that cannot be moved by a bulldozer is likely to seem mystical to them.

I want to speak for the wilderness idea as something that has helped form our character and that has certainly shaped our history as a people. . . .

Something will have gone out of us as a people if we ever let the last virgin forests be destroyed. . . . And so that never again can we have the chance to see ourselves single, separate, vertical and individual in the world, part of the environment of trees and rocks and soil, brother to the other animals, part of the natural world and competent to belong in it.

We are a wild species. . . . One means of sanity is to retain a hold on the natural world, to remain, insofar as we can, good animals. Americans still have that chance, more than many peoples; for while we were demonstrating ourselves the most efficient and ruthless environment-busters in history, and slashing and burning and cutting our way through a wilderness continent, the wilderness was working on us. It remains in us as surely as Indian names remain on the land.

Stegner continued:

Sherwood Anderson, in a letter to Waldo Frank in the 1920s, said it better than I can. "Is it not likely that when the country was new and men were often alone in the fields and the forest they got a sense of bigness outside themselves that has now in some way been lost. . . . Mystery whispered in the grass, played in the branches of trees overhead, was caught up and blown across the American line in clouds of dust at evening on the prairies."

The only wolves I've seen up here were a mile south of the Canadian line, and they were heading north. (I was reminded of the line from the movie *Jeremiah Johnson*, about how "the closer you get to Canada, the more things'll eat your horse.") I want those wolves to come back to my valley. There is enough in the world for us to share. They select for the weak and the slow, all year long, and allow us to indulge in the luxury of so often selecting for the products of their work: the healthy, even the magnificent. When I read about wolves hunting or find one of their kills—where they caught something with their *teeth*!—I am struck with respect; even the best human hunters among us are light years behind the wolves, and always will be.

We keep doing our thing—hunting—and becoming better at it each year, as we learn more, both from the woods and from the prey itself. I like to take pleasure from knowing that, after the snows come and we go back to our cabins or our homes, and turn on the lights or the lanterns, and put a log on the fire, that for others it is still going on, the eternal business of life—of life right at the edge. It gives me a strength, knowing that the wolves are somewhere out there, hunting always with a force and a tension in the world, as I sleep and live my life in the middle ground of sometimes-predator.

And the fact that they are out there, always hunting, gives respect and strength to their prey, too. It makes my own hunting more special. It makes the woods richer.

⚘

The rap on wolves, of course, is that they are "cruel." We've certainly heard that one said of ourselves. And yet wolves kill their prey after a short chase; coyotes—rarely thought of as "cruel," but rather, "cunning"—often kill by wounding: by sinking a tooth in an animal, then following it for a week as the wound festers to gangrene. The coyotes trailing it, staying close, before finally moving in . . .

Neither way is right or wrong; it's just the way the system flows, the way the system's supposed to run. Both ways speak of the wild, and they both speak to me. I do not want to give these things up, if I can help it; I do not want them to vanish from my world and from my children's world. And we're no longer asking for pre–Lewis and Clark conditions—we're asking now to hold on to our last 1 percent.

Think how lonely it would be without the big predators. Every generation of man—which is to say, of hunters—has lived, and hunted, with these fellow hunters.

What would it be like—and what will it be like, I fear—when we are all alone—when we are truly the last hunters?

We would be several leaps closer, I fear, to that very act that we so despair—the simple act of just walking into a store and shopping for our meat, with no wildness involved.

A severance from the natural world that has borne us.

No longer hunters.

The other side wins: the side of prey—which is to say, both sides lose.

Let the predator love his prey, writes the poet and novelist Jim Harrison; but let the predator love, or respect, other predators, too. It was over thirty-five years ago that Stegner argued for the idea of wilderness; and the bears, and the big wild, are worse off today than then. (Grizzlies were listed as a threatened species in the 1970s.)

Where are our leaders now? When was the last time hunters had a Teddy Roosevelt in power?

Even if today's leaders do not have wildness, and the big wild, in their hearts, we can force them to represent us, to act for us. We can explain it to them.

We must. Our representatives and senators are very relieved that we've been quiet on this one, so far. They don't want us to stir things up and make demands that they represent us—that they save wildness. They'd like to keep taking those PAC contributions, unopposed.

But back in the big wild—back in the old forests and up in the mountains—the hunters are watching. And waiting to see which side we will weigh in on.

Waiting, perhaps, to see if we will weigh in at all.

A Failure of the Spirit

❧

Tom Beck

As the state bear biologist for Colorado, my vocation is wildlife management. My primary avocation is hunting. What follows is an appeal to my fellow wildlife managers and hunters.

❧

The philosophies underlying wildlife management have evolved little in the past sixty years, while the philosophies of society have changed greatly. The role of state wildlife agencies has been, and remains, to protect and to provide. We protect wildlife in order to provide for an array of human benefits. Dominant among these benefits is hunting. Ironically, even as we have progressed technologically, we've developed a mind-set and jargon that serve to distance us from both wildlife and the social act we call hunting. Animals are no longer killed; they are "harvested." We measure our success not in pleasant hunting experiences but in dead bodies. Maximum sustained yield has become management's mantra. And therein lies the problem: we have traded our concern for individual wild animals for a preoccupation with an abstract called "total populations." Along the way, we have lost much of the awe, the fascination, and the joy of working with wildlife.

Most state wildlife agencies have developed along a business model, with hunters and fishers their primary "clients." Consequently, these agencies have adopted a restricted circle of information and influence. Wildlife agencies provide a product for which hunters pay. And because they pay, hunters have come to believe the agencies owe their loyalty to them alone. Such a closed system leaves many concerned citizens disenfranchised.

Certainly, the general lack of trust many Americans have for government agencies contributes to the current sad state of affairs in black bear hunting, wherein citizens of more and more states are overruling their wildlife agencies and banning, via ballot initiatives, the use of baits and hounds for hunting bears. But there's more: the main reason bear hunting has become the Achilles' heel of so many state wildlife agencies is that they have never understood how human societies *perceive* bears. In our arrogance, we have ignored the social aspect of our conservation mission. In our stupidity, we have been caught treating bears with less respect and concern than other hunted species.

I've been involved in public debates over black bear hunting methods since 1981, and the most common piece of advice offered to me by bear hunters, usually quite emotionally, has been to "go with biology, not emotion." I've never been sure if these people are truly that ignorant, or if such sentiments are a calculated effort to restrict the debate, knowing their positions are socially indefensible.

Hunting, if it is to persist in America, must operate within two sets of rules, one biological and the other sociological. While the biological rules set the outer limits for *what* we kill, the sociological rules dictate *how* we kill.

The biological rules of black bear hunting relate primarily to survival of the species, welfare of individual bears, and modification of bear behavior. Since unrestricted hunting can lead to major reductions in bear numbers, even to extirpation, methods have been developed to protect against overkilling—including restrictions on the number of hunters, season timing and length, and hunting methods. So long as the annual kill of black bears in an area is less than or equal to the birth rate, the population will survive. Biologically, there are no right or wrong methods to reach this objective. But then, biologically, there are no compelling reasons not to hunt geese in April, elk in July, or bighorn sheep in February. The fact that we *don't* do these things highlights the sociological base of most of our hunting rules.

Wildlife agencies and their hunter-clients have long tried to defend the use of spring hunting seasons, baiting, and hounding as effective methods to direct the kill to certain age and sex groups of bears—primarily large, and presumably older males. Yet little effort has been spent to determine whether this is an appropriate strategy, and if so, whether it can be effectively implemented. I don't believe it is, and I don't believe it can.

Black bears are long-lived animals with low reproductive rates and high annual survival once past two years of age. They are solitary but highly social. In most years here in Colorado, fewer than 20 percent of female bears have cubs. Conservative management would seek to protect these breeding adults, yet selection for large bears tends to focus hunting pressure on this very group.

But for the sake of argument, even if selectivity were a good idea—can it be done successfully? Bear hunters assert that it can *if* they are allowed to use bait and hounds, reasoning that such techniques allow them to get close enough for a good look before they shoot. Wishful thinking.

While I don't doubt that a *few* hunters who have observed *many* bears can be *somewhat* selective, most hunters cannot consistently distinguish males from females or adults from subadults. The experienced hunter is normally accurate in identifying large males, about 10 percent of the population. But for the remaining 90 percent, it's a crapshoot. In thirteen years of black bear kill data gathered in Colorado prior to 1992, when hounds and baiting were voted out of use, there is no suggestion that hunters selected for males or even for larger bears. Why don't the data support the hunters' contentions?

First, because it's so difficult to accurately judge the size, age, or sex of a bear, even at close range. Bear biologists have learned this through the trapping and collaring of thousands of black bears in the last twenty-five years.

Second, because the majority of bears killed over baits are *not* killed at ranges close enough—less than thirty yards—to allow a good look at the animal before shooting. Consider that more than three-fourths of bears killed over baits in Colorado were shot with rifles. Given the natural wariness of bears, how many rifle hunters will choose to hunt within thirty yards of a bait and risk scaring off bears, while holding a weapon that's effective at *three hundred* yards?

Similarly, chasing bears behind hounds is strenuous work, with only about one in five bears "started" eventually being treed. After hiking the mountains for several days, how many of today's hunters will walk away from a small or medium-sized bear in a tree? Moreover, most outfitters work on a fifty-fifty split; half up front, the second half payable only if you kill a bear. Consequently, there's strong financial motivation to convince every hunter that he's looking at a big bear in that tree.

Third and perhaps most important, all bears appear to be larger than they really are. This magnification is a result of their quiet movements, long hair, and the mental images people carry of the power of bears. The adrenaline rush of being close to a bear in the wild has a way of clouding our vision.

✠

With the "selectivity" defense debunked, defenders of baits and hounds turn to the "hunter success" argument, asserting that the kill will decline radically without these methods: the brush is too thick, the mountains too steep, the canyons too deep.

But nary a whisper of the hunter too unskilled.

Granted, the kill rate *will* decrease. But is this necessarily bad? After all, with a lower kill rate, more hunters can participate without endangering bear populations. And why should the kill rate (quantity), rather than the *quality* of the hunt, be the measure of success? How fulfilling is it to shoot a bear with its head in a barrel of jelly-filled doughnuts?

And concerning success rates: Hunters in both Montana and Pennsylvania kill nearly a thousand bears a year without bait or hounds. And three years after the prohibition of baiting and hounding in Colorado, we see that the kill rate declined from 28 percent with, to 21 percent without . . . hardly the "radical" decrease predicted by hunters. Moreover, this lower success rate is still higher than that for bull elk, and hunters *rave* about Colorado elk hunting.

A tertiary defense of baiting is "supplemental feeding"—a euphemism—the claim being that baiting provides a valuable service by buffering bears from poor natural food years (such as 1995, when a widespread acorn and berry failure sent starving black bears into campgrounds and subdivisions in record numbers). Frankly, this argument strikes me as a self-serving rationalization.

While access to human food might improve cub survival or spring birth numbers (a pregnant sow that enters her den undernourished will spontaneously abort), this is a short-term effect having little long-term impact. Bears evolved to absorb periodic food failures and associated changes in cub survival and birth rates, a system that has worked well for thousands of years without the heavy-handed intervention of man. Bears don't need us to protect them from the vagaries of nature.

Furthermore, while baiting clearly improves the nutritional status of individual bears—at least until they're shot—are these lunches really free? Bears are easily hooked on human food, so much so that some will limit their natural foraging. But what happens when the bait is discontinued at season's end? The baited bear is now handicapped by not having been forced to learn the locations of the best natural feeding sites. Consequently, he will roam more and quite likely will wind up near human food again. I firmly believe that baiting creates "nuisance" bears. Black bears are naturally wary, instinctively avoiding close contact with humans. But baiting them with large amounts of tasty food, easily obtained, defeats this wariness. It creates lazy bears who have been rewarded, not punished, for overcoming their fear of humans. All too often, a fed bear is a dead bear.

Finally, we need to ask ourselves what impact the unnatural concentration of bears at a bait site has on individual animals. Are normal seasonal movement patterns modified? Many baited bears become largely nocturnal (to avoid being shot at). Do they transfer this nocturnal habit to *all* of their activities near humans? If people overreact to bears at close range during the day, which they do, imagine their response after dark!

❧

And now to the hottest-potato issue of all: spring hunting as it relates to the orphaning of cubs.

Spring bear seasons, no matter how carefully designed, do result in the orphaning of some dependent cubs. Starvation or predation is their fate. Many nursing females will not bring cubs to a bait site until they have visited the site several times alone. Similarly, when pursued by hounds a mother will leave her cubs in one tree and go find another tree for herself. Consequently, even well-meaning hunters continue to kill nursing mothers during spring seasons.

Hunters argue that orphaned cub deaths have little if any impact on the total bear population, and that the number of nursing females killed annually in Colorado when spring hunting was allowed was usually less than twenty-five. And finally, say the population apologists, half of those dead sows' cubs would have died in the first six months anyhow.

Do not despise them, for they know not what they say. The propaganda has worked. There are no individual *animals*, only "populations."

❧

Finally, bear hunters attempt to defend baiting, hounding, and spring hunting as traditional cultural activities. They contend that as long as they don't overhunt, society should not dictate to them *how* to hunt. They appear to have confused the concept of tolerance of minority opinion, which is strongly rooted in American society, with complete autonomy. Society is a dynamic entity. Arguing to hold to the past without justification in the present and future carries little clout. Not so long ago, baiting waterfowl, the use of punt guns, jacklighting deer, party hunting, basket-trapping and dynamiting fish, and other such "meat gathering" activities were accepted traditions, at least in the South where I grew up. Today, can the wildlife resource bear the weight of such abusive "traditions"? And will society condone them?

I believe the driving force behind hounding and baiting has been to maximize kill rates while minimizing effort, a fact that eclipses the few positive attributes of these methods. Some bear hunters truly enjoy watching large numbers of bears at bait sites while waiting for the "right one." And some houndmen hunt primarily because they love working their dogs. But most hunters sitting over a bait or following hounds only want to kill a bear; the activity is less important than the outcome. Consequently, today's bait hunters have not developed the woodsmanship skills that are so much a part of the American hunting tradition. Instead, they expound on the comparative merits of rotten fish and honey drippers for pulling bears in, and Twinkies versus Jolly Ranchers for holding bears at the bait site. Is this what hunting should be?

We are learning that if we are to coexist with wildlife in a more crowded world, we must refrain from artificial feeding. This may even include a cornerstone of twentieth-century wildlife management: food plots. Today, much of every state wildlife agency's information and education budget goes to convincing a naive public that feeding wildlife is bad for wildlife. Then managers turn around and condone baiting—but only for bears. The inconsistency is glaring to the nonhunting public and to ethical hunters as well. Why is it bad to feed raccoons on your deck, or elk in the winter, but good to feed bears in the spring?

❧

I've spoken mostly of baiting; what of hounding?

Houndmen are quick to point out that not all chases end with a dead bear, proudly declaring theirs a largely "nonconsumptive" activity. But again, there are no free lunches. During their annual fall fattening frenzy, bears often feed twenty hours per day in preparation for hibernation. In poor food years, can an hours-long pursuit by hounds really be harmless to bears? Not only are the hounded bears deprived of critical foraging time, but they burn essential calories in fleeing—and sometimes battling—the hounds. And what of heat stress during a prolonged chase? Bears have a heavy, insulating coat; perfect for hibernation, poor for running. Just because you leave him panting in a tree doesn't mean a bruin is uninjured.

We Americans are enamored of technology, at the same time craving at least symbolic ties to our frontier past. Hunting is a major part of that nostalgia; witness the growth in "traditional" forms of hunting, notably archery and black powder. But look at the equipment! We seem incapable of self-examination and restraint. Technology, its use and abuse, has erupted as a major issue in hounding that employs radio-collared dogs. Proponents say they use the collars only to retrieve lost dogs. Their critics counter that in roaded areas, hunters never leave their trucks until the bear (or lion) is treed. Then they radio-track to the tree and shoot the quarry. Where is the truth?

If the only purpose is in fact to retrieve lost dogs, then there's a reasonable middle ground: prohibit anyone from carrying a weapon while in the field with radiotelemetry gear. I've suggested this often, and consistently receive the same frigid response.

A few years back, the Michigan Department of Natural Resources convened a panel, composed mostly of houndmen, to look at this issue. It came as no surprise when they concluded there was no real problem. What *did* come as a surprise—to me at least, since I've used radiotelemetry for twenty-four years—was their conclusion that telemetry is too inaccurate and unpredictable to be an effective hunting tool . . . while arguing that radio-tracking enables hunters to stop dogs from going onto posted private land!

❧

The root argument among foes of baiting and hounding is that these behaviors are inconsistent with our attitudes toward other wildlife we pursue as game—that is, they run counter to our notion of fair chase. And they're right. I believe the primary reason agencies have condoned a different, less "sporting" standard for bear hunting is based in the antipredator attitudes and programs once widely endorsed by our society. What managers have failed to notice is that society now takes a more tolerant view of predators, especially the large species, and a far less tolerant view of traditional Draconian methods of predator "control."

The notion of fair chase is key to the nonhunting public's tolerance of hunting. These are not antihunters but just concerned people predisposed to object to what they perceive to be *un*fair. It's difficult, for instance, to condone the orphaning of bear cubs in the spring. Anyone (excepting a houndman) who's witnessed a pack of hounds tearing apart a bear or lion cub is going to find it difficult to condone hounding. And where is the sport in shooting a bear in a trash can? The real issue is not bear *hunting* but *hunter conduct.*

Hunters and wildlife agencies defend these practices by explaining that we *can* hunt bears this way and not endanger the species. They never bother to explain whether we *should* hunt them this way. Rather than provide a rationale for their desires, they choose to attack their critics as antihunters. The very term "anti" creates paranoia among many wildlife managers and hunters. But I discern two distinct factions among the antis: those who oppose hunting based on philosophy, and those who oppose *hunters* based on observed behavior. Those of us who are hunters and wildlife managers strengthen this latter group every time we ignore their reasoned criticisms of hunting.

Will hunting still be a part of American society in twenty years? Hunting is currently enjoyed by less than 15 percent of Americans. We are permitted to hunt only so long as the majority of nonhunters

believe we are conducting ourselves in an honorable manner. It is
they who will decide all ballot initiatives and most legislative actions.
Therefore, it seems prudent for us—the hunters and wildlife managers—to critically examine our activities *from the perspective of
nonhunters*. Most hunting can be ethically defended. Some cannot.
It's easy to pick out the bad bits: just listen to the antis, who tend to
throw stones at the most visible and vulnerable targets. Listen to
them and *honestly examine* their criticisms. Change, where necessary, is our only hope for survival. To continually brand all criticism
as antihunting rhetoric and all critics as antihunters only serves to
paint us into an ever smaller corner. Antihunters may hold a spot-
light on our behavior, but *through* our behavior we control what
they see.

Too many managers and hunters believe that problems like those
now surrounding bear hunting can be solved through more, and
more effective, public education. They reframe the question so that
"the poor ignorant public" is at fault and the agencies are their only
hope to see the truth. But hunting issues are not amenable to education (propaganda) as a remedy; rather, they elicit public responses
based on their core values. Providing more data on the health of the
bear population is meaningless. *Hunter conduct*, a social activity, is
the issue.

Wildlife management agencies currently have strong support
from most of the public, who often don't know exactly what these
agencies do yet think they do a pretty good job of it. This is an enviable position in a period of general disenchantment with government. But we risk our credibility as managers if we don't critically
and honestly respond to challenges to the status quo.

Black bear hunting will remain a primary point of attack for critics of wildlife management. Bears hold a unique place in the spirit of
human cultures everywhere, and America is no exception. I seriously
doubt that baiting and hounding, if used to kill skunks or coyotes,
would generate the same level of outrage they do when used to kill
bears. For too long, we managers have tried to distance ourselves
from the spiritual aspects of wildlife management, with species represented by abstract X's in our computer models. But bears are special, and our reluctance to acknowledge this fact is a failure of the
spirit that contributes significantly to the fury of today's bear hunting debates.

There will be other issues: trapping, target practice using live animals, and contest hunts come to mind, all deservedly. Our critics will never disappear. Nor should we want them to, for they keep us from getting stuck in amoral bureaucratic ruts. They force us to look forward. They force us to recognize that social issues are as important as biological issues.

❧

I look back with fondness to 1978, when I first began studying black bears in the wild. I was so dumb: I only wanted to know as much as possible about bears, which I found and still find truly awe inspiring. Knowledge is what I craved. What I've learned is a little about bears and a lot about human behavior. Most days, that makes me wish I were a bear.

Today, much of my energy goes into attempting to reform my profession and my fellow hunters. I do so for many reasons, some of them selfish: I want to keep hunting. I want to keep learning about wildlife. I want to keep living with wildlife. These things can only happen if we bring a stronger social consciousness to our roles as wildlife managers and hunters. We must change, or we will cease to exist. To help steer our way through the coming years, we must adopt a new paradigm: *Biology provides the planks to build the boat, but society steers the ship.*

The Violators

❧

JIM HARRISON

Picture this man on a cool, late summer morning, barely dawn: giant, bearded, walking through his barnyard carrying a Winchester 30/30, wearing a frayed denim coat and mauve velvet bellbottoms. He is broke, and though able-bodied he thinks of himself as an artist and immune to the ordinary requirements of a livelihood. Perhaps he is. He is one of the now numberless dropouts from urban society, part of a new agrarian movement, the "back to the land" bit that seems to be sweeping young writers. But he hankers for meat rather than the usual brown rice. I myself in a fatuous moment have told him of my own two-hundred-gram-a-day protein diet—meat, meat, meat, lots of it with cheese and eggs, plus all the fruit you can lift from neighboring orchards and all the bourbon you can afford during evening pool games. Who needs macrobiotics?

Anyway, back to the barnyard. The killer lets the horses out of the paddock and they run off through the ground mist. This morning is windless and the grass soaked with dew, ideal conditions for poaching a deer. He walks up the hill behind his house, very steep. He is temporarily winded and sits down for a cigarette. Thirty miles out in Lake Michigan the morning sun has turned the steep cliffs of South Fox Island golden. There is a three-foot moderate roll; the lake trout and coho trollers will be out today in all their overequipped glory. Later in the season he will snag lake trout from the Leland

River or perhaps even catch some fairly. He thinks of the coho as totally contemptible—anyone with a deft hand can pluck them from the feeder streams.

About five hundred yards to the east, clearly visible from the hill, is a deserted orchard and a grove of brilliantly white birch trees. Beautiful. He will walk quietly through a long neck of woods until he is within a hundred yards of the orchard. Except in the deepest forest, deer are largely nocturnal feeders in Michigan, but they can still be seen in some quantity at dawn or dusk if you know where to look. During the day they filter into the sweet coolness of cedar swamps or into the rows of the vast Christmas tree plantations. He sits and rests his rifle on a stump. He immediately spots a large doe between the second and third rows of the orchard, and farther back in the scrubby neglected trees a second-year buck, maybe 130 pounds, perfect eating size. He aims quickly just behind and a trifle below the shoulder and fires. The buck stumbles, then bursts into full speed. But this energy is deceptive and the animal soon drops. My friend hides his rifle, covering it with dead leaves. If you do happen to get caught—the odds are against it—your rifle is confiscated. He jogs down to the deer, stoops, hoists its dead weight to his shoulder, and heads back to the house.

A few hours later his pickup pulls into my yard. I am in the barn wondering how I can fix one of the box stalls when my brother has bent the neck of my hammer pulling spikes. I hear the truck, and when I come out into the yard he hands me a large bloody package. Everything is understood. We go into the kitchen and have a drink though it is only ten in the morning. We slice the buck's liver very thin, then drive to the grocery store where I have some inexpensive white bordeaux on order. When we get back my wife has sauteed the liver lightly in clarified butter. We eat this indescribably delicious liver, which far exceeds calves' liver in flavor and tenderness. A hint of apple, clover, and fern. We drink a few bottles of wine and he goes home and I take a nap. That evening my wife slices a venison loin into medallions, which she again cooks simply. During the afternoon I had driven into Traverse City to splurge on a bottle of Chateauneuf-du-Pape. The meal—the loin and a simple salad of fresh garden lettuce, tomatoes, and some green onions—was exquisite.

End of tale. I wouldn't have shot the deer myself. But I ate a lot of

it, probably ten pounds in all. I think it was wrong to shoot the deer.
Part of the reason I would not have killed it is that I am no longer
able to shoot at mammals. Grouse and woodcock, yes. But gutting
and skinning a deer reminds me too much of the human carcass and
a deer heart too closely resembles my own. My feelings are a trifle
ambivalent on this particular incident, but I have decided my friend
is a violator only barely more tolerable than the cruder sort. If it had
been one of the local Indians—it often is—I would have found it easy
to bow to the ancestral privilege. But my friend is not a local Indian.

Game hoggery is not the point. The issue is much larger than human greed. We have marked these creatures to be hunted and slaugh-
tered, and destroyed all but a remnant of their natural environment.
But fish and mammals must be considered part of a larger social con-
tract, and just laws for their protection enforced with great vigor.
The first closed deer season in our country due to depletion of the
herds occurred in 1694 in Massachusetts. Someone once said, "The
predator husbands his prey." The act of violation is ingrained, habit-
ual; it represents a clearly pathological form of outdoor atavism. Not
one violator out of a hundred acts out of real need or hunger. The belief that he does is another of many witless infatuations with local
color.

❧

I have an inordinate amount of time to think and wander around.
Poets muse a lot. Or as Whitman, no mean fisherman, said, "I loaf
and invite my soul." Mostly loaf. I have always found that I can
think better and more lucidly with my Fox Sterlingworth, or any of
a number of fly rods, in hand. I'm a poor shot, but I really do miss
some grouse because I'm thinking. Recently I was walking along a
stream that empties into Lake Michigan within half a dozen miles of
my farm. It was late October, with a thin skein of snow that would
melt off by afternoon. There were splotches of blood everywhere
and many footprints and small piles of coho guts. The fish were
nearly choking the stream, motionless except for an errant flip of tail
to maintain position. And there were some dead ones piled up near a
small logjam. They stank in the sharp fall air with the pervasive
stench of a dead shorthorn I had once found near the Manistee River.
Oh, well. Sport will be sport. No doubt someone had illegally
clubbed a few for his smokehouse. Clubbed or pitched them out

with a fork or shovel as one pitches manure. They are surprisingly good if properly smoked, though you must slice and scrape out the belly fat because of the concentrated DDT found there. But in the stream, in their fairly advanced stage of deliquescence, with backs and snouts scarred and sore and whitish, they look considerably less interesting than floundering carp. How could a steelhead swim through this aquatic garbage to spawn? Tune in later, maybe another year or two, folks.

I walked back to my car and drove west two miles to the stream mouth. This confluence of waters has never produced any really big trout, but it is fine for close-to-home fishing. I rigged my steelhead rod, put on my waders, and began casting into a mild headwind, which required a low-profile turnover. Around here one learns to appreciate anything less than fifteen knots, though if the water is too still the fishing is bad. I am not a pretty caster and my ability to double haul, thus increasing line speed, is imperfect; when you flunk a double haul the line whips and cracks, then collapses around your head and you are frustrated and sad as only a fly caster can be, glad only that no one was watching. I hooked two small fish on an attractor pattern and lost them after a few jumps. Then I hooked a larger fish on a lightly weighted Muddler, and within an asthmatic half hour of coaxing I beached it. I was breathless, insanely excited. A steelhead, maybe six pounds with a vague pink stripe and short for his weight, chunky, muscular, a very healthy fish. Yum. Then a retired contractor from Ann Arbor I know came along and began casting with a small spoon and light spinning tackle. He is a pleasant sort, mildly arthritic, so his sport exacts no small amount of pain—the water is cold, and the wind is cold and moist. He fished for an hour or so before he hooked an ungodly animal, a steelhead that porpoised like a berserk marlin, easily the largest I had ever seen. It made a long lateral run and he followed it down the beach for a few hundred yards before the fish turned and headed out for South Manitou Island and, beyond that, Wisconsin. It cleaned him. We sat and talked about the beast and I could see that his hands were shaking.

Three more fishermen came along and began casting in my spot with huge treble-hooked spoons. One of them quickly changed to a heavy bell sinker to which he attached large hooks. They were using what is known in Michigan as the "Newaygo Twitch"; three easy turns of the reel and then a violent reef. It is a fine method for foul-hooking and snagging coho and chinook, even spawning steelhead and lake trout. The Michigan Department of Natural Resources has submitted to political pressure and ruled that foul-hooked salmon can be kept rather than released, and this ruling has encouraged bozos by the thousands to use the twitch method to the exclusion of all other styles of fishing. I have seen sportsmen snag upwards of two hundred pounds of lake trout—incredibly far over the legal limit—in the Leland River where the fish are in layers devouring their own aborted spawn below the dam. And these people have been led to think they are fishing. Anyway, I left the beach immediately. I stopped into Dick's Tavern to calm my abraded nerves. I often fantasize about bullwhipping these creeps as Mother Nature's Dark Enforcer. When my imagination for vengeance is depleted, I think about moving to Montana where such yuks, I suppose, are as plentiful but seem at least less visible. It is strange to see a government agency sponsoring acts that are a degradation of the soul of sport. It is as if the National Football League were to encourage and promote face-mask tackling. Take a firm grasp and rip his damn head off.

It is a silly mistake, I've found, to assume that rules of fair play are shared. I have met and talked at length with men who harry and club to death both fox and coyote from snowmobiles. It should not seem necessary to pass laws against so base and resolutely mindless a practice, but it is necessary. I suppose that in simplistic terms our acquisitive and competitive urges have been transferred directly to sport—one can "win" over fish or beast, but, unlike what happens in other forms of sport, the violator disregards all the rules. A certain desolate insensitivity persists: I know some seemingly pleasant young men who in the past have gathered up stray dogs to use as target practice to hone their skills. This is not the sort of thing one can argue about. Neither can one question the logic of the hunting club members who bait deer with apples, corn, and a salt lick, and then on the crisp dawn of the first day of the season fire away at the feeding animals. Or marksmen who hang around rural dumps to get their garbage bear. Or those who wander around swamps adjacent to lakes in the spring collecting gunnysacks of spawning pike; usually they are the same people who tell you that fishing "isn't what it used to be." To be sure, the majority of sportsmen follow the laws with some care, but the majority is scarcely overwhelming. More like a plurality with a grand clot of the indifferent buffering the middle. And silent, at best.

Not to mention the chuckle-wink aspect, the we're-all-cowpokes-ain't-we attitude of so many judges who mete out wrist-slap fines to game-law violators.

I think I was about fourteen when the problem first became apparent to me. It was late in November near the end of the deer season, very cold up in Michigan with a foot of fine powder snow, not bad to walk in as it burst around one's feet like weightless down or fluff. I was hunting along a ridge that completely encircled a large gully forming a bowl. At the bottom of the bowl there was a small marsh of tag alder, snake-grass, dried-up cattails and brake, and perhaps four or five slender tamarack. I sat down on a boulder to eat my lunch and watch the swale, thinking it might hold a large buck or even a young spikehorn. Across my lap I held an antique 38/40, the accuracy of which was less than profound but better anyhow than the shotgun and slug my friends used, which was an embarrassment to them. After an hour of sitting and staring, staring so hard that my eye tried to trace the shapes I wanted to see, four deer calmly walked out of the far side of the swale. I looked at them quickly through my peepsight. All female. They picked their way cautiously in single file toward a sumac thicket on the side of the hill, trying to minimize the time spent in the open. But then an explosion, a barrage, a fusillade. The first doe made the thicket and bounded up and over the ridge. The second dropped in her tracks but the third, shot probably in the hindquarters, tried to drag herself back to the swale by her forefeet. Then she was hit again and was still. The fourth doe ran in narrowing, convulsive circles until she dropped.

I don't remember thinking anything. I only watched. Three men walked down the hill and looked at the deer. They were talking but were too far away for me to hear distinctly. I sat very still until their red forms disappeared. I didn't go down the hill and look at the deer. I thought the game warden might come along and think I had shot them, and the fine for shooting a doe would be enormous for someone who earned at best two dollars a day for hoeing potatoes. I hunted without thought for a few more hours, getting a hopeless shot at a distant buck, and then walked to the car where I was to meet my father when it began to get dark. All the staccato noise of the rifle shots had served to remind me of the Korean War and what it must sound like. Pork Chop Hill was much in the news in those days.

🌿

I think it was Edward Abbey who coined the phrase "cowboy con-sciousness" to describe that peculiar set of attitudes many Americans still hold: the land is endless, unspoiled, mysterious, still remaining to be overcome and finally won. So shoot, kill, bang-bang-bang. WOW! And city dwellers, it seems, who come to the country during the hunting and fishing seasons, are now more guilty of these atti-tudes than their rural counterparts, who sense the diminishing wilderness around them, the truncated freedom of movement. Every dentist and machinist and welder and insurance adjuster in Michigan either owns or wants to own twenty posted acres "up north."

But we are hopeless romantics about this imaginary Big Woods—it simply no longer exists in any faintly viable form. Even one of the far corners of creation, the north slope of the Brooks Range, is lit-tered with oil drums. It seems funny, too, to discover that every American in the deepest little synapse in his brain considers himself a natural at hunting and fishing, a genetic Pete Maravich of the out-back, wherever that is. We always tell each other that the deer are on the ridges today or in the swamps or clustered in the grape arbors or frittering away the morning behind the woodpile despite the fact that few of us could identify five trees at gunpoint. And every little rural enclave has its number of wise old owls who have spent a lifetime sipping draft beer and schnapps and are rife with such witticisms as "you greenhorns couldn't hit a bull in the butt with a banjo. Now back in 1938, why . . ." The point is that in the old days the rivers were stiff with giant bull trout and deer wandered the countryside in grand herds like Idaho sheep. You didn't even have to aim. This cow-boy consciousness is so ingrained and overwhelming in some viola-tors that they will suffer any risks. A poacher near here was arrested for the twentieth time, fined a thousand dollars, and given 165 days in jail. An equal punishment was given to two men who dynamited a rainbow holding pond at a weir. I somehow doubt that this will dis-courage them.

🌿

I feel a very precise melancholy when I hear rifle shots in the middle of a September night; the jacklighters are at work after a tepid evening at the bowling alley. Picture this recent local case. A yellow cone of light is shining into a field. It is a powerful beam, and nothing animate within a hundred yards escapes its illumination. Three teenagers are sitting in an old Mercury playing the light against the backdrop of woods and field as they drive slowly along a gravel road. One of them has a loaded rifle. If a deer is spotted, the light paralyzes it hypnotically. The deer will stare without motion into the light and even the shabbiest marksman can pick his shot. But this will prove an unfortunate night for shining deer. A car approaches from the rear at high speed and swerves in front of the hunters to block any escape. It is Reino Narva, the game warden, to the rescue. In this particular instance all of the culprits are juveniles and first offenders and the sentences are light.

❦

There is nothing inscrutable about the matter of violation. I fancy myself an amateur naturalist and have hot flashes when I think of the sins of my own past, harmless and usual though they may be. I think of the large brown trout I caught at age twelve by illegal set line in the Muskegon River. Turtles had eaten all but its head by the time I pulled the line in. I nailed the head to the barn alongside my pike and bass skulls as if I had caught the fish by fair means. Or the roosting grouse stalked and shot with a .22. Or diving into a lake for weeks on end with a knife, handle in mouth, to carve the heads off turtles we had flushed from logs. We thought they were killing our fish. Or shooting crows. Or shooting at deer in midsummer with bow and arrow, though I don't remember ever coming close. All the mindless sins of youth committed in the haze of reading Edgar Rice Burroughs, Zane Grey, James Oliver Curwood, Jack London, and Ernest Thompson Seton; wanting to be a steely half-breed Robert Mitchum type with hatchet, revolver, cartridge belt, and a long mane of hair trained with bear grease.

❦

Gentle reader, rules will never stop the jacklighter and snagger, the violator. It is not so much that enforcement of the law is inept, but that respect for the spirit of the law is insufficient. And in Michigan there are fabulous ironies; a portion of any fine for a game violation is earmarked as "restitution to the state." But you might well be shining your deer in an opening in a forest that has been ravaged by the oil interests—public land doled away for peanuts by conservationists in a state with boggling population and recreation problems. Or you might get caught snagging a trout in Manistee Lake where a paper company belches out thousands of gallons of fluid waste daily into public waters so rank that a motorboat scarcely can manage a wake. Who is violating what? Or as René Char said, "Who stands on the gangplank directing operations? The captain or—the rats?" Not a very subtle distinction, hereabouts. The problems seem, and perhaps are, insuperable. The political-business-conservation relationship in Michigan often reminds one of old-style Boston politics; everyone gets a piece of the action but the pie itself suffers from terminal rot. Of course, this is ho-hum stuff now. Pollution is "in committee" everywhere and government is firming up its stand, à la kumquat jelly, with a lid of yellow paraffin. I have a dreamy plot afoot for a court test to be decided on Saturn wherein the Constitution and Bill of Rights would be made to apply to fish and mammals.

❦

Finally, it is a very strange arrogance in man that enables him to chase the last of the whales around the ocean for profit, shoot polar bear cubs for trophies, allow Count Blah-Blah to blast 885 pheasants in one day. It is much too designed to be called crazy or impetuous.

Those lines of Robert Duncan's about Robin Hood come back to me now: "How we loved him / in childhood and hoped to abide by his code / that took life as its law!" The key word here is "code." Sport must be sporting. We have a strong tendency to act the weasel in the henhouse. At dawn not a single cluck was heard. It might be preposterous to think we will change, but there are signs. Judges are becoming sterner, and people are aware of environmental problems to a degree not known in this country before. Game wardens get more cooperation from the ordinary citizen than they used to. Violating is losing its aura of rube cuteness.

The true violator, though, will persist in all of his pathological glory. Even if there were no game left on earth, something would be devised. Maybe a new sport on this order: ganghooking Farmer Brown's pigs. A high-speed power winch mounted on a vehicle hood is required, and a harpoon with large hooks. You shoot the harpoon over the pig's back and press the winch button. Zap! You've got yourself a squealer. Precautions: make sure Farmer Brown is away for the day, and take your finger off the winch button in time or the pork will really fly.

Dark Days in the Glass House

JOHN WREDE

He knows as well as I do, it's not a harvest. It's a massacre they're doing out there. The hunt itself, as he calls it, it's not a hunt! The people go over there, they pay two hundred dollars if they're within the state, and a thousand for out of state, to mount a buffalo head on the wall and then go home and tell their wife what a big man they are. They are ruthless people. It's a stupid hunt. We saw one buffalo out there try to get to its feet forty-one times. They didn't even bother to go and shoot that [one] until they'd gone on and shot other animals.

—Cleveland Amory, Fund for Amimals

(From an interview on *CBS This Morning* featuring Amory and Yellowstone National Park superintendent Bob Barbee.)

The rhetorical, political, and legal battles continue to rage over virtually every form of hunting worldwide. Hunters and their organizations form battle lines in the trenches of biological fundamentalism, while antihunters fire salvos of explosive rhetoric from their barricades of emotionalism. Each side exchanges its most righteous shots, never considering the impact these disputes have on the wildlife resources themselves. While hunters and antihunters duke it out in the courtrooms and legislative halls, North America's wildlife struggles against habitat destruction, pollution, overgrazing, poaching, and commercialization. As hunters and antihunters amass huge war chests in preparation for political and legal battles to come, wildlife and wildlands—the supposed beneficiaries of all this debate—continue to suffer and in some cases disappear.

Hunters are understandably alarmed by the antihunting movement. It threatens a noble tradition that has supported wildlife conservation for nearly a century, not to mention all manner of businesses and individuals who depend upon hunting and shooting sports for their financial existence. From outward appearances, the adversary seems easily identifiable—but this may be illusory. Is it possible that in haste to rise up in defense of hunting, hunters have failed to recognize the elemental ooze that spawned this antihunting monster? Could it be that hunter misconduct lies at the root of the antihunting mentality? Is it the taking of an animal's life that is primarily at issue—or whether that life is taken with reverence or callousness?

Take a closer look at what Cleveland Amory has to say. There is grudging recognition that a difference exists between a hunt and a slaughter. Amory suggests that behavioral differences distinguish a traditional hunt from a massacre. Several hunters participating in the buffalo harvest publicly expressed emotional discomfort at the conclusion of their hunts. Why? Because the procedures they were required to follow did not fall within their definition of hunting. In essence, the circumstances abridged their ethical standards.

Biological and political justifications mean nothing if a hunter's actions fail on moral grounds, and the hunting fraternity has some serious flaws that require at least as much attention as is currently being focused on the "antihunting threat." Hunters and wildlife management professionals live in a brightly lit glass house, and we can never convince the nonhunter—who represents some 80 percent of the political horsepower in America—that our intentions and practices are honorable unless and until that house is immaculate.

In some cases, errant or unethical behavior may not have a significant biological impact upon the wildlife resource, yet it invites—and deserves—public scrutiny, and will ultimately further restrict hunting opportunities. Greed, competition, ego-driven attitudes, commercialization, or any other behavior that deviates from a high moral standard is a direct affront to all ethical hunters, to concerned non- and antihunters, to wildlands and wildlife. The killer or shooter who hunts to achieve bragging rights or judges his success by body counts is clearly an albatross around the necks of everyone who cares about wildlife—but so, albeit more subtly, is the hunter who is not deeply committed to conservation.

Laws can never replace morals; intimidation is no substitute for education. Nurturing good field ethics falls on all our shoulders. The strongest persuader is not the fear of fines or jail, but one friend encouraging another, through deed and word, to aspire to a higher moral standard. By necessity, law enforcement and the judicial process are often too impersonal to make sure the wrongdoer understands the origin, principle, and reason behind the laws he or she is breaking—and in the larger scope, the principles behind ecology and conservation.

Too many hunters regard wildlife conservation officers with the same mixture of dread and contempt inspired by traffic cops. In recent times, some nationally syndicated writers and spokespersons representing the hunting media and some wildlife conservation organizations have embraced this attitude, characterizing wildlife law enforcement officers as overzealous, antihunting storm troopers. Many of these attempts to discredit wildlife law enforcement stem from covert "sting" operations that netted some pretty big fish.

Fish like an attorney who killed a whooping crane, a judge who baited geese and shot over his limit, a high government official who shot rails from a speeding boat, a museum curator who laundered illegally taken trophies, socially and politically prominent citizens who killed endangered species, and guides who escorted trophy hunters into a national park to kill grizzly bears.

Alleged sportsmen turned on wildlife officers, charging legal impropriety, entrapment, and unprofessional conduct. In spite of the political maneuvering, though, the cases passed all the judicial tests, and the antihunting crowd added a trainload of bad examples to its arsenal.

Some hunters chastised wildlife law enforcement for betraying the brotherhood, but the public record, open for all to see, confirms that the defendants have only themselves to blame. Wildlife is far too important to be compromised by cronyism. Wildlife law enforcement officers ask social, economic, and political leaders to join with them and other honorable and responsible sportsmen in forging an ethical revival in the hunting community. Wildlife law enforcement is duty-bound to expose and prosecute those who abuse wildlife and wildlands. Failing to do so is a direct affront to honest sportsmen and the dignity of wildlands and wild creatures.

As for the name-calling, accusing wildlife law enforcement agents of harboring antihunting sentiments verges on the ludicrous. I am a wildlife conservation officer. Like 98 percent of the men and women who share this field, I hunt and fish. My motivations spring from a deep-seated love and abiding respect for wildlife and the time-honored tradition of hunting. My ultimate goal is to foster ethical and biologically sound behavior in the field.

In one small but critical area, wildlife law officers and the animal-rights crowd have something in common—they expect people to recognize and respect the beauty and dignity of wild creatures. But it's worth remembering that most wildlife enforcement agents were drawn to this often frustrating and demoralizing work out of their love of hunting and fishing and dedication to protecting the wildlife resources we all cherish and share.

Gaining a deeper understanding of ecology and wildlife biology must become every hunter's goal—a commitment as strong as the passion to hunt. We must ask for ethical excellence from ourselves and all with whom we share the field. We must exhibit more than a casual interest in environmental affairs. Buying hunting and fishing licenses is no longer enough. The individual sportsman and -woman must become involved as an activist for improved ethical and legal standards, habitat enhancement and protection, pollution abatement, ending poaching, and finding solutions to problems associated with commercialization of wildlife.

Wildlife law enforcement officers are the staunchest allies of sportsmen in all of these endeavors . . . not a part of the problem, but a part of the solution.

When Not to Shoot

❦

GARY WOLFE

Seven days into the hunt, I finally saw elk, and they were coming my way. When I first spotted them, they were drifting out of the timber about eight hundred yards away, outflanking my hunting partner who was still-hunting an aspen grove on the other side of the canyon. I had set up in a saddle across the ridge from my part-ner, hoping that any elk he pushed from the timber would follow the natural contours and head in my direction. At last one of my strategies was working. All I had to do now was wait. The elk, a dozen in all, looked relaxed as they slowly worked their way up the sagebrush hillside toward me. I tried to match their calm, but my heart was pounding. Anterless elk were my legal quarry, but this had been anything but an "easy" cow hunt. With only two days left in the season, this could be my first and last chance for a shot.

It felt like the perfect ambush. If the elk kept coming, they would be right on top of me. There was just one problem—the wind. Pinecones and small branches ricocheted down through a sieve of limbs, and the big trunks creaked and groaned. I guessed it was gust-ing to at least thirty-five miles per hour. Although I was shooting a 220-grain bullet from my 8mm Remington magnum, those choppy gusts gnawed at my confidence.

While I'm not an expert shot, I'm usually comfortable shooting at distances up to three hundred yards, provided I have a good rest and the animal is standing still—preferably broadside. I'm definitely no ballistics wizard, however, so I had no idea how much drift a thirty-five-mile-per-hour crosswind would cause, but I felt sure it would affect my accuracy. Weighing the unknown effect of the wind, I decided to shoot only if the elk came within a hundred yards and stood still. But I didn't think distance would be a problem. If the elk stayed on course, they would pass within fifty yards of me.

As luck would have it, they veered off to my left, flaring like a nervous flock of geese. When they were about 150 yards out, they paused for a moment, standing broadside. I steadied my rifle on the blowdown that hid me, placed the crosshairs on a fat cow, slipped the safety off, breathed . . . then let her trot over the ridge without firing a shot. Sure, I could have easily hit the cow, but where? When I went back to camp that night I might have carried the burden of a crippled animal instead of backstraps.

I didn't ponder this at length, though. The elk had gone over the ridge toward an old stand of aspen, and I knew a shortcut. I pounded downhill and was again in position to intercept them as they came into the trees. And they came. This time they held their course, passing within fifty yards of me. The dense stand of quakies took the punch out of the wind, but it also wove a fine net of finger-sized branches between me and the legs, necks, and chests that scudded through the trees. The heavy magnum could surely hammer the bullet through to the animal, but any one of those twigs could deflect it from the vital zone. Once again, I quietly lowered my rifle.

I mulled it all over as I hiked back to my truck. Seven days without seeing an elk, then suddenly two chances at a dozen elk within half an hour. Only two days remained in the season, and I could smell a skunk coming. There was a very real possibility that my freezer would not be filled with elk for the first time in fifteen years. But that was much more tolerable than the thought of a wounded elk dying over hours and days and nights. I knew I had made the right decisions, even if I didn't see another elk for the rest of the season.

❧

I am probably more aware of wounding loss than the average hunter. For twelve years, I managed an extensive private big game hunting operation. During that period, hunters took more than three thousand elk, and I had ample opportunity to track wounded animals. Both bulls and cows have incredible stamina, and I soon learned that poor shot placement often results in a lost elk. Most poor shooting hinges not so much on faulty marksmanship as on bad judgment.

Four factors contribute to almost all wounding loss: distance, movement, angle, and haste. The animal is too far away, moving too fast, standing or running at a bad angle, or the hunter doesn't take a proper rest and rushes the shot. Any one of these can spur a bad shot, and they come in many combinations. Behind each of these factors, though, there is one fact: the hunter squeezed the trigger when he should have lowered the gun. More hunters spending more time at the rifle range would surely reduce wounding loss, but judgment and self-control are even more important.

Passing up a big animal requires considerable self-discipline. The temptation is compounded if the hunter is inexperienced, the trophy is unusually large, game is scarce, or hunting time is running out. Take my situation. Although I consider myself an experienced hunter and the cow was not what many would call a "trophy," I twice thumbed off the safety and looked long and hard through the crosshairs. These were the first elk I'd seen after seven days of a nine-day season, and I dreaded the thought of substituting storebought beef for my preferred elk diet. Experience and discipline won out, but what if I'd been watching a trophy-class bull instead? Ten years ago, as a less experienced hunter, I might have chanced a shot at a big bull under the same conditions. Today, I hope, good judgment would prevail.

Webster defines *ethical* as "conforming to the standards of conduct of a given profession or group." I hope that the "standards of conduct" of our group, hunters, are such that each of us recognizes that the decision to shoot at a living creature carries a tremendous responsibility and obligation. In his classic book *Meditations on Hunting*, José Ortega y Gasset contemplates the ethics of hunting: "Every good hunter is uneasy in the depths of his conscience when faced with the death he is about to inflict on the enchanting animal. More than once, the sportsman, within shooting range of a splendid animal, hesitates in pulling the trigger."

To be the good hunter Ortega describes, one has an obligation to his quarry to do everything possible to ensure a quick, humane kill. One of the most effective ways to do this is to pass up marginal shots. Wounding loss can never be completely eliminated, regardless of how conscientious one is, but it can be minimized through improved judgment and self-discipline. Deciding when *not* to shoot is the ultimate test of ethical hunter behavior.

And what about my elk? Patience and perseverance paid off. I found a cow standing broadside in the open at forty-five yards the next day. She died instantly.

Passion, Gifts, Rages

Stephen Bodio

> I think we are in some ways dealing with a language failure listing both baseball and falconry as sports.
>
> —Thomas McGuane

I was born in the city, where I lived until I was four. There, that early, though I could not know it, I was bitten by something and became a naturalist. By the time we moved to what was then still the country, twenty miles south of Boston, I was catching insects, picking up dead birds in the aftermath of a hurricane, and—my parents were artists—sketching the backyard sparrows. When we arrived in the swampy forests of Easton, I kept frogs and toads first, then snakes and baby birds, a perfect example of Edmund Wilson's "biophilic" youth. At eight I began keeping homing pigeons. Having learned to read at three from the pages of 1950s *Life* magazines full of animal dioramas, I became a precocious devourer of books, especially natural history and dog stories. In the halls of the Ames Free Library, I learned that people kept, trained, and "flew" hawks, those remote and dashing killers that sometimes chased our pigeons. And so at thirteen I built a bow net of yardsticks and badminton netting, baited it with a pet store white mouse, and, to my everlasting astonishment and delight, pulled a little kestrel down from the sky.

A week later he flew across the yard to my call, and I was marked for life. As I wrote in *A Rage for Falcons*, "the only thing better than pulling a hawk from the sky by trickery was to return him there and have him come back to your call because he wanted to." I still play with hawks, thirty years later; I have learned many things from them and have worked for them.

✻

Biophilia, I expect, is inherent in every human, a part of our genes and our earliest culture. Hunter-gatherers must notice everything with the loving eye of an artist, the attentive senses of a good cook. But like many behaviors in us and in our fellow animals, it must be stimulated at the proper time or it will wither. If children do not learn to speak at the proper time, they never will. If they never get to touch animals and plants, they will lose their ability to love them. "Hands on" is not a myth. I was fortunate to grow up in a time and place before burgeoning human populations and finicky laws denied children free and easy access to wildlife.

All kids, if left to themselves in a decent environment, go through this stage. Sadly, for most of them it is just a stage. What is it that leads a few of us beyond, through obsession to something more healthy—the acceptance of nature as an integral, necessary, and almost unremarked part of our lives? (I once told a new friend that a hawk in the living room seemed more normal and unremarkable than a television set.) Maybe it could be high-end experiences, like that kestrel in the net, modified by something that is rare today— what we might call "apprenticeship."

✻

Real passion grows alongside growing expertise. Years came along in which I can remember being ruled by hawks. My first wife, from whom I've been divorced for twenty-some years, recently handed me an old book that had been stored in her attic all that time. "How did you know it was mine?" I asked in amazement.

"It couldn't have been anyone else's." She turned it over to reveal a paint streak of snow-white, odorless droppings. "Who else would have hawk chalk on their books?"

Well, I could think of a few other such maniacs in the early 1970s. There was Mark, who drove two hundred miles to show up unannounced on my doorstep with a goshawk and a case of beer. Jim Weaver, who more than any other single individual could be called the Man Who Brought Back the Peregrine, shared his apartment in the Cornell hawk-breeding barn with an aged gyrfalcon, a peregrine's-egg mobile, a buffalo robe, and an Audubon print. Another Jim had a wife who left him for the last time with the admonition that he should make love to his hawks (although that was not quite how she phrased it). And then there was Darcie, a girlfriend who, I now think, was more attracted to goshawks than to me. She once called back a departing half-trained male to a frozen day-old chick clutched in her bare hand and, with her own blood and the chick's yolk running down her arm, grinned through her tears and bragged, "I got him."

Does this sound extreme for an activity that even Aldo Leopold called a hobby? Well, yes, if you consider falconry a mere time-filler for when you're off work rather than something that you structure work around. But consider those often-misunderstood concepts "hunting" and "play." Sport hunting is not (despite an animal-rights brochure I read recently that blandly asserted it was, "of course," sublimated sexual sadism) some sort of aggression against creation. It is a series of rituals that have grown up around the most basic activities: acquiring food—capturing energy to keep us alive. Some of the rituals have come about because of their beauty, grace, and difficulty; others (like the German custom of giving the fallen animal a sprig of its favorite food), because of the sadness and mystery that accompany taking a life.

Hunters who hunt out of physical need still appreciate these rituals; ones who do so out of "play" or out of a civilized desire to personally touch the roots of the flow of energy may elevate the ritual to the end result. The finest kinds of hunting—fly fishing, falconry, upland shooting with pointing dogs—are, and should be, elaborate ways of playing with your food and with the universe, ways that also give you windows into the lives of things as alien as insects (in fly fishing) or into the minds of canine and avian partners. Ideally, you leave the human behind for a few moments and become predator, prey, nonhuman ally.

(Oh, and that food thing. Personally I think that a culinary exam should be part of the elaborate, "If-I-were-king" test for any hunting license. It would remind hunters of the roots of hunting. Hawks leave no lead or steel pellets in their prey, take only a little, and either kill clean or fail. It's not for nothing that the old falconers' toast begins, "Here's to those who shoot and miss.")

Obviously, I believe the passion about these activities is good. T. H. White's preferred title for *The Goshawk* was "A Kind of Mania." Many years later, I wanted to borrow it for my book *A Rage for Falcons* and ran into the same set of editorial doubts that White experienced. But falconry is a healthy mania. As Father Matthew Fox observed, "'Apathy' is two Greek words meaning 'no passion.' The antidote to apathy and acedia is to fall in love. To rediscover our erotic attachment to what is beautiful in the universe. That is where we get our passion. If we fall in love with creation deeper and deeper, we will respond to its endangerment with passion."

And we did fall in love. Many of us were attracted to falconry by the sight of a bird falling from the skies, but by the 1970s birds were falling in a far uglier manner. DDT had nearly wiped the slate clean of the eastern peregrine and was about to do the same with the western and arctic populations. The bald eagle, Cooper's hawk, and osprey were also in varying degrees of trouble. Alarmed legislators passed a ban on persistent pesticides in 1968, but by then the birds were gone. Even if they could reclaim their old sites—by no means a certain prospect, given growing cities, changing forests, and the expanding great horned owl population—it might take centuries.

Enter the Peregrine Fund. In 1971 four falconers—Jim Weaver, Frank Bond, Dr. Tom Cade of Cornell University, and Bob Berry—formed a nonprofit group to oversee the captive breeding and eventual restocking of the peregrine. They took over an old Quonset hut at Cornell, put it under the day-to-day management of Weaver, and waded in. Over the next two decades, they raised hundreds of birds, which were stocked at every old and many new nesting sites throughout the lower forty-eight states and released under the supervision of hundreds of volunteers. The program continued until its own success made it unnecessary. It was the first, and to date the most successful, restocking of an endangered species. Probably everyone knows this. What the publicity never mentions is that this was done almost entirely by falconers. Not only were the founders falconers, but most of the hack-site attendants during the first decade were too. Where else would you get people with both the expertise and dedication to spend two months on sunbaked or freezing rock ledges, for little more than food (the average mid-1970s "salary" was seven hundred dollars for two months), in order to babysit a clutch of obnoxious baby birds?

John Tobin and I were probably as typical as any. He was a Vietnam veteran, an ex-medic, who had just completed his master's in biology at the school where I was engaged in one of my periodic not-very-serious attempts at getting a degree. He had a two-year-old son and a beard so red it was almost orange and was on the short list to become a Massachusetts game warden. I was a freelance writer and part-time editor who was getting published with some regularity in the sporting and "alternative" press while trying to write fiction. We had in common a taste for whiskey, ancestors in the Maritimes, a passion for training goshawks, no money, and a devotion to peregrine restoration that bordered on the maniacal. We were assigned to Mount Tom, near Holyoke, Massachusetts, where a historic aerie had survived the clearing of the forest and the building of a city only to succumb to DDT in the early fifties.

It was a strange summer—exhilarating, exhausting, illuminating, and finally (we thought then) depressing. Our birds, with some others, disappeared soon after they became strong fliers. Before that, we endured bugs (including a near-lethal sting that I, seriously allergic, received from a yellow jacket that was feeding on chicken remains under a nest), mud, freezing rain, and not one but two lightning strikes within two hundred feet of our flimsy orange tent. We saved a rare New England timber rattler from the terrified park staff, nearly getting bitten in the process. We raised hundreds of half-grown chickens and coturnix quail in cages behind our camp, herds for our screeching charges, and when a flash storm wiped out half of them, we buried them in the mud and packed hundreds of those still alive up a ski lift and then in backpacks to the camp. Each day before dawn we'd sneak the day's supply of freshly killed meat down thirty feet of nearly vertical granite and across a traverse that always contained hundreds of sleepy wasps and might shelter rattlers. We couldn't let the young ones see us lest they associate us with food and end up following humans rather than acting like proper birds. We got severely sunburned from light reflecting off bare rocks and answered what seemed like thousands of dumb questions from hikers, the most common being "Why?"

And somehow we had a great time. Our first reward came after the anxious time when the four birds first flew. After a couple of awkward days during which they flew into rock walls and clung to outcroppings for dear life or got stuck in the center rather than the top of a scrub pine, they suddenly owned the air over the mountain. They showed their mastery by chasing doves, flickers, and butterflies. They were not in deadly earnest yet. If a hang glider passed by overhead, they'd climb to meet it, then circle it companionably; we often wondered what the pilots thought. (This was before city releases made the peregrine project famous.) Once they did the same to a passing wild peregrine, an old bird that swiftly drove them, screaming, to the shelter of the rocks. They were more aggressive with turkey vultures. The buzzards had taken to patrolling the ledges below for chicken scraps, but if any of the peregrine gang were present, they would sail out screaming gleefully and fall hundreds of feet to cut at the terrified scavengers, who would flare and flap and speed off as fast as vulture wings could carry them.

And then, after a week of rain that kept them bored and near the ground, came a clear, blue, high-pressure day. All four young falcons soared up into the blue and never came back. We went through apprehension to fear to sadness. But though they left a hole in our summer, we came to realize we hadn't lost a thing. That summer now stands as a kind of turning point, a time when I realized that there was no going back to a life in which such days were not possible around every bend.

And whenever I see a peregrine in the East, I do still wonder . . .

✻

So we learned, as others did, to give back to the birds. What but passion causes anyone to give that much? There are people I know, devotees of television nature programs, who disapprove strongly of my hunting. They do not spend much time in the rural world, nor do they convert their own energy from life to food. They think themselves more moral than I am.

And maybe they *are* more moral, if moral means selfless. I have received more from the birds than they have from me, though they neither know nor care which way obligation flows. Birds have—falconry has—taught me to be polite to an animal, to have manners toward the wild, to listen and move slowly, to watch and keep my mouth shut. These lessons—emphatically *not* morals, but almost Zen disciplines and "ways"—have now permeated my life; I am kinder to dogs, horses, and humans than I was before I learned to carry a bird on my fist, to walk smoothly, to face it into the wind, to keep heedless friends from walking behind its back, not to stare rudely in its face while it ate. I swear that some of my odd, primitive, eighteenth-century ideas—that legal dueling rather than lawsuits would improve manners; that if women were armed we'd have fewer crimes of violence against the weak and a lot fewer rude bigots—somehow come from getting to know these mannered creatures from the skies, these fierce but fair visitors in human society.

Birds have improved my perceptions too. I know that when a falcon "weathering" on the lawn cocks her head momentarily sideways, something significant is passing overhead, often so high that I need binoculars to see it. I can read the cliffs of the West, and I know where the nests of falcons are likely to be. I can go to the woods and almost without conscious observation know when the slope, the height of trees, the nearness of water, the calls of certain songbirds mean that soon I will find the feather-littered "plucking post" of a goshawk or hear her sudden *KUKKUKKUK* of challenge as I approach her nest. I can look down a barrier beach in fall and recognize the rolling flush of shorebird flocks that means an arctic peregrine, a merlin, even a gyrfalcon is making its way toward me. Hawks have molded me more than I have ever influenced any hawk.

❧

Is this too abstract? Let me take anther tack. I know a place in southeastern New Mexico, once nearly destroyed, that is home to one very rare species that is being reborn. Its location—well, I won't be too specific; let's just say it's a good drive south from the little agricultural and college center of Portales, not too far from Texas. These plains were once home to the legendary "southern herd" of bison, to the great lobo wolf, to the Comanche. For a few years settlers tried to subdue this place, to divide it into small farms. When drought came, as it always does here, the broken soil just blew away, forming long ridges where it piled up in the tumbleweeds caught in the mile-long section fences. Eastern New Mexico is the western edge of what came to be called the Dust Bowl. Most of the homesteaders gave up and moved on west, leaving battered graying buildings and maybe a few Siberian elm trees to mark the graves of their dreams.

There are no buffalo out there now, no wolves. Coyotes still howl and giggle, dawn and dusk. There are a lot more deer than you'd think and more doves and cranes and quail and birds of prey than anyplace else I know. The rare trees are hung with nests like Christmas ornaments.

Fewer people live here today than in the first two decades of the century. The homesteads that still stand are inhabited by barn owls and ghosts. When you walk on the prairie at dawn, the sun comes up out of the ground the way it does out of the ocean. At such a time, the sight of a band of Comanches might scare but not surprise you.

Once, flocks of pinneated grouse, better known as prairie chickens, lived here. The latest research indicates that they were nomads that came in when the buffalo left, living on the fertile margins of grazed and ungrazed land. They have spiky black headdresses and dance like the plains tribes. When the pioneers broke the sod, the grouse population first boomed with the new food sources, then crashed as their last nest sites disappeared. Nobody seemed to understand that birds who once followed the great herds need edges. Though they hung on through the Depression and the Dust Bowl, their numbers continue to diminish.

But native open-country grouse—the sage grouse, the sharptail, and the greater prairie chicken, as well as these "lessers"—are the noblest of all falconry quarry, the most difficult and beautiful and (when you can catch one) the most delicious. To hunt them, you walk or ride your horse in the sky; you are often the tallest thing you can see. You follow wide-ranging point dogs that run in quarter-mile casts ahead of you. When they "make" game, they turn to stone. You cast your gyr or peregrine to the wind. She circles and works in it until she stands overhead, "waiting on," sometimes a thousand feet above you, looking as tiny and insubstantial as a swallow. You run in, and the grouse burst up and race for the horizon. The hawk falls through the clear autumn air, her bell slots whistling with a demon's scream, and hits with a burst of feathers. Or misses, rebounds, and tail chases over the horizon. Later, there may be Mozart and braised grouse breast and wine, or whiskey and worry and early-to-bed.

Grouse brought my friend Jim Weaver to this place; first, as rumors, twenty-some years ago, then, as quarry in a nomad's true home and favorite camp, through eighteen years of raising young birds at Cornell, and as many banding young arctic birds in Greenland. He would return here for rest and recuperation after countless hours in his plane checking the hack sites and their attendants, or after mapping populations of rare hawks in Zimbabwe.

A couple of years ago, with peregrine reintroduction an official success, he came here for good. He is buying land, reseeding native grasses, banding all the raptors from barn owls to Swainson's hawks to migrant prairie falcons. He is restoring the land's capacity to hold water. Although he does not share the fashionable equation of cows with evil, he has removed them from many overgrazed pastures. Until and unless the land recovers, he'll keep them off. He spends days on his tractor, dawn to dusk in his fields, planting, building fences, putting in water points, studying the land. He is showing his neighbors by example and hard work, rather than by preaching, that you can graze and grow grain and still provide a habitat for wildlife. He has inspired in the more thoughtful among these farmers a new interest in their most unique "crop," the prairie chicken, not to mention other more common game animals. They are beginning to realize that if your product is more diverse, your topsoil won't blow away—and then you won't have to blow away either when the lean dry times come again.

Which is why Jim and I are not hunting this year. It has been a dry year, and young bird survival was low. So we stand beside his mile-long dirt driveway at dusk, with no hawks, no guns, and no dogs. We are as still as the almost freezing air—silent, waiting, watching. The sun is almost down.

In the last moments of light, I see a flicker, a vibration of molecules almost, on the horizon. It turns into a flock of birds, resolves into individuals, tacks like a bunch of ducks. They set wings, curve down, drop into the stubble against a background of darkly luminous sky, raise their heads for a moment, calling, and then disappear.

The light goes. A coyote yaps, and I hear sandhill cranes, their eerie bugling falling from above, though I can see nothing in the darkening sky. I'm grinning like a maniac because it has just occurred to me that all these things—our friendship, the prairie chickens' restored habitat, this ranch, and everything on and above it—are still more gifts from the hawks.

All Birds Flying

✤

DAN CROCKETT

In Hemingway's *Fathers and Sons*, Nick Adams muses, "When you have shot one bird flying you have shot all birds flying. They are all different and they fly in different ways but the sensation is the same and the last one is as good as the first."

For years, I regarded Nick's words as a good truth and an oblique invitation to flush more birds. The simple phrases resonated in my mind while a German shorthair broke the immense geometry of Kansas wheat fields into points and lines of scent. I heard those words as a ruffed grouse splintered the stained-glass light that filtered through Minnesota birches. Gradually, though, my confidence that the last bird was as good as the first began eroding.

The first was pretty good. Having inherited a compulsion for fishing from both my father and mother, I cheerfully gave myself up to it at age three. But nobody in my extended family hunted. Statistically, I was on the road to a life of softball. Or, in my case, a year-round fishing jones. Then one afternoon when I was seventeen, I went dove hunting on an impulse with three high school friends. Though it was only mid-September, a cold snap in southeast Nebraska, our home, had nudged most of the doves down into Kansas. But my friends had located a pond near uncut soybeans that lay beyond slowly rolling hills. They figured we could still ambush a few birds there. Two on each side, we set out along a brushy fence line toward the pond. Carrying a borrowed single-shot twenty-gauge, slightly bewildered and edgy, I nonetheless felt the tug of a vague predatory urge.

Ten minutes from the rig, we stumbled into a big covey of quail. For a moment, there was the brilliant chaos of a meteor shower, then they were gone, faint trails lingering in the air, tracing trajectories toward a distant plum thicket. With opening day for pheasants and quail still six weeks away, my friends still shouldered their guns, swinging with the birds and fantasizing.

At the pond we spread out and crouched beside ragged clumps of sumac. Only a handful of doves whistled past, all flaring well out of range. Ennui set in among my friends, and they were soon blasting at bullfrogs in the pond. Still awed by the unfamiliar power of the shotgun, I didn't shoot. This was due in part to an irrational fear that the pellets would somehow ricochet off the pond's surface and boomerang into my eyes. There was also an instinctive notion that this was horseshit behavior. Mostly, though, I couldn't stop thinking about those quail.

Five days later, knowing nothing of shotguns, I eclipsed most of my savings account and bought a 1962 Savage-Fox side-by-side twelve-gauge. I resolved to hunt alone for a while, partly to achieve some level of comfort with the gun, partly to avoid any buffoonery with bullfrogs or songbirds. But mainly it was greed. I wanted to be able to shoot freely, 360 degrees, at any quail or pheasants I might encounter.

Quail enticed me, but cock pheasants were the birds I craved. Big and bright, they seemed more tangible (more hittable) than a little brown bird with the same flight pattern as a two-stage Silver Jet (my favorite black-market pyrotechnic). And there was something in the rooster's swagger and sudden *Shit, let's get out of here* escapes I could identify with. (I had not yet learned of his prankster's sense of timing and his tenacious will to live, but I would come to appreciate these, too.)

Dogless and alone, I shunned the daunting expanses of milo and corn stubble and kept to draws and fence lines. On those occasions when a rooster would rise up nearby, I instantly unhinged into a pandemonium of undiluted panic. I would fire twice, as rapidly as possible, then listen grimly as strong wings drummed toward the horizon.

After half a dozen empty-handed ventures, I had speculated a correlation between pheasants and cattails. So on a bright November afternoon I stepped into a boggy expanse at the base of an earthen dam the state had constructed to corral a small creek. The bird flushed as I approached the far edge of the cattails. All iridescence, waggling tail, and clamorous cackle, he groped aloft like a hod carrier straining up scaffolding, wings detonating the overpuffed seedheads. Then he bore straight away in a line drive that could be hit without swinging.

Where the rooster had flushed, cattail parachutes drifted on the breeze. Where he had flown, a few feathers did the same. I galloped hollering through the muck. Holding the bird, I was astonished by his big gaudiness and that I had stilled his wings. Moments before, he had been vigorously alive, all tension and motion. Now he lay loosely in my hands, smooth and solemn as the flight of a great blue heron. Traditional Ojibwa people in northern Wisconsin believe young men should give away the first deer they kill. This reminds young hunters that the deer was a gift to them. Lacking any such heritage, I wasn't about to relinquish this bird. But I did begin a personal tradition of speaking to the animals I kill. This first soliloquy consisted of "Thank you, Pheasant." Unwilling to rumple the rooster's feathers by stuffing him in my game pouch, I grasped the thick, collared neck and carried the bird to my 1966 Plymouth Valiant. I laid him in a state of repose on the backseat, then headed for another cattail patch.

❧

I've been drawn toward the next patch of bird cover ever since. But, as I say, a sense that the next bird might not be as good as the first began to seep in. Simultaneously, the groundswell of places where people pay to flush and shoot pen-raised birds caused me to reconsider just how encompassing Nicholas Adams's "all" really ought to be. Should it include shooting "preserves" where birds that have known the keen of wind siphoning through chicken wire since they were embryos are set free an hour before the gunners show up?

In a magazine ad for one of these outfits, rows of groomed plumage hang against a cedar plank wall, glinting in slanting sunlight. Three men stand beside them. They look satisfied. Maybe one of these guys basks in the afterglow of connecting on a particularly sweet spiraling left-to-right crossing shot. Has he ever prospected the margins of a wild rose thicket, pausing to chew a puckery rose hip and wonder if the great sweep of land that will describe the remainder of the afternoon is indeed grouseless as Uranus? If he has, then perhaps a shadow of unease tinges his mood.

To fend off this prickle, maybe he tells his partners that preserves sure stretch out the season and give the dogs a chance to work. Could be he speaks of the frustrations of finding a place to walk up a rooster in a dwindling landscape increasingly punctuated with For Sale signs and splashes of orange paint. He probably just shrugs, thinking how nice it is to get some shooting. But I can't help wondering if maybe he murmurs, "It was almost like hunting."

Hemingway was an aficionado of pigeon shoots. Yet nothing in his words suggests he confused the purely athletic pleasures of dropping pigeons inside the wall with the five-sense baptism of hunting. Catapulted into the 1990s, Nick Adams might be bemused by the moral evolution that has (with a few sordid exceptions) replaced the pigeon arena with courses where clay disks are ingeniously launched to simulate loping lagomorphs and arcing fowl. Who knows, maybe he would conclude that using animals as targets was a dark arrogance long overdue for purging. But about rousting pen-raised birds from designer food plots and cover strips as a surrogate for hunting, one can imagine only Nick's hard sorrow.

What do such places preserve? Do shooters perpetuate the magic of the hunt by enacting an elaborate charade, with chukars, bobwhites, and pheasants filling in for pigeons? Do they feel any more reverence for the lives they take than the cretin who blasts the decrepit tiger sold off by a two-bit circus to die seventy-five yards from its cage on some Texas ranch?

Apart from my rancor toward those who would forfeit the mystery, challenge, and wonder of hunting, there is something else. I have come more and more to feel that the sensation Nick Adams speaks of *isn't* always the same. On a visceral level, I learned this long ago in one of few moments still vivid in memory from the shimmer of my sophomore year in college.

I was hunting alone through a mix of gooseberry tangles, sycamores, and pin oaks on a friend's farm in southeast Kansas. Having lucked into the scant, ephemeral woodcock migration, I was lathered by the rare opportunity. Twice that morning, woodcock whirred up almost at my feet. Both times, brush veiled their flight and I didn't fire. Then a small bird lifted and went lilting toward a screen of cedars.

Doubt descended immediately after the shot, and I walked over to find the delicate body of an eastern screech owl. Numbed, I laid down the gun and knelt beside the bird. After constructing a burial platform of sticks and bark in the low branches of a redbud, I arranged the owl in a bleak semblance of flight. Walking out of the woods, I turned back and withdrew one of the owl's variegated flight feathers. I keep it to remind me that done in haste, or without respect, hunting can deliver the most profound regret conceivable.

❧

During the two falls I lived in Colorado, my efforts as a mountain bird hunter were lukewarm and tenuous. With the utopian pheasant fields of western Kansas just five hours away, I remained, at heart, a creature of the plains. I did discover the pleasures of walking ridges for blue grouse. But these hunts were almost always marked by a visual dualism. My orientation to midwestern grainfields fixed game birds either on the ground or in the air. I was never quite able to reconcile this with the fact that blue grouse spend much of their lives loafing in trees.

Intent on weaving a flush-provoking course through old blowdown, I would suddenly ratchet my head back in the manner of the neighbor's basset giving voice to the moon. Positioned thus, I would gape at the underside of a bull blue grouse clattering from its perch fifty feet up a spruce. Then I would pivot and attempt to cover it as it swept downslope with the conviction of a kamikaze. Subsequently, I would stumble along peering up into the latticework of branches in a vain effort to isolate the telltale silhouette. And a pair of birds would roar up from spearing grasshoppers in the bunchgrass.

I hunted ptarmigan once. The birds lived above twelve thousand feet in a great cirque striated by hogbacks and avalanche chutes. This basin cradled a lake in which swam cutthroats of palsy-inducing size. It was while crawling an olive scud among these fish that I first noticed ptarmigan browsing on a nearby slope. Gradually, I conceived the idea of returning in September when the state allowed a person a daily limit of three of these birds that only descend to timberline in deepest winter.

Carrying shotguns, our fly rods strapped to our packs, a friend and I stood in the thirteen-thousand-foot saddle above the basin, exhilarated by the climb and curious about the birds. It soon became apparent the only challenging part of hunting ptarmigan was finding them. Trusting their mottled rock-lichen-snow camouflage, they allowed themselves to be approached almost to petting range. Once airborne, they had an unsettling tendency to land again before you could shoot without feeling you were in cahoots with ground sluicers. Eventually, we hit on the idea of driving them off the small hogback ridges. This involved some clownish footwork but resulted in sustained flight. My first shot reverberated around the cirque, seeming loud enough to trigger avalanches, unwelcome as a sonic boom. Still, we persisted until we had killed six birds. When I bent to pick up my last ptarmigan, I was visited by the image of a crumpled screech owl.

Grilled hot and fast over Osage orange coals several weeks later, the heart-dark birds had the succulence of a meadow filled with columbines and the tang of a pika's whistle. Even as I savored the meat, I knew I wouldn't shoot another ptarmigan, though I wasn't quite sure why. These birds had spent their lives in country less altered by man than any I had ever hunted. I could taste the wildness of that high basin with every bite, and it sharpened my hunger for wilder country still—all a person could ask from a meal. But hunting is so much more than simply gathering meat. The ptarmigan had asked something of me, and I had no answers.

Maybe the birds were too naive. Maybe it was something more base, the way a cat disdains an inert moth, but when its wings suddenly flutter, the paw flashes out. Whatever, it simply felt wrong. I had shamed the ptarmigan, myself, and this place that had been so generous with alpenglow and cutthroats. I knew I had no business hunting unless I could find the discipline to shoot only when it felt right.

❦

Seven years ago, my wife and I moved to western Montana. We came for two things: the presence of wild rivers where spotted fish swam, and the absence of people (an illusion propped up for a while by the contrast between the gluttonous desecration of Colorado's Front Range and the cavelike cabin we rented on Rock Creek). Long bewitched by trout, we now entered a period of delicious mania.

So when September arrived, we knew almost nothing about the local possibilities for game birds. But it was time to hunt. We walked long, south-facing ridges stippled with great ponderosas and Doug firs. My eyes caromed between branches and earth. We had moved a thousand miles north, and still blue grouse toyed with my head as if it were a yo-yo.

Despite the fishing and the country, visions of early fall in Colorado lingered. Conjuring whole mountainsides covered with yellow leaves and white trunks, I mourned Montana's lack of aspens. Through this nostalgic fog, I slowly perceived that the bottomlands and foothills were, in fact, laced with fine patches of aspen. And as it turned out, where there were aspens, ruffed grouse—*ho!*—were seldom far away. Then in October, the larches did their Roman candle routine, needles eventually falling to form amber halos around thick trunks. I stopped looking backward.

The next spring, I drove east over the divide and north toward Blackfeet country. Like many people before me, I saw what a seventy-nine-year-old rancher later described as the "cardboard cut-out skyline" of the Rocky Mountain Front and promptly went out of my head. Even from the highway, I could hear a thousand miles of prairie crashing into limestone. The rock rose almost straight up to form jagged serrations in the manner of a stegosaur's dorsal. Gesturing toward this skyline was a sign on which someone from the state highway department had honed laconic irony to a fine point. It read "Rocky Mountains."

I tried to imagine how it would feel to be a tumbleweed or a coyote or a curlew sailing toward those great stone reefs across the sweeps and folds of the land. The country spoke in the mother tongues of wind, light, and water, and murmured in dozens of other languages. One of the things it said was, Birds.

Since then, I've returned to the Front often to hike and camp. In the best moments, I think I'm learning to listen. And on these burnished plains, I've flushed pheasants from irrigation ditches, mallards off winding jump-across creeks, snipe out of seep-bogs, and Hungarian partridges from windbreaks of Russian olives. They all flew well.

But for me, sharp-tailed grouse define this land of short grass and tall walls. In the spring they dance, strutting and spinning, tamping the earth with feathered feet, thumping out a staccato rhythm. With the quiet browns and whites of winter prairie checkered boldly across back and wings, lavender air sacs puffed, yolk-yellow eyebrows vivid, tail stabbing sky, they dance. And when they fly, I feel grizzlies following snowmelt down the creeks and out onto the plains. I feel the sloppy flakes of a late blizzard that surprises the great bears and drives them disgruntled into willow tangles. I feel the first gust of a chinook.

Sharptails insist I comment on plans to sink more shafts into the much-shafted earth, probing for the petroleum mother lode that lies pooled somewhere along this syncline. They urge me to write letters seeking reauthorization of the Conservation Reserve Program, so swaths of prairie won't be upended like an hourglass, topsoil sifting away in the scouring wind. They make me wince as the edges of great working ranches crumble into ranchettes and vacation homes. They nudge me to become part of this community, to come to know these ranchers, to join them in keeping open the Old North Trail, where mule deer and people and short-horned lizards have walked at the feet of these mountains for thousands of Septembers.

Maybe if I still lived in southeast Nebraska, pheasants would push me to question the fertilizers, herbicides, and pesticides that poison the soil and water there. Perhaps those hardy immigrants would challenge me to advocate dryland farming techniques, providing real alternatives for all the Ogallala Aquifer junkies who economize by bulldozing shelterbelts and farming cleaner. Pheasants might send me into country cemeteries and old railroad rights-of-way, seeking relict populations of native plants, hoping to resurrect small corners of the tallgrass prairie that so astounded the pioneers not long ago.

But Montana is my home now. So I'll fight for grizzlies, pronghorns, and sharptails. Last November, my wife and I walked quietly among wind-gnarled aspen, our young daughter riding in a pack on my back. We had hunted and played together throughout the day. Now it was twilight, and the guns were put away. Moistened by a skiff of snow that had shrunk deep into the shadows, the leaves underfoot gave off an aroma so faint and good it could have been the scent of northern lights. I glanced up at a branch and sensed, *knew*, it was about to bear the weight of feathers. Presently, an immature great horned owl grasped the pale bark and folded its wings. For an instant, there was the intimacy that comes from knowing a place well. I realized I had been hunting for an ecosystem in which to participate. At last, I was learning how to reciprocate with this land. And I knew once more that the last shot could indeed be as good as the first. If it's a wild bird in wild country, a place where I walk humbly and with an open heart, it may be the best of all. Or I might not even raise my shotgun.

          ✻

Say it's the fall equinox. Cottonwoods pulse with the radiance of your three-year-old daughter's eyes as she releases a tiger swallowtail freshly unfurled from its chrysalis. The wind that any day now will tear these glowing leaves asunder and hurl them at North Dakota is almost quiet. Calf-high grass the color of knapweed honey flows with the grain of the light breeze, eddying around little clumps and great tangles of willows. Your partner whistles and points. A sharp-tail zags through the sky, wings pumping like a jigsaw. Thirty feet behind it, a northern goshawk echoes every move. For ten thousand years, these birds have carved one another. With your big, booted feet you suddenly feel grounded and graceless as a telephone pole but also filled with wonder. You think, Why not ten thousand years more?

Moments later, five sharptails flush. You stand with the gun at your side and watch them fly until all you can see is an occasional shard of light flung from a wing tip. Then they are gone beyond the curve of the earth.

Paying for It

❧

TED WILLIAMS

What is NAGB & SPA?

This is a legitimate question, one that is asked in the subtitle of a foot-square, mustard-colored pamphlet—entitled *Get Acquainted with NAGB & SPA*—which was thoughtfully, if anonymously, mailed to me this past summer.

"An alliance between the Non-Asthmatic Glass Blowers and the Society for the Prevention of Animals," I hypothesized, having read the document and having noted, to my surprise, that it never got around to answering its own question.

But later, a grand, silver-haired gentleman, James (we'll call him), told me that I was wrong, that NAGB & SPA stands for North American Game Breeders and Shooting Preserve Operators Association. "What happened to the 'O' for 'Operators'?" I asked. James said that they probably just forgot it.

NAGB & SPA seeks to better the preserve experience—for proprietor as well as client. Article one of the "Code of Ethics" reads, "I possess faith in and look forward to a greater game breeding and shooting preserve industry." In addition, NAGB & SPA "has fought some of your battles (even though you were not a member), saving you from many restrictive rules and regulations."

James's friend, Guido (we'll call him), is proud of his membership in NAGB & SPA and proud of the Red Lantern Pheasant Farm (we'll call it), which he owns and operates and which is probably the oldest and most respected of America's more than three thousand commercial shooting preserves.

When I had phoned to ask him if I could come out to Red Lantern to watch and photograph a Sunday tower shoot for an article I was doing, he had startled me with his enthusiasm. Several times thereafter he had called back to firm up details, and once had even offered to put me up for the night. The last preserve operator I had spoken with had granted me a grudging invitation to a tower shoot on Long Island—until I told him that I wanted to write a story about it. Whereupon the invitation had been promptly retracted, with the explanation that the written word cannot convey what tower shoots are really like.

✻

On the appointed Sabbath I find myself under a red dawn, jeeping out of the thickly wooded Berkshires where they slope down from Massachusetts into the rolling gold-brown corn country of eastern New York State. It is beautiful land, but it is something of a painted beauty. The farmhouses are too white, the hedges and lines of spruce too straight. Look closely at the brooks. They are milky with broken dirt from sagging banks. Between the corn stubble the fields are cracked and wrinkled. The earth has been had by too many.

Guido meets me at the pheasant pens, which sprawl over several acres on both sides of the road as you enter Red Lantern. The pheasants—about ten thousand of them—see the world through blue plastic glasses wired to their nostrils. These, Guido explains, prevent them from plucking each other's tail feathers. On our approach they labor into the air, raising an eye-watering stench of guano, and bash drunkenly, again and again, into overhanging chicken wire.

These birds are a triumph of selective breeding, combining all the virtues of forty-two of the world's best pheasant stocks. They are plump with long, streaming tails. The cocks are brilliant, almost garish. So desirable are they that the state once saw fit to commission Guido's father, Salvatore (we'll call him), to raise them for public stocking. Salvatore, one of NAGB & SPA's most revered presidents, successfully fought off a public movement against shooting preserves in 1937—the first year in Red Lantern's fourth decade of operation. In one newspaper editorial he noted that a sportsman had reported shooting one of his birds over a hundred miles from Red Lantern. Such escapes, he wrote, clearly illustrated the shooting preserve's role in sustaining public hunting. (The second article in NAGB & SPA's Code of Ethics reads, "I believe that the game breeder can insure the future generations a plentiful game supply.")

The air in the clubhouse is rich with the scent of pipe tobacco and leather. The walls are a confusion of yellowed photographs of bygone hunts, old guns, and peeling, brittle-skinned trophy heads. Guido offers me coffee and doughnuts, which I decline, and hands me a Red Lantern brochure to sign for his grandson. It is my first autograph, and I am proud as a cat with a rat. I have been writing for the national market for barely two years. His grandson must be an exceptionally discerning young man, a voracious reader (he'd have to be to find my lightly and widely scattered bylines), and, no doubt, a fellow ecofreak.

Guido pulls down a window-shade map—an idea he got from the military—and explains how the tower shoot works. The concept did not, as many believe, originate at Red Lantern. Nor is it anything new. It is an Old World tradition that has been adapted only slightly to satisfy an element of the American sporting psyche. There is a forty-five-foot-high tower with a high-walled six-foot-square platform perched on top. The tower is ringed with blinds. About an hour before the shoot, crates of mallards and/or pheasants are winched aboard the platform. Clients, having drawn their blinds earlier, surround the tower. The proprietor and an assistant climb a ladder and hoist themselves into the platform through a trap door, which they shut and latch behind them. One toot of a horn means get ready. Every thirty seconds or so a bird is tossed skyward and shot at as it breaks for the perimeter of the circle of blinds. After five birds, two toots means proceed to the next blind on your right. It ends when you reach the blind you started out from.

This morning's shoot is an exceptionally small one. There are only thirteen "guns" (often there are twenty) and only 110 birds—100 pheasants and 10 mallards. Guido says that just the other day he had thrown out 288 birds for a sportsmen's club. Occasionally he has thrown out 300. Clients pay eight dollars per bird released, so, with tips, a big tower shoot can cost $2,500. You are guaranteed at least ten fair wing shots, and at the end of the hunt you can exchange your ducks and pheasants for frozen, processed birds.

The clients begin arriving at nine. Guido introduces them to me as they enter the clubhouse. Almost all are from New York City. There is a handsome, wistful boy of nine or ten in a tweed suit and matching tweed hat with brush, three slender, stylish girls, and three young men—one of them the boy's father, another an Englishman elegantly attired in shooting coat and breeches. The rest are old men. They carry their age well, but they are very old. They look at and into you through cataract glasses and speak in pleasant, lightly quavering voices of their practices in the City and of bygone hunts. Several have shot in England in parties smaller than this and have been top "guns" in kills of over a thousand pheasants in a single day.

All—young and old—are glowing with this sudden release from the pheasant pen of New York City into a bright, warm November morning and earth that still lives. How wonderful, they say, to be here on this morning. How fresh the air, how pleasant the uncluttered countryside.

The guns are unsheathed at a quarter to ten. Most are straight-stocked English side-by-sides, undefiled by butt-plates. Purdeys, Webleys, Churchills, and the like. The young carry light-gauged, plastic-finished Browning over-and-unders.

Charles, the boy in tweed, tells me that he's just been given a very fine twenty-gauge double, but that he's not sure what kind it is. He goes to school in New York City and should be in the fifth grade, but his mother kept him back last year. This is his third tower shoot. I ask him how he likes them, and he says he guesses they're okay.

Blinds are drawn at 9:55. At 10:00 the troop marches toward the tower. A late flight of robins has settled in. It is bright and warm under a high, thin overcast. Frost drips off dead grass and loose clouds of crane flies hang in the air like milkweed. The cover, five hundred acres of it, is voluptuously birdy—a beckoning blend of low grass, planted corn, multiflora rose and brambles, all laced with close-cropped, two-foot-wide paths for easy walking. We move toward the tower through this pseudo-spring, robins flushing ahead of us, roosters—penned and loose—crowing seductively.

When we reach the tower Guido and his helper, Joe, climb the ladder to the platform and seal themselves in. Only the tops of their heads show above the barricades. The "guns" embrace their blinds. And I—goggled, swaddled in blaze orange, terrified into a trance of calm efficiency—take my position on a rise in the middle of it all, fifty feet sunward of the tower. If a bird flies low at me, I will jettison my newly strapless Nikon and bellyflop.

Breeches click shut. Guido holds back the gas horn, teasing, tantalizing. At last the horn grunts, and a rooster is hurled aloft, trailing feathers as it sculls away . . . *low and at me*. I sit down quickly, unable to drop the camera. Silence. Has he slipped the defenses? I look up, holding the lens lengthwise in front of my eyes. The bird is still out there, still sculling. Six fast shots, and six little puffs of feathers that drift like smoke in the morning breeze. The bird hovers at fifty feet, flapping crazily. Six more shots, and he crumples. Pellets slap down on my neck and shoulders, but they are spent and sting barely more than sleet.

Instantly another bird is airborne, a hen. I remember the camera and focus, too late, on the tower. A dozen more shots—deep-throated twelves and squeaky twenties in harmony—and she crumples. Another bird is up. This time I catch him in the viewfinder, but even before I release, I know the picture has been spoiled. The camera is shaking too much for even one one-thousandth. Two more birds, one box of ammo. The horn grunts twice, signaling allemande right.

I am ready for the next round, steeled to the sleet and thunder. Up in the platform I can hear a game-farm mallard quacking. He is a *smart* game-farm mallard—almost a contradiction in terms. At the sound of the horn he simply unfurls his wings and parachutes to my feet. He pulls it off so quickly, so adeptly that I do not immediately grasp the hideous peril of my situation. We stare at each other, and I taste five-hour-old coffee.

"Get away from me," I croak. "No! Don't! God no! Stay right there!"

"Quack," declares the duck.

Another game-farm mallard is catapulted into space. The behavior of this bird is less aberrant. He finds the perimeter and circles twice, drawing unspeakable fire. At last he loses altitude and pitches into a patch of aspens.

And so it goes—five birds, two grunts; one grunt, five birds. A very few make it past the perimeter and streak toward the highway or the pond, none with all its feathers. A few crippled pheasants ditch near the pens, apparently with the hope of getting back in. One, gravely wounded, pedals down out of the sky in slow motion, lights briefly in an oak, and is slammed to earth.

At the beginning of round fifteen the tower exudes an all-white pheasant. I had seen a few in the pens earlier and noticed that their rumps were stained brown. If you shoot the white bird, you win a handsome china plate bearing the Red Lantern logo. Thirteen guns speak and the white bird explodes in a shower of feathers like a pillow slashed and shaken out an attic window.

At the end of round nineteen, I yell to Guido and scurry up the ladder. The view from the platform is lovely—brooks catching the sun, patches of woods, rolling fields. I can see the clients coiled in their blinds. Two grunts, and round twenty begins.

Presently, Joe takes a pellet in the cheek, and there is momentary disorder until he announces that the skin is only bruised.

Then there is only one hen left in the top box. She is thrown up and shot. And it is done. Breeches click open, and the troop marches back to the clubhouse for lunch.

I walk with Guido. "It's a lot of fun, isn't it?" he says to me. I nod and thank him for letting me be part of it. He says that it is nothing, that he is always glad to cooperate with the press. (The third article in NAGB & SPA's Code of Ethics reads, "I believe that the general public should be awakened to the need for shooting preserves and game propagation.")

"They did pretty well," says Guido. "In fact, they did very well." He is all lit up, and suddenly I realize that I like Guido and that he is one of those rare people that everybody likes—instinctively, without asking why.

※

Waiting for me in the clubhouse are a thick roast beef sandwich, coleslaw, and potato salad. The clients are less fortunate. This shoot, unlike the larger ones, is not catered, and most people have had to bring their own food. I sit on the leather couch, eating the sandwich and staring into the fire. My ears are ringing, and the fragrance of gunpowder is still in my nostrils. The old men talk of the morning's shoot and of bygone hunts.

❧

"Given up on the Miramichi, eh, what?

"Hurumph . . .

"Given up on the Miramichi, eh, what?"

It is the Englishman. He is speaking to me.

"Why, yes," I answer, startled that he should know. My exploits on the Miramichi had hardly been front-page material. Two Augusts before, Bob Daviau and I had whipped the river for three dog days—over the scornful gaze of tough-scaled salmon who had been stewing in their lies since June. I had gone in over my waders and nearly drowned, we had been ignominiously routed from two private pools, and we had each taken one six-inch brook trout.

The Englishman smiles a quick, thin-lipped smile, and turns crisply to mix a drink.

Dogs bark. Time for the "walk-up hunt." This follows every tower shoot. Since the clients have paid eight dollars for each bird released, Guido lets them conduct a mop-up operation for possible survivors. (Article four of NAGB & SPA's Code of Ethics reads, "I pledge my earnest and sincere cooperation in securing and maintaining the confidence of the public in the honesty and integrity of game breeders and shooting preserve operators.")

The walk-up hunt is more informal than the tower shoot, the clients more festive, less purposeful. Sleek German shorthairs grin and dance around their handlers. Bells ring. Whistles blast. The young men lounge against their cars, smoking, guns broken and resting in the crooks of their arms. The girls are sitting on the clubhouse steps, talking and laughing. The old men, glowing again, are pointing, mapping, planning. This is how it must have been in bygone hunts.

The Englishman and a bone surgeon choose up teams—one is to hunt east, the other west. I go west with the bone surgeon.

Twice we hear shots from the Englishman's group, but for half an hour we move no birds. At the men's urging, the girls stop by the trap to shoot skeet. They have been bragged about and try hard not to disappoint. Their expressions say they enjoy it, but their guns are mounted before they say "Pull," and they flinch when the trap snaps. They break three for nine.

We step across a stream and push up toward the tower, each of us on his or her own manicured path. A hen gets up at a young man's feet, and he slows it with the first barrel, dumps it with the second. At the top of the hill we stop to let the old men rest. Presently, one of the dogs begins to snort the ground and beat his tail stub. He pauses with a front leg cocked, then races down into an open stand of oak. In a few seconds he returns with a crippled hen.

No sooner has the dog dropped the bird and been congratulated than another dog, bounding through golden two-foot grass, turns to stone in midair and lands looking at his feet, eyes glassy. The young man who just shot the hen approaches, and no one says a word. He walks crisply, with confidence. He stops. Two seconds of silence is all the bird can stand. It is a big rooster that churns up almost under the dog's nose and flashes straight away, low and cackling, sunlight on his tail. The dog throws his head back, but follows only with his eyes. The gun comes up smoothly, almost slowly, and the bird dies cleanly in the air.

❧

Back in the clubhouse, Guido is apologizing for the unproductive walk-up: two days ago he released forty birds; he loses 35 percent of all the birds he puts in the field; he's got an awful predator problem; just yesterday one of the guides shot a hawk stealing a pheasant. "What kind?" I ask.

"Ringneck," he says. I tell him I mean what kind of hawk, and he says he doesn't know but that "he was a big bastard." "Hate to shoot them," he says, "but what are you going to do."

"What are you going to do," someone echoes.

An old man shuffles toward me, smiling, and stands a foot beyond the socially acceptable discourse line. "How you hitting 'em, Ted?" he asks. I force a chuckle, having heard the joke before, and move back a foot, bumping my head against the stone chimney. "Do you miss baseball, Ted?"

"Actually," I say, "I detest baseball; it's a game for people who like to talk—'Hey, Pitch, Hey, Pitch. Lay one in there, Pitch.' Tennis is my game."

There is polite, nervous laughter from four corners. All eyes are on me. The realization starts in my face and seeps down my chest and into my armpits the way the cold does when you step coatless from a hot living room into a January night. My God. They really think

I'm *Him*—the Splendid Splinter! Who, *the year I was born*, had distinguished himself in the American League to the extent that my father argued I not be named "Ted" ... until his mother-in-law assured him that the ballplayer would be forgotten in five years. These people had come not just to shoot, but to see me. And I was a fraud, a fake, an *impersonator*.

I watch the door like a redtail watches a pheasant in brush, but there is no escape. The next hour is a nightmare of handshaking, posing for photographs, answering questions with mumbled fiction. I am in way too deep and getting deeper by the second. I can't come clean.

At last, on the pretense of scrutinizing a crusty caribou head, I slip out the door and edge around the corner, my back scraping the old boards. As I draw my breath for the sprint to the jeep, I can hear Guido telling about the hawk. And I hear someone say, "That's funny, I thought they'd all flown south."

From *A Hunter's Road*

Jim Fergus

I crashed the opening-night barbecue of the National Grouse and Woodcock Hunt in Grand Rapids, Minnesota (a town best known as the birthplace of the late Judy Garland, although town fathers prefer not to call attention to that fact because in later years the singer made unkind remarks about the city and then, of course, there was the matter of her suicide: "It's not the way a girl from Minnesota is supposed to end her life," said a censorious local spokesman in an interview).

I'd been driving all day and I was hungry—thirsty, too—so I stepped up to the buffet table at the local gun club, which was hosting dinner, and helped myself to some quite passable barbecued beef and sausage, and then I filled a large plastic cup at the beer keg and sat down alone at a table to enjoy my meal.

The RGS puts on quite a winging for their invited guests, an exclusive group of contributors to the cause. In an ideal world, wildlife would be protected and preserved for its own sake, no strings attached, simply because it deserves protection on fundamental moral grounds. In this world, it is sportsmen's organizations like the Ruffed Grouse Society, the Izaak Walton League, Trout Unlimited, Ducks Unlimited, Pheasants Forever, Quail Unlimited, et al., that provide the economic incentive and the vast majority of the funds to protect and improve habitat and ensure continuing game populations. Ironically, as Gordon Gullion pointed out, the efforts of anti-hunting groups, ostensibly formed to save wildlife from the hunter's gun, actually encourage its decline. If polled, surely every garden-variety environmentalist, conservationist, or animal-rights activist would vote to protect the ruffed grouse, the prairie chicken, or the duck. But the sportsman puts his money where his mouth is. He buys wetlands; funds the work of such dedicated professionals as Gullion; cajoles, woos, threatens, and pays off lumber companies to initiate better timbering methods; bankrolls subsidies for farmers and ranchers to maintain and improve wildlife habitat degraded by poor agricultural practices.

For all that, some of us are not joiners of groups and would prefer to be sons and daughters of the forest; we would prefer the natural world to be still wild and free, and for humankind to cultivate a reverence for nature that extends beyond economic interests and remains independent of them—although this seems an increasingly farfetched and romantic notion these days. As Aldo Leopold pointed out over forty years ago in *A Sand County Almanac*, without an ethic of this kind, we are doomed to deplete everything for our own purposes, and the best efforts of any organization or government become mere fingers in the dike. For all the thousands of acres of wetlands saved by Ducks Unlimited, how many more have been lost? For all its dedicated work in the field, millions of dollars poured into the cause, and hundreds of paper-miles of conservation legislation initiated, who can honestly say that waterfowl habitat and populations are not still in precipitous decline? National Wildlife Federation statistics suggest that half of the original wetlands in the continental United States have already been destroyed and that we continue to lose an additional three hundred thousand or so acres per year. The Audubon Society has the figure even higher—four hundred thousand acres per year. Scare tactics, the developers and boosters will tell you; so what? ask the growth junkies. Who needs swamps and marshes when you can have parking lots and shopping malls? In any kind of economic footrace, the natural world always loses, and too often the same people who are backfilling wetlands to build the shopping mall with one hand are bidding on bad sporting art at a Ducks Unlimited banquet with the other.

I considered these grand ethical, moral, and economic arguments as I, uninvited guest, stuffed my face with Ruffed Grouse Society barbecue and swilled its draft beer. I felt a bit conspicuous among the invited guests, a little nervous at being such a shameless party crasher, though no one appeared to notice me. Maybe they just assumed I was one of them and that I had forgotten my name tag. Halfway through my second plateful of barbecue and another draft beer, someone "made" me.

"Gordy sent me," I hastened to explain to the fellow who came over to my table, and whose tag identified him as Dan Dessecker, a biologist with the Ruffed Grouse Society. He was a ramrod-straight young man, with a quick, efficient stride, eyeglasses, a clipboard, and a chopped professional manner. He looked kind of like Clark Kent in khakis.

"Gordy sent you?"

"Yeah, I saw him yesterday down in Cloquet. He said to say hello to everyone. He said to tell you that he was sorry that he couldn't make it this year."

"How's he look?"

"He looks pretty good. But today he started another round of chemo. He hated to miss this hunt."

"I know."

I explained to the biologist that I was researching a book about upland bird hunting, and that at Gullion's suggestion, I'd come up here to have a look around. He excused himself, crossed the room purposefully, and relayed this information to a couple of large, beefy fellows in close conference over cocktails by the bar—one, I later learned, the executive director of the Ruffed Grouse Society, and the other the local host of the event who owned the motel in town where the participants were being lodged. They eyed me suspiciously. I ate like a dog whose bowl is about to be taken from him, and drained the last of my beer.

I was just getting up to leave when Dan strode back over to my table. He didn't ask me to leave, after all; instead, he told me that he had been assigned to look after me, show me around, answer my questions, and even take me out hunting tomorrow if I so desired. "First we'll have to get you a name tag," he said. Evidently Gordy's name opened doors. Also, as I was beginning to learn, if you want to get invited on a lot of interesting hunts with interesting hunting companions, it doesn't hurt to tell people that you're writing a book about bird hunting. You see? One minute I'm a party crasher with barbecue sauce on my chin and beer foam on my upper lip, and the next I have my own biologist and I'm getting an official name tag.

I drove back to the motel, found a spot to camp in the lot, and arrived at the meeting room in time for the prehunt briefing and an inspirational film about ruffed grouse. My biologist stayed right at my elbow. I got the feeling that he had been charged with keeping an eye on me.

The hunters enter the event in teams of two and almost all of them bring their own dogs. Each team is assigned a "huntsman," usually a local familiar with the country, who serves as both guide and scorekeeper. The competition is scored on a point basis—with points awarded for dog work (birds pointed, flushed, retrieved) as well as for total number of birds killed. (The legal limits are five grouse and ten woodcock per day per hunter.) I believe that any such competition runs against the grain of a true hunting ethic, and there's no point in trying to obscure the fact that the points awarded for dog work are largely a matter of ceremony, as the winners are invariably the team that kills the most birds in the course of the three-day hunt.

Grouse hunters tend to be a solitary lot; aficionados of other kinds of hunting might even accuse them of a certain elitism. Heir to the grand tradition of such American sportsmen as William Harnden Foster, Dr. Charles Norris, and George Bird Evans, they admire elegant pointing-dog work and double-barrel shotguns and are notoriously closemouthed about their favorite coverts. Many of them are more than willing to hunt hard all day, busting for hours through dense, briar-tangled undergrowth in order to flush one grouse, to hear the deep sound of wingbeats in the forest, and perhaps catch a glimpse of the bird through the trees. These are hunters who pursue their game more for the intense aesthetic value of the sport than for the killing.

I will not bore the reader with further tales of the cocktail dinner parties of the next few evenings; no more descriptions of well-appointed buffet tables or tiresome auctions and raffles. Suffice it to say that nearly all the hunters I spoke to salved their consciences with the rationalization that they were participating in important scientific studies, collecting invaluable data for the team of working biologists who at the end of each hunting day sexed, aged, and examined the crop contents of all the birds killed. For the biologists, this is a strange kind of symbiotic relationship; conscientious professionals, generally underpaid and overworked, they enjoyed the hoopla attendant to the hunt, schmoozing with the wealthy sportsmen, and grazing at the lavishly laid buffet table. Who wouldn't? I liked it myself. It becomes harder and harder to be a son of the forest.

"Gordon was an eloquent defender of the hunt," explained Dan over beers in the bar that first evening after the briefing. "He understood that you have to put a dollar value on something before people are going to support it."

"But don't you ever worry that by overpromoting the sport, you might also do harm to the resource, to the very thing you're trying to protect?"

"No, I'm not concerned at all with that. Hunting is not a factor. We know that."

"Gordon told me that he had the results of a study that clearly indicated that hunting pressure can suppress grouse populations."

"That study was done in a relatively small refuge near a large urban center [Minneapolis/St. Paul]. Up here we have over a million acres to hunt. Fifty teams of two hunters hunting for three days can make no significant impact on bird populations."

"He said that the Ruffed Grouse Society didn't want to hear the results of his study. That it was too hot politically."

"Gordon said that?"

"Yes."

"Well, we can ask Sam about it [Sam Pursglove, the executive director of the Ruffed Grouse Society], but I certainly don't think we would ever ignore Gordon's findings. He was instrumental in getting the hunt up here started."

"Let's put it this way then: Do you think that a competition like this is somehow counter to the spirit of grouse hunting?"

"How do you mean?"

"I mean aesthetically. That you're turning the essentially solitary and esoteric tradition of the sport into a kind of grand 'promo' affair."

"You mean, do the means justify the end?"

"Something like that."

"Well, you tell me. We've proven to the lumber companies via the community and the chamber of commerce that there is a real economic value attached to grouse. Without that there would be no reason for them to spend the extra time and money clear-cutting in a way that is beneficial to the birds and other wildlife as well. It isn't just a question of aesthetics."

"It so rarely is."

"Look, one of the biggest myths in this country is that of the American wilderness. There is no wilderness left in North America. Period. As soon as fire suppression became official federal policy back in the 1930s, we altered the natural balance. We became land managers. That's our responsibility now."

"Not a very romantic notion, is it?"

"I'm a scientist."

Touché.

❧

The dogs woke me the next morning before daylight. The camper was surrounded by trailer and pickup truck kennels, whose occupants began to fidget, whine, and bark, anxious to get on with the day's hunt. When their masters came out of the motel rooms to feed and walk them at daylight, my dog Sweetz and I peeked through a crack in the curtain to watch the activity. It was another gray, overcast, drizzly fall day in the northwoods. Hunting weather.

Nearly every hunting breed was represented at the affair—English setters, Gordon setters, English pointers, German shorthairs, German wirehairs, vizslas, Brittanys, weimaraners, griffons, springer spaniels, Labs, you name it. It was great fun watching them all mill about excitedly, their owners talking to them, hollering at them, chasing them, scolding them. Small harmless turf skirmishes broke out among some of the more aggressive dogs, while the rest went about their business—lifting legs, squatting, dragging their owners along at the ends of their leashes. Dozens of dog poops steamed on the motel grass in the misty dawn.

I was feeling a bit logy and disheveled from several too many beers with my biologist, and I got up, put the coffee on, and quickly got back under the comforter while it perked. I'd almost forgotten our hunting date when Dan rapped smartly on the door. Where at first I thought him to be rather humorless, as I had gotten to know him over beers I found that he just had one of those senses of humor so dry that it sometimes passes nearly undetected. This morning, dressed in hunting clothes and orange cap, with clipboard in hand and dog whistle on a lanyard around his neck, he looked as crisp and efficient as the evening before, almost annoyingly so.

"Morning, Jim," he said, chipperly, as I peered around the door of the camper. "I thought you'd be ready to go by now. I thought you'd want to get into the woods before the hunt participants shot every grouse and woodcock in northern Minnesota."

❧

My father used to take me on fishing trips to the northwoods when I was a boy. He died a quarter of a century ago and I haven't been back much since. Now the midwestern trees seemed all new to me and yet vaguely familiar, like running into old acquaintances whose names you have forgotten. The forests here are lush, dense, and close, particularly to one accustomed to the open, Spartan aridity of the West. Though there are no vistas here, no "views" to speak of, and the closeness can seen claustrophobic at first, I was beginning to lose my prejudices about this country, to give up the chauvinism that so many westerners, native and adopted, feel about the big open. This was good country, too, only different—impossibly damp, verdant, and rich, with a remarkable diversity of flora. The trees—aspen, white birch, red maple, sugar maple, black ash, white ash, green ash, all in different stages of their poignant fall dance—had begun to shed their leaves, opening up the canopy and leaving a carpet of color on the forest floor—reds, yellows, golds, and greens—a kind of hunter's autumn cliché.

My biologist lined me out on the flora as we hunted, identifying plant species and explaining good grouse cover, food sources, and general habitat requirements. Sweetz worked the dense cover well for a rookie, though sometimes ranging a bit too far out. This was an entirely new game for us, and when I saw the first grouse flush wild out of range through the trees, it occurred to me that there was an excellent chance that I would never actually hit one. How can you shoot them with all those trees in the way?

Dan had his German shorthair, Jute, hunting out ahead. A slightly hardheaded dog, he was giving the biologist fits by busting grouse out of range; we could hear their wingbeats reverberate through the forest, even if we couldn't see the birds. Then Dan would chase the dog down and punish him. He would pick him up off the ground by the ears and shake him until Jute made piteous howling noises, terrible sounds as if he were being murdered. All the while, Dan would be patiently lecturing the dog, explaining to him with the calm, articulate, precise diction of the scientist all the things he had done wrong and all the things he must not do again lest they have to repeat this unpleasant business. Sweetz and I would wait out these disciplinary sessions, like listening in on a domestic dispute, looking at each other with faintly embarrassed expressions. We're afraid we had been through a bit of it ourselves, our looks seemed to say, and it isn't very pretty, is it?

Now we walked leaf-covered roadsides and paths through the forests and worked the edges of clearings and clear-cuts. As you can never get up high enough to find out where you are in this country and as I was born with a poor sense of direction, I'd have been hopelessly lost in under five minutes if I hadn't had Dan along as my guide.

We came upon an old abandoned farm site, slightly elevated on a rise where finally I could have a look around. I breathed a sigh of relief and didn't want to leave it right away. If I had a farm in this country a hundred years ago, this is just where I'd have put it, too.

Jute pointed a woodcock in a wet alder thicket and Dan killed it. Woodcock are easier to shoot than grouse; they hold well for a point and when flushed tend to fly straight up in the air, pausing at the apex above the cover before leveling off and flying away, making a startled, plaintive cry. All game birds may have roughly the same level of intelligence, but some species clearly have better personalities than others, and woodcock are nice little birds with their chubby bodies, long beaks, and large soulful eyes. I know a number of hunters who have difficulty killing them. It has something to do with their portly carriage and those big prescient eyes looking up at you, a certain feeling of wrongdoing to shoot something so sweet and trusting who will sometimes hold so tight to a point that the dog and bird will be facing each other, inches apart, nose to nose. Dog handlers prize "timberdoodles," as they are sometimes called, for their quality of holding for the point, but if I ever see the bird on the ground first I simply can't shoot it when it flies. This is one advantage in using a flushing dog, where the flight comes as a surprise, the shot as a reflex.

And I do love to eat the woodcock—a large-hearted, rich, red-meated migratory bird.

So we killed a couple of woodcock, and later Dan killed one grouse. I had an opportunity to shoot a double on a grouse and a woodcock that flushed milliseconds apart out of the same thicket, but I fell apart and missed them both. We decided to call it a day.

As we were driving back down a dirt road in the national forest, we happened upon a car of road hunters. A favorite method of the locals, road hunting is usually pursued on weekends or in the evenings after a hard day's work. Frequently it involves beer drinking, and can be an outing for the whole family, as well as a good way to obtain dinner. In the mornings and evenings the grouse often come out onto the road to gravel or to dust themselves, or just to loaf and feed along the edges; road hunting can be an effective technique to find birds and easy on the legs, too, and it infuriates and disgusts traditional grouse hunters.

As we approached the road hunters, we watched the driver lever his gun out the car window. "I can't believe it," Dan said. "He's going to dust that bird right in front of us! He's breaking at least three laws: carrying a loaded firearm in a vehicle, discharging a firearm from a vehicle, and discharging a firearm from within twenty yards of a public road."

The driver squeezed off a shot, jumped out of the car, and picked up his dead grouse on the side of the road. A small child tumbled into the front seat from the back, and an enormously fat man in the passenger seat took a long swallow from a tallboy can of Old Style beer.

"And his partner's drinking beer," I pointed out.

"Four laws."

"Why don't we make a citizen's arrest?"

"No, you don't want to mess with these people. But I'm going to get his license plate number and turn him in to the game warden."

As we passed the road hunters, the driver beamed and proudly held the bird up for us to see, the passenger tilted his beer can toward us hospitably, and the child, a little girl, waved. They didn't look so dangerous to me.

"Let's stop," I said. "I'd like to talk to them."

Dan was stony-faced and tight-lipped. "Absolutely not," he said, angrily. "I'm afraid I'll lose my temper if we stop."

So I just waved back to the happy road hunters as we passed.

&

The next morning, I went out early by myself and parked along the road until I spotted a car of road hunters. You can't miss them because they drive so slowly, no more than five miles per hour, scanning the roadside. I got out of my car and flagged them down.

I explained to the driver, a stocky, bearded man who introduced himself as Merlin, that I was writing a book about bird hunting, and I asked if I could ride along with them for a while, see how they went about this. Merlin, an auto mechanic in town and a very friendly fellow, said sure, and he seemed pleased at the opportunity to hold forth about his sport; he clearly fancied himself to be something of an expert. He told his passenger, a big man in coveralls named Carl, to get in the backseat and let me ride up front. We all got situated.

"You want a beer, Jim?" Merlin offered. It was nine o'clock in the morning.

"Only if you're going to have one, Merlin."

"Why not? It's Saturday, isn't it?"

"Sure is."

"Carl, hand us a couple of beers there."

"Merlin, let me ask you something," I began. "You know they've got that group of Ruffed Grouse Society people staying in town this weekend. Some of them would say that the way you hunt here, ground-sluicing birds from the car, besides being illegal is also unsportsmanlike—that it violates the traditions of grouse hunting."

Merlin smiled a wicked smile. He had small, twinkling eyes. "The *traditions of grouse hunting*?" he said, mimicking me disdainfully. I could see that Merlin had a sense of humor.

"That's right."

"You want to know something, Jim? *This* is my tradition of grouse hunting. This is how we've always hunted partridge. This is how my father hunted partridge, and this is how his father hunted partridge—hey, lookit there, there's a partridge!" Merlin stopped the car and slid a single-shot .410 shotgun with a short sawed-off barrel (the gun of choice for road hunting) from the floorboards between his legs. The bird was poking around in the brush at the side of the road. Slowly, Merlin maneuvered the gun out the window.

"Aren't you going to get out of the car?" I asked. I was certain we were going to get arrested and that I'd have to go to jail with Merlin and Carl, as an accessory to a crime, even though I was just an innocent spectator.

Merlin sighed and looked at me with a tolerant expression and addressed me as if talking to a child. "Jim, if I get out of the car," he explained patiently, "the partridge will fly away."

"Oh, yeah, of course."

Merlin took careful aim and dusted the partridge.

"All right!" Carl said from the backseat.

Merlin retrieved his grouse, and we went on creeping down the road.

"Doesn't it bother you that this is illegal?" I asked.

"They haven't caught me yet." Merlin smiled. "Getting back to those grouse people, Jim. You know they all come here from out of state? They bring their fancy dogs—did you know that some of those dogs cost five thousand dollars? Yeah, that's right, *five thousand dollars*! You think I can afford a five-thousand-dollar dog? Well, Jim, I sure as hell can't. I can't afford a five-thousand-dollar car! And anyway, I don't have time to train a dog. Then they got their fancy ten-thousand-dollar shotguns. You know how much this shotgun cost me, Jim? Forty dollars. So these rich assholes come out here every year; they run all over the woods with their five-thousand-dollar dogs shooting *my* partridge with their ten-thousand-dollar shotguns; they shoot hundreds of them, and then they complain that they don't like the way *I* hunt? Hell, I admit it, I'm a meat hunter. I like to eat partridge. So maybe I kill twenty birds in a whole season this way. Is that so terrible? Mostly we come out here just to drive around, get out of town, have a few beers. What's so wrong with that? And it really *pisses me off* that these rich guys from out of town turn their noses up at me when they see us out here. This is *my* home, not theirs, and I'll hunt however I goddamn well please.

"Hey, Jim, up ahead on your side of the road! There's a partridge. See him? I'll pull up a little farther. You get the gun ready. When I get in position, blast him."

"Oh, gee, I don't know, Merlin." I'd read all the sporting literature about the mythical ruffed grouse, and this was not precisely the way I wanted to shoot my first one.

Merlin looked at me with his thin, wicked smile, his hooded, twinkling eyes. "You one of them, Jim?"

"Does it come down to that, Merlin?"

Dust to Dust

RUSSELL CHATHAM

Late one night in the fog, just before Labor Day of 1984, upstairs in a hollow old summer home in the northern California beach town of Bolinas, the author Richard Brautigan let himself have it with a .44 Magnum. What was left of him was found four or five weeks later because, according to the papers, when he failed to arrive in Montana for the hunting season, worried friends up there called the Bay Area and sent someone over to check out his house.

I was a friend of Richard's for nearly twenty years, which was long enough to have watched him shoot to smithereens any number of unlikely items including an entire wall of his Montana home, clocks, telephones, dinnerware, sport jackets, and, his favorite target, television sets. It was enough to make me feel downright effete for shooting at the stars from the yard of my house just a few miles away.

In any case, during all the years I knew him, in both California and Montana, I can never remember him going hunting, or even talking much about it except in passing. Once he presented a gift of a sixteen-gauge double-barreled shotgun to Jim Harrison, inscribed "Big Fish," to commemorate a four-pound brown trout Jim had landed in the Yellowstone River, but that was it.

The word "macho" appeared in the postmortem press just as it so often does when journalists turn in a report on a man reputed to like the blood sports, and who happens to live someplace other than in a condo or co-op apartment on one of the Dream Coasts.

Webster gives macho a certain amount of negative weight by defining it as "a virile man, especially one who takes excessive pride in his virility." Interestingly enough, there is no correlative word that unflatteringly describes the female who is feminine and who "takes excessive pride in her femininity." Even the archaic term "feminie," which means womankind (especially the Amazons), is largely meaningless to us. The closest female equivalent of machismo may be what some modern women—secretaries and shop clerks in particular—refer to among themselves as femme femme. This term describes a woman who is preoccupied with feminine sexuality as well as perhaps the coy and stereotyped behavior usually listed under the heading of the Feminine Mystique. Unlike the obviously macho male who is scoffed at by nearly everyone, the femme femme woman is disliked only by bull dykes, resentful spinsters, and certain humorless members of the clergy. This is true even in San Francisco, where the board of supervisors recently declared the three-dollar bill legal tender.

The media, with the exception of that small part of it devoted specifically to the blood sports, tend to view hunters as people of imperfect character; macho, overly competitive boors who are boisterous, boastful, uncultured, rude, insensitive, and violent.

The sad truth is that probably 80 percent of those who go afield with a gun or rifle fit the above description. These people aren't hunters in any true sense of the word. They're gunners trespassing in the woods under direction of some very suspect motives.

One often hears, especially from nonhunters, that men confuse their guns with their penises. This has never happened to me, and so it seems absurd, something like confusing your nose with a car wash. The confusion might have been started years ago, the first time an army recruit mistakenly referred to his rifle as his gun during boot camp, and the outraged drill sergeant made him parade around the grounds with his rifle in one hand and his dick in the other, repeating over and over, "This is my rifle, this is my gun, one is for fighting, the other's for fun."

In a similar vein, psycoanalysts love to make inferences and draw conclusions by relating real events to hypothetical ones. For instance, a friend of mine told his therapist he had always wanted to make love to his aunt. The doctor explained what that really meant was he wanted to make love to his mother. "No I don't," my friend replied. "My mother was a dog. My aunt was beautiful. Nobody in his right mind would want to screw my mother." So much for Freud.

Richard Brautigan was not a macho man. He was unyielding and often infuriatingly obtuse, but he had a certain defiant dignity and great personal strength because of his strict literary convictions. At the core he was essentially fragile and sensitive in a society that tends to reward those virtues with poverty and an early death.

✖

The California ranch my great-great-grandfather established during the 1860s is part of what was once an enormous Spanish land grant in Monterey County. In an odd way, it's a curse to have been born and raised in one of the most sublime places on earth. I've been around the world and have never seen another place of such sensuous, languid character, or where the climate is so benign.

From the ridges above our ranch house, on a clear day, you can see Salinas and Monterey Bay. Up there the sea breeze is always surprisingly fresh and its voice is soothing as it sweeps across the tall yellow grass and through the sorrowful, scattered oaks.

Down in the canyons, on the flats beside Chupinas Creek, it is always warmer. In August and September it can be very hot, and that's when my father and I went dove hunting.

During the Depression my father said there were a great many birds. He sometimes shot thirty in an afternoon with relative ease. By the time I started going along, which was soon after the Second World War, we were very happy with ten or less.

We walked around the hay fields looking for birds on the ground. We never shot them there, you understand, but this was how we found them. You could see them bobbing and strutting, while they fed for quite some distance, so there was always suspense as to whether they would hold long enough for us to get within range before they flew. Sometimes we were surprised by doves jumping up out of the creek bed or out of a patch of tocalote weed. Or else there were singles or doubles simply flying by, wings whistling on an erratic, swerving course. My father was a good shot, and he didn't often miss.

Hunting dogs have no fear of the sound of a shot; the noise itself suggests the excitement of the hunt, creating a demeanor of extreme happiness. A gun-shy dog often cowers even at the sharp clacking of a shell being chambered into a pump gun. This timidity, or caution—call it what you like—can be genetic or due to remembered trauma.

I was a cautious, rather timid child, yet the sound of gunfire didn't frighten me. I cannot recall even hearing it. My recollections of hunting in those formative years concern the smell of sage and tocalote, the forlorn, soft sound of the mourning dove in the distance, the song of the quail, again in the distance, the odd, rather rhythmic cries of the redheaded woodpecker, breezes rattling the dry oak leaves, the silent circling of buzzards, the muffled tinkling of the creek's diminished riffle, the afternoon sun diffused through the sycamores, the presence of my father just beside me or else whistling his familiar whistle behind a stand of trees. I saw birds sometimes falling, but I never heard the shots.

This notion occurred to me when I recalled the first time I ever discharged a firearm. We weren't hunting, but there was still the simple distraction of place, and being with my father.

Several things about the incident make it easy to recall. The first was we had a giant bag of fireworks illegally procured for us by our Chinese housekeeper. Second, it was the only time I ever recall being in the vicinity of the Mission Dolores, a district of San Francisco where only Mexicans were supposed to go. We had gone there to borrow a .45 automatic pistol from a serviceman my father had met. The war was over, but it still carried tremendous weight as an immediate, historical, exotic event. The man was a captain and my father informed me sternly, "We are going to shoot the captain's pistol."

We drove down the coast to what is now Pacifica, shot off all the fireworks (mostly giant firecrackers), and repeatedly fired the captain's pistol from the cliffs down onto the beach below. If you've ever shot a .45 automatic, you know how powerful they are. And if you have ever lit an old-fashioned four-inch Chinese firecracker, you know how loud they are. Do you know what I remember about that afternoon? Seagulls hovering on the breeze and the sun glinting off the ocean. I remember only peace, quiet, and happiness.

My father's first rule of hunting was "never point a gun at anything you don't intend to shoot." His second rule was that I could only hunt alone because "that way there is only one person you can shoot accidentally." He meant this in reference to peers, naturally, not adults. The second rule was inviolable.

If you shoot something when you are alone, there is never any secondary reason for it, no pointless sense of competition or triumph. You must deal realistically with the act itself. An easy shot can sometimes appear difficult to someone else, and the temptation is to keep quiet.

I wasn't allowed to take the shotgun out by myself, only the .22; therefore real bird shooting, which is to say dove or quail on the wing, was out. So, I had bluejays, magpies, crows, cottontails, and squirrels. Dove and quail were fair game if I could get one on the sit, but this was ethically complicated because only a poor sport shot those birds when they weren't flying. It was much better to save them for "real" hunting.

In order for the emotional tension to be fully stressed and functional in a real hunting situation, it is necessary to understand and love your prey with a force precisely equal to your desire to kill and eat it. The business of emotional tension rides on a sliding scale, with the desire to hunt and kill rising and falling due to any number of variables. The question of honor is important as well. To kill anything without an apology is unconscionable.

Doug Peacock, the grizzly bear expert, told me he survived numerous attacks or "rushes" from grizzlies by holding his ground, averting his eyes, and cowering slightly. Aggression or flight would both have been fatal. The desire to shoot certain birds or animals is heightened by their flight and dissipated by their immobility.

Speed and stamina are two of the qualities that make certain game birds and animals exciting to shoot, but excitement alone, uncomplicated by regret, becomes a negative, like the word "macho." Neither is such a crime, really, merely flawed character in the latter case and a sign of a one-dimensional mind in the former. Neither is like child molesting.

❧

I went on a controlled pheasant hunt in California recently. As we were uncasing our guns, a young boy, hunting nearby, accidentally shot the man who had taken him out. I saw how it happened, and it was clearly not the boy's fault. The kid became hysterical and was largely ignored in the confusion that followed. The man didn't die, but it was close. The boy had not been instructed on how to use the gun, and the man foolishly and carelessly stepped in front of him to flush a bird that was being pointed by the dog.

There were many reasons for the accident, all of them having to do with lack of proper teaching. The boy didn't know exactly how the gun worked physically, and he was not prepared to deal with the excitement of the flush or the ease with which the trigger could actually be pulled. Most of all, because of the casual, commercial, obvious, easy way these birds were dumped in the field only to be harvested hours later, he had no reason to adopt an attitude of wonder, reverence, and respect for the incomprehensible mysteries of a real hunt. I suspect that boy will not want to hunt again for a very long time, if ever.

Richard Brautigan's last published book was called *So the Wind Won't Blow It All Away*. It is, in part, about a family who sets up a living-room group of furniture on the shore of a lake.

> I had become so quiet and so small in the grass by the pond that I was barely noticeable, hardly there. I think they had forgotten all about me. I sat there watching their living room shining out of the dark beside the pond. It looked like a fairy tale functioning happily in the post–World War II gothic of America before television crippled the imagination of America and turned people indoors and away from living out their own fantasies with dignity.

It is also about how he, Richard, accidentally shot and killed his best friend with a .22 while out pheasant hunting.

> "What happened?" I said, bending down to look at all the blood that was now covering the ground. I had never seen so much blood before in my entire life, and I had never seen blood that was so red. It looked like some liquid flag on his leg.
> "You shot me," David said.
> His voice sounded very far away.
> "It doesn't look good."
>
> *So the Wind Won't Blow It All Away*
> *Dust . . . American . . . Dust*

I love you, Richard, and although hunting has saved my life more than once, and I don't want to go on without it, I understand perfectly why you wanted to shoot Sonys rather than roosters.

For a Handful of Feathers

❧

GUY DE LA VALDÉNE

No one can have the part of me I give to my dogs, a gift as safe as loving a child; a part of me I guard carefully because it bears on my sanity. My dogs forgive the anger in me, the arrogance in me, the brute in me. They forgive everything I do before I forgive myself. For me, the life and death of a dog is a calendar of time passing. I dream about my dogs, but recently the dreams have been turning into nightmares. One recurring scenario finds me hunting with Robin, the spaniel, on the ridge of a steep talus slope overlooking the Snake River in Idaho. The bitch runs after a cripple and follows the bird over the edge of the cliff. In my dream I watch Robin fall away, seemingly forever, a small, tumbling figure against a mosaic of sagebrush, wheat, alfalfa fields, and water thousands of feet below. More recently I dreamed that, without warning, the same dog began shrinking, shrinking and barking and running in tiny circles around my feet, her eyes huge and brown and imploring. I threw my hat over her mouse-sized body but missed, and when she was the size of a fly she flew away.

I don't know what these dreams mean, but if they are meant to prepare me for my dog's eventual death I would like to remind my psyche that the bitch is only five years old. On the other hand, perhaps these dreams are preparing me for my own death, or are fed by the guilt I feel when I kill something as beautiful and enviable as a bird. In any case, I'm sure that the communion I have with dogs should be channeled to my peers. However, since I think of man as the creator of desolation and not the center of reality, I don't; and as a by-product of that choice I accept the longing of loneliness, and the dark dreams that follow.

✕

December 1, 1989: I wait in the front seat of my car, next to a four-month-old puppy, for ducks to fly out of a flooded hardwood marsh on the edge of Lake Jackson. A cold fall morning without a gun. This time I hunt with a different perspective on life after spending time in southern Florida. I do this by sitting and watching wild things pass by. The sun, which broke quickly into the pale, gray sky, now hangs a few inches above the lake, shedding clouds until the water turns red. When the clouds burn off, the white sun resumes its ascent. The desperation I feel every time I venture into cities passes, even though not a duck creases the sky. The young dog, Robin, sits next to me with her head out the window, her ears opened to the fecund sound of the marsh.

Back at the lake by 5 P.M. The puppy sits on my lap and stares out the front window, trembling. When the darkness gains weight the wood ducks fly back from the open water of the lake to roost, and Robin follows their outline until the upholstery blocks her view. The ducks become long-winged shadows falling from the sky. In the backwater under the hardwoods, the ducks squeal and stir the mud, exciting the puppy. Wood ducks are my favorite table duck, and my least favorite to shoot because they are beautiful and dumb: male-model ducks.

Lake Jackson has turned purple, purple water supporting a red horizon. Robin stares through the windshield at mosquitoes as big as birds. I am at my best when the sounds of civilization are at their lowest decibel, and I envy the fellow who, along with his Nagra tape recorder, hunted for and found all the places in the world where the sounds were purely natural and nonhuman. He found only a hand-ful, but there he made beautiful music.

A cold wind pushes night into the car. Robin shivers and curls up on my lap. On my way home the headlights play under the pine trees. Rock and roll fills the cab. I feel young again for having been alone with the dog, the birds, and now the music. At home, just be-fore I fall asleep, the puppy lays her head on my chest to let me know our day together is over, and then she moves as far from my restless turning as she can and still share the bed.

My second dog, Mable, is a seven-year-old lemon-and-white English pointer I bought four years ago as a broke bird dog. Mable lived in a kennel before I bought her and now sleeps in a chair in my bedroom. I have spent four years hunting for Mable instead of hunting for birds; four years of howling at her to come and watching her run 180 degrees away from me into the quagmires of neighboring counties. The dog doesn't mean to run away, but the moment the terrain is at odds with her ability to see me, she becomes confused and lost, incapable of figuring out from which direction I am calling. This happens because Mable is dumb, dumb as a knot, dumber than the dumbest human being I have ever known, and a graduate of Spark College, the modern, electrically oriented school of dog training.

I should have sent her back to her previous owner, or at least given her to a retired social worker. The dog loves children and women; they, in turn, enjoy dressing her up in their clothes. I persevered in thinking that because she loved me she would one day recognize the sound of my voice as a rallying point and not the echo of dementia. She never has, and now that she is middle-aged she has taken to peeing in the puddle of water she drinks from, licking the fertilizer in the flower beds, and eating toads. I, of course, have taken to feeling sorry for her.

It has been said that a pointer that comes when called is rarer than an honest judge, to which one should add that compliance is not the compelling reason for owning a bird dog in the first place. Bred and trained to hunt with their senses screwed to the bone, they are designed to raise the level of quail hunting to an art form, and when things are right, they do. A breeze ruffling a handful of feathers carries enough weight to enslave a dog to a bird in a covenant of uneasy immobility. Setters, Brittanys, and German shorthairs face quail as if their lives depended on it, but when a good English pointer faces a bird, he does so with all but one foot on the coals of hell.

To counteract two demanding and jealous bitches, I have recently brought into the house an eight-week-old equalizer—a roan-colored male with white whiskers, a black nose, and black eyes. His name is Carnac, the first male dog I have owned since I was sixteen years old. Carnac is a French Brittany that looks like a suckling pig, a roan-colored suckling pig that keeps its eyes on mine or on my hands, the hands that feed him and smack his butt. The little man-dog already likes to bite the females' behinds and then run like hell, barking with joy. Once in a while the bitches catch him, pin him down, and make him pay, but because he is a male they mostly put up with his puppyhood. Carnac is a happy dog, willing and able to pee on any carpet, and hump a woman's leg, displaying via the abandon of his grasp the keenness of his will. Now, if he will only hunt . . .

I remember when southern quail were abundant and time was cheap and hunting was an honorable diversion; when bird dogs spent most of the year as glorious bags of teats and bones, raising their pups under slat-board porches until the sounds of acorns crackling under the tractor tires snapped them to their feet, fired up their genes, and drove them to the woods. Dogs were bird dogs, English pointers whose real reason for being was to stop the instant the scent of a quail crossed their olfactory paths. What actually happened in terms of training between the time the bitch rose from her eight-month slumber to the time she addressed covey after covey of bobwhite quail, forgetting everything except the birds and the men she was hunting for, was not specified, leaving me with a picture of synergetic aplomb and grace.

Once in a great while, albeit not for very long, I have a desire to own an all-age, field-trial dog, a crackerjack flamenco dancer with quick feet, a flaring nose, and a whalebone rib cage; a dog that owns the ground on which it runs and the wind on which birds fly. I want a dog whose cast gives reason to the landscape, a dog that shakes at the delirium of discovery and imposes on birds the fortitude of its resolve. I covet the bag of bones that each fall metamorphoses into a greyhound. I covet the magician, the trickster, but I also want it to come when I call, and that is asking too much. All-age dogs are the savants of the field-trial world, and asking them to do something as mundane as coming on command is like asking van Gogh to add a cow to the landscape.

Twenty years ago, I hunted bobwhite quail from horseback behind those kinds of dogs. Memories return in the shape of thin, black men riding fast southern horses, men who worked the flanks and signaled points by raising their caps above their heads, and uncanny dog handlers who smelled birds before the dogs did. I remember galloping to points with my heart in my throat for fear of not getting to the covey before it blew up. I hunted behind all-age dogs that had competed in, and in some cases won, national championships; dogs that trembled at the mere mention of birds; dogs that presented to the guns a quarry whose head they were given to eat. Memories of those days also include races between horsemen and deer across broom sedge fields; old dogs found pointing swamp-birds under the radiance of a cold winter moon; and gentlemen who killed only male quail.

A quote from the guest book at Sehoy Plantation, Alabama, December 13, 1967:

> Flushed twenty-seven coveys of quail, shot over twenty-three. Filled two limits. My companion missed all but one bird. Pointers, stretched to a beautiful attitude. Kennel mates backing in perfect unanimity of opinion. Tipped a bobwhite or two out of each covey rise. Moses [name of black dog-handler] exclaimed, "Gents, the covey's powerful close." Ate fried quail, collard greens with pepper vinegar, lima beans, hot rolls and French wine. Port with dessert, cognac later. Bid six hearts, finessed the jack, and made the slam. A day to remember.

Dogs, like men, lose their range and enthusiasm for life from having the wildness in them questioned. In the case of dogs, trainers these days ask the questions with single-digit probes of electric trauma, trauma that reaches its destination faster than the trainer's thought. When sustained, and with the range to reach across field and dale, this bolt of bionic inhumanity will scramble a dog's brains and walk him to hell and back. In the hands of most men the electronic collar serves a number of purposes ranging from suppressed hate to a genuine training tool. The obvious shortcut electricity provides is not unlike sound bites and fast foods, and allows questionable trainers to postpone working a client's dog almost indefinitely. In the hands of a good man the collar removes the boot and leather strap from the routine of training, and when it's applied just right the dog can be made to believe that God is watching and its salvation rests with its trainer. A thin line. One application too many, and the client owns a round-eyed dog that pees in the water it drinks.

I am a terrible dog trainer because the traits I like in a dog are the same as those I like in men: namely, civil disobedience. Training is repetition, hell is toeing the line. I have witnessed extreme punishment applied to dogs with instruments ranging from a thirty-second hold on a number-five (full-power) button to a two-by-four. When I was much younger and fresh out of Europe, where field trials were, and still are, thought of as civilized sporting contests between reasonable men and women and their dogs, I sucker-punched a dog trainer at a field trial in Pennsylvania for jerking a full-grown Labrador off its feet by its ears. The dog had swum the wrong course at a dead duck. I drilled the trainer in the ear, and he pitched face-first into the mud. My British host, without so much as raising an eyebrow, patted the dog on the head, looked down at the man, and said, "Well, as he's in no position to answer you, we might as well be moving along. Cruel bugger, what?"

✻

The best dog is the one that adapts to its master's temperament and style of hunting, and while I marvel at the English pointers and setters, such dogs have always tiptoed beyond the reaches of my hearing within hours of my owning them, and from that moment on I have had to blow my face up to get their attention. Now that I have retired my sneakers, this type of dog is no longer right for me. I want a dog that comes about a hundred yards or so on either side of me and passes within gun range each time it checks in. I usually have an idea where the birds are and would just as soon have Biff go where I tell him to. Not a workable agenda when dealing with the tightly strung violins of dogdom.

Now, when I hunt, I like to think about things, like how the trees have grown, the last time I slept with a woman, the direction of the wind, what wine I'm going to drink with dinner. Killing is a formality. When I hunt with another person, I want to listen to and talk with that person—otherwise I wouldn't be hunting with him. I want to stop if I choose to without losing the dog or having to hack at it to keep it on a level course. I have done all these things, and after a decade of getting just as frustrated as I did when I played golf, I bought the Brittany with the hope that I won't feel the fingers of retribution crawl up my backside each time the dog is out of sight. It all comes down to the man and what he wants from his dog. In my case, I plan to hunt behind pointers and setters until the day I retire my guns, but they will belong to someone else.

❧

One can argue that, performed with a measure of dignity and restraint, hunting is just as important an issue now as it was three hundred years ago, but for opposite reasons. Hunting is no longer a survival issue for man, but it has become a survival issue for the game; while we have multiplied like rabbits, the game has dwindled tenfold. Our importance as hunters lies in the fact that we as individuals, having no affiliations with anything or anyone other than the sport, witness and assess the condition of the game and habitat in this country. Our credentials are that we are out there, in nature, when others are not, and that we are out there because we want to be, not because we have to or are paid to be. Our eyes solicit the traceries of spoors on the earth and of birds in the sky. Our spirits are conscious of ravens and long for the restitution of wolves and bears to the land. We are the wildlife thermometers, poling about in rivers and swamps, in the shadows of forest canopies, under the flashes of desert suns, and the force that drives us is our soul.

We hunters, more than any other group on earth, should understand the symbiotic relationship between species and how it has come to pass that, thanks to our destructive meddling, the reflection of a teal on a pond is no longer free of charge. Those of us who understand the complex nature of a teal's life—and what it takes, in terms of protection and food, to grow the feathers that send that image darting over the water—also understand what the chase and the kill do to the spirit of man, its rewards and its shames. Because we understand and feel these things more acutely than our peers, it is sacrilegious of us not to protect with all our might what resources remain to be saved. If we neglect our obligations, we stand to incur the contempt of generations to come.

❧

I have done some shameful things in the name of sport in the past forty years, and recognize in my not-so-distant past the genetic chimpanzee in me. When Robin wasn't quite a year old I picked her up by the scruff of the neck and, with just enough anger in me to make the act sickening, threw her to the ground. The dog had been running around in a dove field enjoying her youth, the sounds of gunfire, and the sight of falling birds while I, infuriated at her disobedience, wanted her to sit by my side. When I threw her, Robin fell wrong and screamed like a baby. She wasn't so much hurt as she was terrified that the one being in the world she loved unconditionally had suddenly and for no apparent reason turned on her. It scared me for all the appropriate reasons, not the least of which was that I recognized in me the dog trainer I had knocked to the ground years before, and nowadays when the little bitch lays her head on my shoulder in the dark of the night it is because I have called her to me, waking from the nightmare of that act; waking from the dream in which I had broken her neck.

The same crass and impulsive behavior incited me to shoot sparrows and swallows as a child, crows and hawks when I should have known better, and, more recently, a bobcat in the back and a raccoon in the face. My unbecoming and violent nature as a child doesn't concern me anymore. I have forgiven myself for being a young man with a young man's rules. But now that I am, for better and for worse, tired—no, exhausted—from witnessing the insipid violence in men, these questions of ethics so easily dismissed a few years ago weigh me down for reasons of principle, age, and change. I fully understand the nature of hunting and being hunted, eating, sleeping, and procreating. In fact, my inclination toward reclusiveness nudges me closer and closer into the world of animals, and I have to be constantly on guard not to let myself regress into a state that functions with even less thought than the one I see in the streets and watch on television. On the other hand, I know deep in my heart that there is something basically wrong about killing for pleasure.

The day I shot a bobcat instead of a turkey I altered the natural progression of life by killing for no reason. The cat walked out of the woods, I raised the gun and pulled the trigger. The act was simple. A response to the knowledge of the cat's predilection for turkey, but one I deeply regretted when I ran my hand over the tawny-colored coat of the adult female, tough and sinewy from making a living and dropping litters, but now lifeless and flat on a bed of dirt in the shade of a sweet-gum tree with a .22-caliber Hornet hole in her heart. There was a time when killing the bobcat would have pleased me. I would have felt like the protector, the benevolent despot of the forest. Now I question what it means to meddle in things that are so much more natural than what I see on the news. I feel like a half-wit to possess the same senseless traits I reproach in others, particularly as I am no longer convinced that I am better than the cat. Killing for no reason is killing with malice.

A month later, driving down a dirt road overlooking a pasture, I stopped and, from inside the car, shot a raccoon in the face while it watched me from inside the fork of a dogwood tree. The raccoon fell slowly, raking the bark with its claws, holding on until gravity took hold and pulled it to the ground where it would eventually rot. I had just finished reading an article about how raccoons rob quail nests.

The seduction of the scope made for simple killing and emotional ambiguity. Physical magnification had stolen the life from the image and left me with a sharp target. The precision of glass is finite but the consequence of a senseless death is not, except in how it takes its toll on the psyche of man. Could it be that those unnatural killings—I didn't eat or use either animal—were attempts at killing the wildness in myself?

⚘

By winter, Carnac, the roan-colored Brittany, didn't look like a suckling pig anymore. He was thin and fit, the bones in his face had sharpened, his nose had swayed and lengthened, and his hindquarters had filled out. Carnac had graduated from looking like a pig to looking like a jackal, a twenty-four-pound jackal with a long nose, and at twenty-four pounds the perfect poacher's dog, built to jump into a game vest at the first sign of trouble. At a year old he enjoyed life to its fullest, at the expense of everyone else, particularly the bitches. Not knowing anything about kennels, shock collars, or leather whips, Carnac has had no contact with the darker side of a hunting dog's life, so when I say "birds," stretching the *b*'s and the *r*'s, he looks at me, sits up straight as an arrow, and tests the air. His cheeks puff and unpuff, his nose checking the azimuth, and his eyes follow his nose. He is stationary hunting.

Carnac was a natural from the first day in the field. He loved the grass, the briers, the smells, and the sound of a gun—a sound he was taught to relish early on, beginning with the feral pigs that I sometimes shot in the rear with a .410 to move them out of the yard. Carnac has hated pigs ever since the morning he and Robin ran out of the lake house into the legs of a sow and her four piglets rooting up the grass for worms. The sow cornered Carnac against the side of the house and tried to eat him, scaring the stink out of both dogs, and me. I hit the pig over the head with a shovel, hard, until she finally turned on me, allowing the dogs to get away before rending any meat, but it was close. Carnac does not have a problem with guns.

He pointed a quail wing within a minute of watching it fly at the end of a fishing pole, but that doesn't mean too much. I bought some pen-raised quail, built a call-back pen, and began training the puppy. The only thing that didn't work was that the quail that were supposed to return to their plywood home before dark never did, choosing instead to join the wild ones. Can't say I blame them.

Carnac learned to run through a field chasing birds that smelled good, and one day, just like my trainer friend told me he would, the puppy realized he couldn't catch them and pointed. Pointed, solid as Excalibur.

A week after that the dog pulled a check-cord through the woods and learned to whoa, which he did only to please me. By late summer he began finding a few wild coveys and learned about the sound of a dozen wings. Carnac began to follow his long shovel nose, which rarely deceived him. If he smelled birds, he trailed them until he found them. The dog is stubborn.

Meanwhile, my doltish pointer, Mable, managed to fall asleep under a truck and, oblivious to the engine noise, allowed herself to be run over, dislocating her hip. Once it was mending she did what she had always hoped for: she never left her chair. So much for her vacuous career. Mable has since moved in with a lady who doesn't hunt but enjoys dressing her in Victorian clothes. The age of big-going dogs is over for me. Now I sneak around with a tiny dog that walks on his hind legs to see over cover and looks goofy when the smell of feathers passes his way.

I introduced a blank pistol into the picture a few weeks into fall, and Carnac is now convinced that life is one big bowl of food, field, and birds. When the sounds of wings and gunfire became inseparable entities in Carnac's mind, and I was able to hold him on point through the flush without raising my voice, I started calling friends up, praising the poacher dog's abilities. I lied a little, too, just to make sure they knew what a fine animal had graced my jubilee year, the dog that will hunt me to my sixties.

At home, Carnac missed few opportunities to display the flip side of his character. He kept right on eating rugs, shoes, the springer's tail, and whatever else was handy. Carnac is not popular with those who don't know or care about his split personality. He is with me.

Graduation day came on an overcast winter morning, full of fog and pale shadows. I released him into a section of the farm I had seen, and watched proudly as the little dog cast back and forth, looking at me for direction, moving with a special eagerness, as if his instincts were telling him that this was what all those weeks of training had been about. The terrain sloped down through a mixed cover of grass, year-old oak saplings, and myrtle bushes, leading to a small cornfield cut into an open bench in the middle of the woods. Half the corn was standing. The rest had been mowed down. There was grain on the ground. The deer had taken to the field, as had the turkeys and at least two coveys of bobwhite quail. The wind was right, it was early in the day, and wild smells sprang out of the dew.

Carnac worked on, fifty yards ahead of me, looking pretty sure of himself. Quail had always been easy for him to find before, and he saw no reason why they wouldn't be on this day.

When he stopped, he had a face full of bird scent, and, except for a speeding tail and his cheeks that puffed, he stared ahead and didn't move. The scene warmed the cockles of my heart. This was the first of our salad days together. I walked up behind the dog, quietly reminding him to stay, walked to a piece of low cover, and watched a good covey of bobwhite quail hurl itself off the ground and fan over the cornfield. No doubles today, I thought and, assuring the shot, dropped a bird twenty-five yards away.

"All right, little man," I said. "Fetch it up." I was feeling pretty good about the developments.

The Brittany broke for the bird while I reloaded and thought about having a glass of wine for lunch, a big one, to mark the occasion and adjust my personality. Carnac ran behind a stand of tall dog fennel. I must have crippled that bird, I thought, heading his way. What a good dog I have. I encouraged him from the far side of the fennel stand, and when I got around to where I could see, there he was, facing away from me, muzzle in a bush, tail wagging. It looked to me that he had the bird, so I told him to fetch it back. He didn't, so I told him to sit, which he did in his ramrod fashion. No problem, I thought; he pointed, held, and then found the bird. I didn't expect as much on his first day out; after all, perfection is elusive. I broke the gun, walked up behind the puppy, and reached around his head for the quail in his mouth. The only thing my fingers encountered were two scaly feet that, when pulled on, surrendered, and came free.

The rest of the bird shot straight down Carnac's throat.

Restoring the Older Knowledge

❧

TED KERASOTE

In America, and in general, we dislike hunters. We dislike them because they use tools of destruction. And we dislike them because they kill beings who win our affections—mammals and birds rather than fish. Even those who want to engage the values of primalness often dislike the hunter because he insists on getting blood on his hands whereas most of us are satisfied with less graphic measures—songs, drums, a simple walk through the trees. Most important, though, we dislike hunters for their dishonesty—for how their actions do not live up to their claims that hunting is a noble and conscientious activity.

Some hunter advocacy groups claim that these accusations are no more than perceptual problems, rooted in animal-rights literature and urban people's diminished connection to tools like firearms, to land and animals, and to natural cycles. Such arguments have a shade of validity as well as a great deal of smoke screen behind which to avoid the truth: the hunting community has denied the character of many of its members and until very recently has refused to address—deeply, with commitment, and spiritually—what constitutes appropriate behavior toward animals.

This denial is no longer being tolerated, just the way our nation, in fits and starts, will no longer tolerate racism, the actions of the alcoholic behind the wheel, abuse within the home, or the unsustainable use of the commons. Intolerance of the hunting community comes about not only because trophy hunters make headlines when they're prosecuted for violations of the Endangered Species Act or hunters in the pay of sporting goods manufacturers are convicted of shooting elk in Yellowstone National Park while making hunting videos. It is not only these egregious violations of the law that infuriate the public. Additionally, it is how, on a thousand days in a thousand ways, we witness what Steven Kellert has called the "dominionistic/sport hunter" act with a callousness that debases everything hunters say about hunting's being a sacred connection to our Paleolithic roots.

Kellert's 1978 survey sampled hunters across the nation and found that 38.5 percent were what he termed the "dominionistic/sport hunter." Often living in cities, these hunters savor competition with and mastery over animals in a sporting contest. Another 43.8 percent of the sample Kellert called "utilitarian/meat hunters"—people interested in harvesting meat much as they would a crop of wheat. And 17.8 percent of the survey he termed "nature hunters." The youngest segment of the hunting population, these individuals know the most about wildlife, and their goal is to be intensely involved in nature through hunting.

Unfortunately, it has been the dominionistic/sport hunter, even though he represents less than 40 percent of American hunters, who has often set the image for the rest of the hunting community. Despite hunters' best efforts at educating the public about the hunter's role in conserving habitat and species, it is this group's behavior that the public remembers when they hear the word *hunting*. Not only are this group's actions highly visible, but as a group they may very well represent more American hunters than Kellert's study leads us to believe.

Indeed, they may represent a great many nonhunters. The developer who fills a wetland, the homeowner who spreads toxic herbicides on her lawn, every one of us who continues to support monoculture forests, agribusiness, and animal factory farms—all participate in a type of dominionistic mastery over wildlife and nature. Often, because the effects of such practices occur far away from our daily lives and in the form of what economists call "externalities"—birds, small mammals, and reptiles gobbled up by combines and poisoned as nontarget casualties of pesticides—we can ignore their enormous destruction. On the other hand, the dominionistic hunter's actions are visible, premeditated, and often discomforting, but they are in keeping with the fundamental beliefs of the culture that has bred him. When his worst colors show, he can easily become our scapegoat, one who, like an oft reprimanded child, seems to revel in ever more unruly behavior.

As a committed hunter, I say this with regret. I say this with embarrassment. And I say this with frustration. Whereas the hunter was once the teacher and shaman of his culture, he is now the boor. And I'm forced to emphasize this point because on so many days in the field I myself have seen the average hunter bend the rules of fair chase and even the laws of the land—spotting game from aircraft, chasing animals with vehicles, or shooting on the evening before the season opens. On so many occasions such dubiously taken animals end up in the record books, our record-keeping organizations paying only lip service to the standards they have set. I have seen downed hen mallards left to float away so they wouldn't be included in the day's bag limit, and the hunters I have been with only grudgingly retrieve them when their obvious disregard has been pointed out. Some of my own neighbors have taken bucks on their girlfriends' tags; around my home two mule deer, an elk, three antelope, and a black bear with triplets were poached during the last few years; several coyotes were hung on a fence to rot because they were, well, "just coyotes"; and most recently one of Yellowstone's reintroduced wolves was shot because it was "just a wolf." But these aren't real hunters, goes the hunting community's old saw, these are the lawbreakers, these are the people who indulge in inappropriate behavior.

On the contrary, I believe that these individuals are hunters and that their attitudes are founded in the same values that Americans have held about the commons: namely, take as much as you can before it's used up. For a century and a half, starting slowly with the writings of Henry David Thoreau and gathering speed with the forest and park campaigns of John Muir, the American conservation movement has tried to alter the consciousness of use-it-up-and-move-on. For hunting, this change in consciousness was initiated by Theodore Roosevelt in 1887, with his founding of an organization of ethical hunters called the Boone and Crockett Club. Their invention of the idea of "fair chase," while needed to stop the indiscriminate slaughter of wildlife for the restaurant and millinery trades, only began to create a genuine hunting ethic, the rough design for what Aldo Leopold would later call "the land ethic," and what I'm calling appropriate and compassionate behavior toward nature.

However, a hundred years after Roosevelt transformed the nation's leading hunters into some of its most effective conservationists, the most compelling ideas about our evolving relationship with animals come not from hunters but from nonhunters and even antihunters. Indeed, the story of the modern hunter as the best of conservationists often seems, at least to this hunter, like an exhausted myth.

In part, this myth says that it is hunters who are active and fit, and who know nature and wildlife best. However, if you visit the forests during hunting season, you find the roads full and the backcountry largely empty, many hunters "camped" in RVs full of amenities. When hunters are asked to support the creation of legally designated wilderness areas in which hardy recreation takes place (and the places that are irreplaceable wildlife habitat), they often choose to side with the so-called wise use movement and others who want to build roads through the last remaining wild country.

The old hunting myth goes on to say that the hunter is a disciplined, reluctant taker of life. Yet if this were the case, why are so many of my nonhunting neighbors afraid to go into the woods during hunting season? Perhaps it's because there are too many hunters who resemble the fellow I met several years ago on a trail. I asked how he had done. He replied that he hadn't seen any elk but that he had taken "a sound shot." His disregard for the suffering he might have caused was borne out a few years later when, not far from my house, one elk hunter shot and killed his good friend when the friend bugled.

The myth goes on to say that hunting is a courageous and sometimes dangerous activity. The sporting press has been particularly fond of painting this picture. However, with the advent of nature documentaries and adventure travel, millions of people have witnessed the behavior of wildlife that is not being threatened. After you have fished fifty feet from several brown bears in Alaska, and come to no harm, it is difficult to believe that shooting one is either a courageous or a dangerous activity.

It is often said that hunters hunt to return to a world of origins, simplicity, and honest interaction with nature. But when you look at hunters, especially bowhunters, in the pages of sporting magazines, in the equipment catalogs, and in the woods, they look like a cross between Darth Vader and a commando. If you go to one of the annual trade shows that display new outdoor equipment, a hundred people a day will try to sell you a new hearing aid, a new camouflage pattern, a new scent, cartridge, or bow that will improve your chances of getting game, and too few hunters question the replacement of skill and intuition by gadgets.

Of course, using improved technology to enhance survival has been one of the hallmarks of our species since ancient times. Does this inventive tradition mean that we are permitted no room to discriminate between laser sights and atlatls? Developing codes that distinguish appropriate from inappropriate technology is one of the challenges hunters need to face and have not.

All these examples show the discrepancy between who hunters claim to be and who their actions demonstrate that they are. Many outdoor people, including backpackers, canoeists, climbers, and skiers, have noticed that the hunter hasn't cornered the market on nature lore, woods savvy, or hardihood. In fact, he is frequently lacking in them.

Actions also speak louder than words when it comes to the hunter's relationship with the animals he kills. When the hunting community, believing that it can't lose any form of what it calls "hunting," refuses to denounce such activities as shooting live animals for target practice or for competition, its moral stature vanishes.

The image of the hunter as a farseeing conservationist also comes into question when hunters and agencies that represent them refuse to consider the idea that some wild species, not typically eaten as food, might no longer be hunted. These would include brown bears, wolves, and coyotes. Hunters tend to reject such proposals as radical thinking, yet they are increasingly being floated by sportsmen themselves. Indeed, they evolved out of the ideas of some farseeing hunters at the end of the nineteenth century who suggested that certain bird species should remain immune from pursuit. In its time, this suggestion seemed ridiculous to some of the hunting community. It is now unquestioned.

Finally, the American male hunter has been resistant to incorporating women into his activities, mostly because women have stricter rules about which deaths are necessary for the procurement of food, and which are no more than gratuitous, based on fun or the gratification of ego. Men fear that women hunters would close down the sorts of hunting that can't be morally justified.

Given this list of grievances, is it possible to reform hunting? One must also ask the larger question: Is hunting *worth* reforming? The first question is one of logistics, the second one of sentiment. Logistically, hunting can be reformed, given what reforms most things— energy, time, and money. However, whether hunting is *worth* reforming depends on how you feel about animals. If you believe that humans can exist without harming animals—that we can evolve to the point that death is removed from the making of our food— then hunting is indeed a relic. If you believe that human and animal life is inextricably linked, and that the biology of the planet demands and will continue to demand that some life forms feed others, then hunting not only is part of that process but also has the potential to serve as a guide to how that process might be most conscientiously and reverentially undertaken.

I believe that hunting can be reformed and is worth reforming, and I offer these suggestions on how to do it.

First and foremost, the hunting community and wildlife agencies need to find money and staff to provide more rigorous hunter education programs. Biology, forest management, expert marksmanship, and ethics would be covered in far greater depth, and a stiff field and written test passed before a hunting license was issued. Part of this course would examine the pros and cons of ecosystem management and wilderness designation, so that hunters might become a constituency for keeping habitat undeveloped.

This will be an extremely difficult task, given that a more stringent program will eliminate some hunters, which of course will decrease funding for agencies and profits for the sporting industry. If more stringent hunter education is to succeed, agencies will have to find additional funding besides the current bargain basement prices of licenses, and objections from the hunting and outdoor equipment industries, not eager to lose customers, will have to be met.

Nonetheless, there are ways to overcome the loss of revenue associated with a reduction in the hunting population. A hunting license remains one of the most inexpensive forms of recreation in North

America today. If, for argument's sake, the number of hunters in the United States was reduced by half, couldn't license prices be doubled to make up the difference? A deer license that was seventeen dollars would become thirty-four dollars and still be a bargain.

Could gun, clothing, and outdoor equipment manufacturers raise their prices twofold and maintain sales? Unlikely. But outdoor equipment could be taxed, as guns and fishing tackle now are, to produce revenues for wildlife that isn't hunted. As well, a small income tax could be levied for wildlife care and research.

Second, de-emphasize the record book and the pursuit of trophies for the trophy's sake. This is not to say that animals will no longer be admired and that taxidermists need be put out of business. Rather, we would stop valuing animals by so many inches of horn or antler. I would also suggest that if records must be kept as a way of honoring animals, only animals are listed, not hunters. In addition, hunters might initiate a completely new form of record keeping, one that honored the greatest amount of wildlife habitat conserved.

Third, hunters need to speak out against competitions that involve shooting animals—deer, pigeons, coyotes, prairie dogs, you name it. Such gaming shows a gross disrespect for animals and has nothing to do with hunting.

Fourth, managers and communicators need to consider reshaping the terminology they use. *Sport* and *recreation*, the terms that distinguished conservationist hunters like Roosevelt from the market hunters who participated in the decimation of buffalo and waterfowl, have become pejorative terms when used with reference to killing animals. They are unacceptable to many in the environmental movement, who are not opposed to hunting if it is done with care, and many nonhunters, including vegetarians, who have been ambivalent about hunting but who can understand the activity as a "least harm option" when compared to agribusiness and the domestic meat industry. Perhaps hunters can call themselves simply *hunters*.

Likewise, the words *consumptive*, which has been used to describe hunters, and *nonconsumptive*, which has been attributed to birdwatchers and backpackers, need to be discarded. They are divisive terms, and *consumptive* is increasingly going to have a negative sign over it. Besides, *consumptive* and *nonconsumptive*, like *sport* and *recreation*, aren't the most precise terms with which to conceptualize these issues. Should the hunter who hunts a deer ten miles from his home be called a *consumptive* resource user, and his neighbor who flies ten thousand miles to Antarctica to watch penguins be termed a *nonconsumptive* user of the planet's resources? The entire hunting debate needs to be reframed in terms of an individual's impacts on regional, national, and global wildlife.

Fifth, the hunting community must open the doors of hunting to women: in its practice, in its ideas, and in its administration. "Man the Hunter" has been a great sound bite for anthropologists who believe that hunting has been one of the primary shapers of human character, but women—helping to stampede bison and mammoths over cliffs, skinning animals, making clothing, and gathering vegetables and herbs—worked just as hard, if not harder, to keep the species alive. Indeed, if women anthropologists had been doing most of the research, hunting peoples over most of the temperate globe might have been more accurately labeled "gatherer-hunters" rather than "hunter-gatherers." Either way you choose to read it, both genders contributed to the evolution of our species, and it would be healthy if, today, they participated more equally in all the tasks of living, from raising children to growing and killing food. Until women restore their sympathies to hunting's fundamental life-giving, life-respecting aspects, and have a hand in reducing its elements of machismo and competition, hunters will be fighting an uphill losing battle. It is women who will vote hunting out of existence.

Sixth, hunters need to participate in more realistic population planning and immigration policy. At current birth rates, and along with legal and illegal immigration, the United States will have four hundred million people by the year 2080. There will be almost no room left for wildlife. We need to examine our policies on tax credits for bearing children, on teenage sex education, and on the availability of birth control. The United States has one of the highest teenage pregnancy rates in the developed world. Denmark, with equally sexually active teenagers, has one of the lowest. Ignoring the issue of population control, as most everyone in North America does, will lead to the inexorable loss of wildlife habitat, wildlife, and hunting as we know it.

Seventh, hunters need to publicize a more accurate cost accounting of American diets. Millions of North America's hunters hunt locally and put a substantial amount of food, in the form of venison and birds, on their families' tables. In terms of their consumptive effect on the total environment, some of these hunters—who don't use large amounts of fossil fuel to go hunting—can have less impact than supermarket vegetarians whose entire diet consists of products from America's intensively managed and fossil-fuel-dependent industrial farms, where wildlife gets killed from pesticides, combining, and habitat loss.

To illustrate this idea, one must compare the kilocalorie cost of different diets. An elk shot near a hunter's home in the Rocky Mountains incurs a cost to planet Earth of about eighty thousand kilocalories. This includes the energy to produce the hunter's car, clothing, firearm, and to freeze the elk meat over a year. If the hunter chooses to replace the amount of calories he gets from 150 pounds of elk meat with rice and beans grown in California, the cost to Earth is nearly five hundred thousand kilocalories, which includes the energy costs of irrigation, farm equipment, and transportation of the food inland from the coast. It does not include the cost to wildlife—songbirds, reptiles, and small mammals—killed as a by-product of agribusiness. Their deaths make the consumer of agribusiness foods a participant in the cull of wildlife to feed humans.

Even when we understand these trade-offs, it's not always easy to make clear or compassionate choices about our diets. The elk in the forest, the tuna at sea, the rabbits lost as the combines turn the fields to provide us with our natural breakfast cereals, as well as the Douglas fir hidden in the walls of our homes and the wildlife displaced to light and heat our buildings with fossil fuels or hydropower—all are foreclosures. Every day, consciously or not, we close down one life after another, a constant, often unwitting choice of who will suffer so that we may continue living. Given this reality, what one animal-rights scholar has called "the condition of being an imperfect being in an imperfectible world" and the difficulty of escaping from it completely, we may attempt to do the least harm possible to other life. Virtually always, this means finding our food more locally. In some home places such a discipline would still include hunting, in other home places organic farming, in some places both.

No matter our sentiments about animals, hunters and nonhunters remain in this dynamic system together. All the accusations that may be fairly leveled against the American hunter—greedy, thoughtless, lazy, consumptive, sexist—can also be brought against our culture at large. How can we expect more of the average American hunter, or for that matter inner-city gangs or junk bond dealers, when they are a product of a society that, in its films, politics, work ethic, and recreation, frequently displays these very negative characteristics and in the main has lost a sense of attention, discipline, care, practice, respect, and quality?

This impoverished state exists because we have lost our teachers and our holy people. Hunters ought to be in the ranks of both, but unless they find impeccable ways to restore what was a sacred activity, it will be, in its depauperated condition, rightfully disparaged and lost. Going out to have fun, I'm afraid, will no longer cut it. In fact, it never did. The humble, grateful, accomplished emotions that surround well-performed hunting cannot be equated with *fun*, that which provides amusement or arouses laughter. If hunters are going to preserve hunting, they must recreate it as the disciplined, mindful, sacred activity it once was for our species. They will also need to help redeem the culture in which they have grown and which finds fun at the expense of others. This is a job for hunters not only as hunters but also as citizens—an ongoing task to define what is appropriate behavior between both person and person and between what Black Elk, the Oglala Sioux holy man, called the two-leggeds and the four-leggeds. I would say that this definition will have much to do with the notions of kindness, compassion, and sympathy for those other species with whom we share this web of life and on whom we depend for sustenance . . . the very notions—and I might add restraint—that informed the lives of many hunting peoples in times past.

Such a reformation—or rather, return to older principles of mutual regard between species—will be a profound undertaking, for it is based on the pre-Christian belief that other life forms, indeed the very plants and earth and air themselves, are invested with soul and spirit. If we must take those spirits, it can only be done for good reason and then only if accompanied with constant reverence and humility for the sacrifices that have been made. Whether we're hunters or nonhunters, meat eaters or vegetarians, this state of heart and mind compels us to say an eternal grace.

Facing up to this basic and poignant condition of biological life on this planet—people, animals, and plants as fated cohorts, as both dependents and donors of life—wasn't easy ten thousand years ago and won't be easy today. Of course, we can back away from the task, but I think the result will be either a world in which people continue to dominate nature, or a world in which simplistic notions of how to reduce pain sever the bonds between people and nature. In either case, hunters will still be distant from the complex burdens and daily sympathy that ancient hunters considered the basis for a loving community of people and animals.

Can this reformation really be accomplished without the participatory context of gathering and hunting that informed our species for thousands of years? Can we know the old knowledge of hunting times even though many of us spend lives far from the animals and plants that sustain us? I doubt it, unless we attempt to restore participation. Many of us may never have the privilege to thresh wheat we have grown, skin a deer we have killed, or filet a fish we have caught. Virtually all of us, though, have a window and a piece of sky. We can choose to grow salad greens or a few herbs. Though a small gesture of participation in the world that feeds us, putting one's hands in a small pot of dirt, emblem of the original ground from which we have sprung, is a powerful thing to do and a beginning. If we are hunters or anglers, I will suggest that it is our first duty to introduce nonhunters and nonanglers to the participatory context. In short, take a child, a friend, a spouse hunting or fishing, and don't be ashamed to show that reverence for life goes hand in hand with the taking of it.

It is time to stop the rhetorical protection of hunting. It is time to nurture and restore the spirit that informed it. Such a commitment, if followed diligently, would certainly close down hunting as a sport. It would maintain it, though, as one of our important and fundamental weddings with nature.

Another Country

❧

John Haines

To be nothing and nowhere. Shreds, particles adrift, a little pallor spun in the dark.

A blankness, a gray film over the eye that saw . . . shadows and a moving brightness. A last deep sigh exhaled from the troubled lungs, and then no breath. Blood stopped and pulse still. In the warm tissue beginning to cool, already a damp decay. And the mosses and the small plants of the soil upreaching, ready to claim the nostrils and the lips.

And so I have stood by and watched a great animal die. And in the stillness that followed the last heave of the flanks, a bloody froth blew from the nostrils, staining the snow. And I who was practiced in death could sense in that silence, that stillness into which a few faded and yellowing leaves were falling, that the hunt was over. I breathed in the damp, rich odor of mortality and stood for a moment in my own coming death, on the ground of death itself.

It was not clinical death—the sudden stopping of pulse and breath, a gradual rigor in the limbs. It was something else: a sudden space and peace that came to the woods. Before I put rifle and pack aside and prepared for the long job of butchering, I stood for a moment in the oldest stillness on earth. And in that moment, when for this one creature life ceased and its flesh settled into the fixed transience of decay, I could believe in the passage of the soul into another country.

And then there was no time to stand and muse upon the mystery; the animal was down, there was meat to save and work to do.

When the carcass had been gutted and skinned, and the meat cut into quarters, carried off, and hung in the air to age and keep, a stained and matted place in the moss kept for a while the imprint of death in life. Blood, body fluids soaked into the snow and the soil beneath; some stray whiskers—hairs that were long and hollow, shading from gray to brown at the roots, and black at the tips—these persisted, along with scraps of trimmed flesh, of fat encrusted with dried blood, freezing in the cold air.

After the kill, and the work of skinning and cutting was over, an odor remained—a warmth, a sweetness of blood and inner membrane, smelt on the hands and clothing, on the knife and ax. That which emerged steaming and hot from the interior of the killed creature cooled to a faint displacement of the dry woods air. And now that I think of it, I cannot dispel completely the persistent odor of death that clings to the woods I have known and hunted.

❧

One morning late in April, after a hard, snowy winter, I climbed to the potato patch on the hill overlooking the river. As I gained the top of the rise, I turned for a moment to look back down the way I had come. On the cleared slope the winter-matted growth of last summer's grass lay warm and yellowed in the sun; here and there some slender, dark twigs of birch and alder sprouted from an old stump. A few yards away, in the shaded woods, patches of snow still lay on the ground, but these were rapidly melting.

Just below me, in a sheltered hollow of the hillside, lay a drift of deeper snow. In the center of the drift I saw a dark brown stain like a shadow, and the snow around it appeared to be discolored, as if the stain were spreading and becoming vaguely pink. Something about that stain in the snow drew my attention, and I climbed back down toward it.

When I stepped off the path and into the knee-deep snow, I discovered the reason for that stain. Half buried in the drift, and half exposed to the spring sunlight, were the remains of a yearling moose calf. It had obviously been dead for some time, and until recently covered by snow. A pair of foxes had been feeding on it, and their well-marked trails led in and out of the drift. The thin hide of the moose had been torn open, parts of the stomach and the intestines were spilled and matted, the snow around was threaded with brown moose hair, and scattered about were pink ice crystals of blood. Much of the half-grown, wasted body had been consumed; what remained had collapsed upon itself like a sodden brown envelope.

A shoulder blade, gnawed and beginning to bleach and dry, was exposed to the sunlight; still attached to it under a flap of hide I could see a part of the rib cage and something of the spinal column. There was very little meat on any of these bones. Even that part of the body so far untouched by the foxes showed me how poor and thin the calf had been. I reached down and pulled from the snow one of the slender leg bones; it was cracked open, and looking closely at it I saw what remained of the marrow: it was thin and bloody, a sign of starvation.

I remembered then that for a brief period during the winter just past we had seen a cow and calf feeding on the hillside below the house and above the river, the two of them in single file treading the deep snow. It was very cold at the time, at least fifty below zero, and the high shoulder ruff of the cow bristled with frost. Severe as the cold was, the cow looked fit and strong, but I thought the calf moved slowly in the troughed snow behind her. Sometime later, when the weather had moderated, I saw the cow alone one day on the hill above the house, not far from where I was standing now, but I did not think then of the missing calf.

A hard winter, deep snow, and maybe a weakness in the calf, so that it could not pull down sufficient browse to feed its growing body; weaker and weaker, it failed to keep pace with its long-legged mother in her travels through the woods. One night the calf lay down in the snow and did not get up. Frost drove in through the brown coat of hair, chilling the weakened body. Slowly the blood cooled and the breath came less often. The long ears drooped and stiffened, a cold sleep invaded the bones and stopped the breath.

A vague sadness claimed me as I stood there in the wet, soiled snow, looking down at the pitiful remains. The sun was bright and warm on my shoulder, I could hear a few geese far out on the river, and from somewhere close by came the drowsy, interrupted drone of a bumblebee. I turned away and stepped out of the snow and onto the dark, matted soil of the footpath. Facing the strong sunlight, I climbed back uphill to look over the potato ground for the coming season.

Washed by the spring rains, the snowdrift in the hollow soon melted. Of the young moose, hide and tissue slowly disintegrated, and by midsummer only a stray bone remained in the vigorous new growth of underbrush. Close to the ground, perhaps, in the tangle of grass and flowering plants, there lingered a faint sour odor of late spring and early death.

Survival of the Hunter

✤

Peter Matthiessen

Qaanaaq, on the north shore of Whale Sound, appeared as a bright rash of small buildings on a sloping tundra strip at the foot of a stony ridge, which climbs inland no more than a mile, then vanishes beneath what Peary called the Great Ice, looming like a frozen wave over the village. Like most Iñhuit communities, Qaanaaq is composed mostly of cottages in dark reds and greens and blues and mustard yellows, trimmed in black, that are scattered in random rows along the shore, which offers an awesome prospect of white sea and glaciered mountains. Though a few walrus hunters and their families camp at Siorapaluk, beyond the dark cliffs farther up the coast, this village is considered the northernmost human settlement on earth, only 850 miles from the pole.

Offshore to the southwest rise two high, dark islands, each with its own glacier and ice sheet, which shelter Qaanaaq from the winds of Baffin Bay. Beyond those islands lies that region of north Baffin Bay known to the early seafarers as the North Water—a polynya, or ice-free reach of sea among the ice floes, open even in winter—which keeps the Avanersuaq region more temperate than the frozen coasts to north and south. The polynya is formed by the prevailing winds and ocean currents, and its upwelling of nutrients, which supports the food chain, attracts multitudes of seabirds, and also polar bears, whales, walruses, and seals. It is the North Water that permits human

299

beings to remain all year in a region where temperatures may fall below minus-fifty degrees Celsius in the deep winter.

Our plan had been to accompany the whale hunters to camps farther up the fjord, but for the moment a heavy fog kept everyone
stuck in Qaanaaq. I had brought a fly rod, and I asked our Iñhuit
innkeeper, who had introduced us to the hunters, if arctic char were
to be found within walking distance. He said yes, and I asked "How
far?" Without a semblance of a smile, he replied "Three or four
days"—no distance at all in a community where time is measured by
the hunting seasons.

I left my fishing rod behind and went for a walk. On the tundra between the shore and the rocky ridge, I found a few rare
notes of color—hard, flat green and orange lichens, white florets of
Labrador tea, a tiny crimson mushroom tucked in bright-green
moss, tiny lavender blossoms of moss campion, a fragment of
rose quartz, a dull-orange moth. A swift glacial stream of ancient
blue-gray water descended a rocky gorge, and I followed it back
inland a ways, seeking to touch the Greenland ice sheet. Streaks
of blue appeared in the eastern sky, but soon the fog rolled down
again off the Great Ice, and I made my way down the steep and
stony ridge. In the fog over the surface of Whale Sound, the elements
of sea and air and ice all came together. Turning minutely on
the tide, the icebergs, changing shapes, loomed mysteriously and
vanished.

❧

In September of 1897, Robert Peary returned to New York City
with a group of what he called "my Eskimos," who were put on display at the American Museum of Natural History. Lodged in the
basement of the museum in an early October heat wave, they soon
became sick, and within a few months four of the six were dead. The
first to die was the great walrus hunter Qisuk, known to Peary as
"the Smiler" because of his ever-cheerful disposition. A few years
later, Qisuk's son Minik, who survived, discovered that, following a
mock burial, staged for his benefit, his father's body had been dis-
sected by medical students at Bellevue Hospital and the skeleton
duly cleaned and mounted for public display at the museum. Minik,
frail and bitter, died in 1918, in his late twenties, after seeking in vain
for years to have his father' bones returned to him for burial. Not

until the summer of 1993—seventy-five years after Minik's death—
were the bones of the four Iñhuit finally returned to Avanersuaq and
buried in Qaanaaq.

Since we were still trapped by fog the next morning, my son Alex
and I visited the cemetery east of the village, where the bones of
Qisuk the Smiler are now interred among white crosses of white-
bordered graves smothered in plastic flowers. Beyond the cemetery,
in a cove under the bluffs scarcely a mile from the village, were three
tents of a hunting camp and a small boat with an outboard motor.
Alex assumed that the hunters were from some outer settlement such
as Siorapaluk, but we were later told that they were men from
Qaanaaq, so eager to go hunting that they had camped within sight
of home while awaiting the opening of the ice pack that would permit them to follow narwhal up Inglefield Gulf.

The Iñhuit live in such shore camps in the summer and in seal-
hunting huts out on the ice during much of the fall and spring. They
are at Qaanaaq mainly between November and early February, hud-
dled against the perpetual darkness and harsh winds and snow. From
mid-February until the end of April, the polar world turns in unbro-
ken twilight. In spring, harp seals, whales, and seabirds will appear at
the edge of the fast ice, waiting for the icebound fjord and snow-
bound cliffs to open. The sun is high all day and all night from early
May through mid-July. Only during this period does new ice stop
forming, but open water will persist until the first hard freeze of
mid-October.

From May to August, hunters from Qaanaaq, armed with long
pole nets, climb the scree slopes of Siorapaluk to sweep the little
auks, or dovekies, from the air. Before the reintroduction of the
kayak, in the 1860s, these quail-size seabirds, dried and frozen in
hundreds of thousands, were the mainstay of the people's diet, and
perhaps a quarter million of them are still netted every year without
discernible diminishment of their population. The immense bird
colonies along the coasts also provide thick-billed murres, fulmars,
and kittiwakes, all of which live far out at sea during the remainder of
the year. Birds are much more precious to the Iñhuit than either land
mammals or fish, but cod, capelin, and the Greenland halibut are also
taken.

In spring, the narwhal that have wintered in the North Water
move into the sounds and then follow the retreating ice into Ingle-

field Gulf. A few beluga, or white whales, are also taken at this time
of year, when they may join the narwhal in these waters. At Siorapaluk, the walrus is the foundation of subsistence, whereas at
Qaanaaq, halfway up Whale Sound, the hunting varies according to
the season. The small, fat ringed seal, hunted at all seasons, is the
most important quarry, contributing nearly half the meat consumed
in Avanersuaq, and its lustrous gold-and-silver fur has been the
foundation of the Iñhuit economy since Peary traded on these barren
coasts a century ago.

❧

The sea mist remained heavy, and the whale hunters, who could not
spot whales even if they could reach them, did not go out. No Iñhuit
carries a compass, since the shifting labyrinth of ice that covers most
of the sound makes it impossible to maintain a course. I recalled
some astonishing charts shown to me by my friend the arctic explorer Edmund Carpenter. They were drawn from memory by
Iñhuit hunters, with every point and cliff and headland on this coast
in sure perspective. Miles offshore in the mist and shifting floes of
Avanersuaq is no place for error or forgetfulness.

   Two days later, the weather cleared, but the morning tide was too
low to launch the boats. We finally got off in the early afternoon, in
two sixteen-foot open outboard skiffs belonging to Iñhuit hunters.
The older hunter, weathered, and wearing glasses, was called Lars,
and the younger one, very quick and handsome, was called Gedion.
(Like most Greenlanders, they had been given Danish names.) The
boats were built of thick, ice-resistant fiberglass, and each carried a
light canvas kayak (only two or three sealskin kayaks are left in
Qaanaaq) lashed to the port gunwale, and extra gas and stores and
tents for a few days' camping. Because neither man spoke English,
we were accompanied by a translator—Navarana Kavigak, a lively,
sharp-tongued woman whose great-uncle, the famous hunter and
dog driver Oodaaq, traveled with Peary to the Pole.

   Breaking the great northern silence, the boats headed east, into
Inglefield Gulf, passing the camp we had seen the day before under
the bluffs. Near the mouth of Bowdoin Fjord (where Peary had
made a winter base camp), the drift ice had closed into pack ice.
There was no way through, so Lars led the way west again, thread-
ing a labyrinth of floes for twenty miles, and barging through, or

even climbing, the thin ice, with a loud, harsh scraping. Kittiwake and fulmar picked along the ice edge; a pair of ivory gulls like snowy pigeons perched on a floe; the auk species hurtled busily in all directions. Heads of seals gleamed here and there along the leads between the ice floes, and the hunters took out rifles, but seals are rarely hunted hard in this fleeting season when the ice pack is opening and the full attention of the settlement is focused on the whales.

Gedion's sister and her family and kin had a whaling camp—four snug tents perched on rocks under the cliffs at the east end of Qeqertarssuaq, the nearer of the two islands off Qaanaaq. They had crossed to the island by dogsled in May and had since taken several narwhal that had been working their way slowly up the fjord. The tents, whose floors consisted of bedding and piles of clothes, were warmed by cookstoves, and the family welcomed us gladly, offering tea and some smoked whale. We waited there while the hunters kept their vigil on the rocks. Soon the tide swung the ice open to the south and east, and our boats were off again—this time toward the glaciers on the south shore of Whale Sound.

In the distance, a hunter and kayak were poised, dead still, along an ice floe, awaiting a chance to strike a pod of narwhal whose dorsal gleams, barely visible through binoculars, were rising and falling in the open lead beyond. But they passed on unharmed, and the kayak returned toward its boat. Our skiffs continued southeast to a former settlement at Narssaq, on the far shore, and there we made camp. Lars and Gedion climbed a ridge behind the camp to a lookout point, where long ago ancient stone seats for the hunters had been placed in such a way that the whole vast bay at the meeting of two sounds could be surveyed, not only for whales but for movements of the ice and for coming weather. Such lookout stations, Navarana told us, are called *nasiffik*—"the place where everything becomes clear."

By now, it was close to midnight and still broad daylight. Since we had been traveling the ice floes for ten hours and no whales were in sight, the hunters told us to get a little sleep.

✼

Toward 8:00 A.M., a large pod of narwhal appeared offshore to the west. Lars and Gedion ran to the lookout point and soon spotted the narwhal between our camp and the mouth of Bowdoin Fjord, across the sound. The hunters ran down and jumped into their kayaks, which lay ready on the beach. The big pod was well scattered across a long, smooth reach of open water, and four or five narwhal were rising at a time, the arctic sun shining on their black heads, glistening in the mist of their warm breathing, and silvering their wakes in the parted water.

Oddly, in this land of violent storms coming down off the ice cap, there was no wind, not a whisper. The island cliffs at Qeqertarssuaq, twenty miles to the west, and the high red portals of Bowdoin Fjord, perhaps ten miles to the north, were reflected so minutely in the glassy water that the mirrored rock shimmered like a reddish mist rising mysteriously from the slowly drifting ice. In the foreground, pale glaucous gulls harried the arctic terns carrying bright fish in their bills; and in the background, in wait along the floes, each hunter sat motionless in his still kayak, in a long and silent meditation, the half man and the boat all one. The elegance of these light, quick craft is stirring. Even the long paddles are designed to shed a minimum of water and reflect a minimum of light that might flash in the eye of a seal or a whale.

Since the hunters could not overtake the moving pod, they were poised to glide outward if the creatures should pause to rest on the still surface, but the narwhal did not pause and were soon gone.

In the afternoon, from a cairn of stones high on the steep headland above camp, I observed the astonishing prospect to the west. In the distance, past the two high islands, the drift ice vanished in a blue sea inset with giant icebergs—the North Water of Baffin Bay, the great polynya. Below me, just in front of our camp, five harp seals surfaced, lifting sleek, shining heads and necks high out of the water to peer at the intruders on the shore as they moved along. The hunters, staring out to sea, ignored them, for their fur is not so valuable or their flesh so prized as the fur and the flesh of the ringed seal.

In the 1970s, environmental organizations joined an animal-welfare campaign against the slaughter of the "whitecoats"—the white pups of the harp seal—on the ice off northeastern Canada, and these "seal wars" were recorded in propaganda films. In one, a man represented as a Canadian sealer taunts a mother seal with her dead pup. Another film portrayed a hunter skinning a whitecoat alive. Why professional commercial hunters would waste time taunting adult seals in the short winter work hours on cold ice and why they would

skin young seals alive when it would be ten times as easy and as prof-
itable to skin them dead were troubling questions, but the innocent
red blood on the white snow brought outraged new members and
thousands of dollars to the cause, while penalizing the hunting communities, including those of the Iñhuit, with an international boycott
of sealskin products. The Canadian sealers protested that their liveli-
hoods had been taken away from them by ruthless trickery.

The seal wars, which started out as a British animal-welfare operation, had nothing to do with conservation or ecological imbalance,
since the harp seal is a common animal throughout the North Atlantic. Yet the Green groups themselves exploited the whitecoats for
publicity right from the start. Some of the same footage depicting the
"atrocities" of Canadian sealers turned up more than a decade later
in a Swedish documentary about Norwegian harp sealers on Jan
Mayen Island.

Harp seals of the West Atlantic throw their pups at the south end
of their migrations, on the winter ice off Labrador and Newfound-
land, so whitecoats are never harvested in Greenland. But because
the harp seal is known also as the Greenland seal, those bloody
scenes off Labrador, faked or not, have done severe harm to Greenland's hunters.

❦

Descending the scree slope in the late afternoon and coming back
along the shore, I was startled by a strange, soft blowing sound and
turned in time to see the pale head of a beluga whale parting the water not fifty feet away, and leaving a wake thin as a knife slash on the
shining surface. The hunters ran for the beached kayaks, but once
again the pursuit was to no avail.

An hour before midnight, the polar sun was high and strangely
warm. Two of Oodaaq's grandsons—Navarana's cousins—visited
our camp to join Lars and Gedion at the lookout, but they soon went
away toward the east.

At the campfire, Navarana sang a song about some unfortunate
little auks that had to fly south without their young, because jaegers
and gulls had taken all the eggs. But the Iñhuit are nothing if not
pragmatic in their harsh and unrelenting struggle for survival, and so
she added, "We children cried and cried for those little auks, because
we were afraid we would not get any to eat." And it seemed to me

that those words could be an answer from traditional societies to those animal defenders who have never had to wonder about where their next meal might come from, and to whom it may never have occurred that the traditional hunter "loves" the hunted creature more than they do, without the smallest trace of sentimentality, because it is not separate from his own existence.

Our frustrated hunters, teased by Navarana, were still watching the water when the rest of us crept into our tents to get some sleep. Around midnight, with no whales in sight, the hunters walked down to the water's edge and shot for breakfast a small flock of thick-billed murres that had drifted close to shore. Then, two hours after midnight, narwhal were seen in the bright sunlight off to the west. The pod appeared to be moving slowly, and the kayaks streaked away again, two miles or more across the shining sea. This time, Gedion threw his harpoon, the barb struck home, and the line that was coiled carefully on the kayak canvas went spinning off as the narwhal sounded and the sealskin float bounded across the water.

While Lars followed the float and evaded the rushes of the wounded narwhal—"They can be very dangerous," he told us later—Gedion returned to fetch his rifle, which is ordinarily kept in the kayak's bow but had been left on shore in the frustration that followed the failure to kill the beluga. Though he moved quickly, he was a long way off, so, to save time, Navarana grabbed the rifle, I cranked up Lars's engine, and we went to meet him. The Iñhuit are thought to be the oldest whaling society on earth, and Gedion's methods and his tools are essentially identical to those described by the Danish missionary Hans Egede in his description of Greenland of 1745, but firearms are used these days to finish off the whale.

Like most pods during the summer months, this was a cow-calf group, and the harpooned narwhal was a female with a young one alongside. At one point, the panicked cow, still attended closely by the calf, swam close beneath our boat, her beautiful black-and-white marbled hide alight in the clear black water. Every few moments, she surfaced to breathe. Gedion dispatched her at close range with rifle shots, amid much blood and thrashing, and then quickly harpooned and killed the calf. The hunters rigged lines to the carcasses and towed them back to the Narssaq beach. On the shore, the younger hunter, performing an ancient ceremony, cut slices of skin and blubber from the back of his whale's neck and offered one to each of us.

The hunters, using heavy knives, butchered the young whale first—its bronze skin was of an eerie smoothness—and then expertly divided the adult into sections, taking pains with the good cuts, which were to be consumed by human beings, and hacking the rest into crude chunks for the dogs. Since not all the meat could be carried in the boats, some of the poorer cuts were cached high on the beach under big stones, but before we left Narssaq, late that day, gulls were already squalling and fluttering around them, picking and pulling.

✤

I first wrote in condemnation of commercial whaling in 1959 in *Wildlife in America*, a history of rare and vanishing species, and again a decade later, after a voyage on a sperm whaling vessel out of Durban, South Africa. But commercial whaling is not the same as whaling by traditional people for subsistence purposes, which seems acceptable when the hunting methods are as humane as possible and when the species harvested is not endangered. Alex and I had been disturbed by the killing of the nursing calf (which could not have survived without its mother), but we agree that this harvest of sea mammals is necessary if Inhuit culture is to survive. Otherwise, centuries of adaptation to the most uncompromising human habitat on earth will disappear into the listless monoculture of the concrete tract housing that rises above the old cove at Nuuk.

How astonishing it must seem to the Greenlanders (and to the Icelanders and the Faroese), who have managed their marine resources so much better than the United States and Britain, that the English-speaking countries, which only recently desisted from pursuing the great whales to near extinction, and then did so only when the slaughter became unprofitable, have awarded themselves the sovereign right to determine acceptable types of hunting for these peoples. Because of Greenland's harsh topography and climate, and the small land area that protrudes from beneath the ice, the great island's sparse human population of fifty-seven thousand continues to subsist on hunting and fishing. For various reasons, including the introduction of industrial fisheries, most of the fishermen now work for conglomerates, but in Avanersuaq the old methods of hunting persist. Throughout Greenland, it is sea mammals, birds, and fish that permit the ongoing existence of human beings, so the people's life depends on responsible harvesting of marine creatures, which are the basis not only of their diet and their livelihood but of their myth, tradition, and culture. Since this has been true throughout their history, the Greenlanders will never recognize the right of foreigners to interfere with their harvest of wild food, seals and whales included.

The Greenland whale hunts have frequently been challenged by animal-welfare groups, and representatives of Greenpeace and other organizations have criticized what they view as the excessive cruelty of the native hunters' methods. Although not formally aligned against aboriginal subsistence whaling in Greenland, where aborigines, unlike the Icelanders and Faroese, are of appropriate size and color, the environmental groups would doubtless prefer to see it done by men in native costume, using primitive tools. That aborigines use outboard motors, fiberglass skiffs, and rifles to kill whales is barely tolerable and leads to the argument that Iñhuit hunting will "escalate and become commercial and industrialized"—a fear based on the fact, unavoidable in the modern cash economy, that some of the meat must be sold to pay for the hunter's boat and gear and fuel. However, it is the hunter's family, not the market, that takes care of the products of the hunt, which are often shared with relatives or with families unable to hunt food for themselves. This ancient custom has not changed in Avanersuaq.

In traditional hunting, land and life belong to every member of a community. Greenland's mute sea ice and empty land are not an "environment" in the Western sense—a human "habitat," to be exploited. They are the ground of a hard life, and a realm of memory and cultural renewal, providing a sense of continuity and tradition which lies at the heart of Iñhuit well-being. Hunting is the vital nerve of Iñhuit existence, and for outsiders to come and remove that nerve from the spine of a culture so much older than their own—a "green" culture, what's more, which has always lived in balance and harmony with the world around it—would be to do great harm to other human beings without any significant benefit to whale populations.

❧

By afternoon, the drift ice over the fifteen miles between Narssaq and Qaanaaq had once again gathered in broad floes, solid enough so that seals had hauled themselves out and were scattered here and there across the whiteness. The hunters went up to the lookout "where everything becomes clear" to work out a homeward route through the narrow leads.

We went quickly to the laden boats and set out on a labyrinthine passage across Whale Sound, skirting the icebergs, grinding through patches of skim ice that separated one lead from another. Halfway across, Lars's motor quit, and Gedion returned to help him drain and clean his carburetor and wipe the spark plugs. The hunters were quick and adept with the old machine, and I recalled what I had been told when I first went among Iñhuit, in Alaska—that they would take home an old outboard, the only one the family could afford, and, with even the youngest and the oldest in rapt attendance, dismantle it to the last nut and spring to make sure everyone understood the working of the smallest part that might have to be replaced with a bit of bone or sinew when out at sea, beyond reach of help.

The next day, narwhal were seen from the village, and three hunters—Lars was one—went out through the ice in kayaks, but at the sound of the helicopter on its way from Thule the thin craft turned back. The narwhal are made nervous by the sound of rotors and become too wary to be approached, the hunters say.

From where I sat, on a lichened rock above the cemetery, the metallic chattering of the helicopter had been audible out of the south for ten minutes or more before I saw it, and the machine was still thirty miles away when it appeared, as black as a fly, descending a silver glacier from the ice of Steensby Land.

On the return flight across Whale Sound, a wintry sun struck dull facets on the icebergs, and all around was a white jigsaw of broken ice and undersea clouds, drifting beneath the windless green-black mirror. The machine circled with a fearful clatter over a large pod of narwhal, which drifted serenely in silver-glinted water of such clarity that Alex was able to identify a solitary male by its six-foot tusk of whorled ivory. Perhaps it had been the hunters who were unnerved by the helicopter, for the beautiful whales "lying aloft upon the water" seemed quite unbothered. Then we were over the Great Ice once more, bound south for Thule.

From *Arctic Dreams*

❧

BARRY LOPEZ

The mountain in the distance is called Sevuokuk. It marks the north-west cape of Saint Lawrence Island in the Bering Sea. From where we are on the ice, this eminence defines the water and the sky to the east as far as we can look. Its western face, a steep wall of snow-streaked basalt, rises above a beach of dark cobbles, riven, ice-polished, ocean-rolled chips of Sevuokuk itself. The village of Gambell is there, the place I have come from with the Yup'ik men, to hunt walrus in the spring ice.

We are, I believe, in Russian waters; and also, by a definition to them even more arbitrary, in "tomorrow," on the other side of the international date line. Whatever political impropriety might be involved is of little importance to the Yup'ik, especially while they are hunting. From where blood soaks the snow, then, and piles of meat and slabs of fat and walrus skin are accumulating, from where ivory tusks have been collected together like exotic kindling, I stare toward the high Russian coast. The mental categories, specific desires, and understanding of history among the people living there are, I reflect, nearly as different from my own as mine are from my Yup'ik companions'.

I am not entirely comfortable on the sea ice butchering walrus like this. The harshness of the landscape, the vulnerability of the boat, and the great size and power of the hunted animal combine to

310

increase my sense of danger. The killing jars me, in spite of my regard for the simple elements of human survival here.

We finish loading the boats. One of the crews has rescued two dogs that have either run off from one of the Russian villages or been abandoned out here on the ice. Several boats gather gunnel to gunnel to look over the dogs. They have surprisingly short hair and seem undersize to draw a sled, smaller than Siberian huskies. But the men assure me these are typical Russian sled dogs.

We take our bearing from the far prominence of Sevuokuk and turn home, laden with walrus meat, with walrus hides and a few seals, with crested auklets and thick-billed murres, with ivory and Russian dogs. When we reach shore, the four of us put our shoulders to the boat to bring it high up on the beach. A young man in the family I am staying with packs a sled with what we have brought back. He pulls it away across the snow behind his Honda three-wheeler, toward the house. Our meals. The guns and gear, the harpoons and floats and lines, the extra clothing and portable radios are all secured and taken away. I am one of the last to leave the beach, still turning over images of the hunt.

No matter what sophistication of mind you bring to such events, no matter what breadth of anthropological understanding, no matter your fondness for the food, your desire to participate, you have still seen an animal killed. You have met the intertwined issues—What is an animal? What is death?—in those large moments of blood, violent exhalation, and thrashing water, with the acrid odor of burned powder in the fetid corral smells of a walrus haul-out. The moments are astounding, cacophonous, also serene. The sight of men letting bits of meat slip away into the dark green water with mumbled benedictions is as stark in my memory as the suddenly widening eyes of the huge, startled animals.

I walk up over the crest of the beach and toward the village, following a set of sled tracks. There is a narrow trail of fresh blood in the snow between the runners. The trail runs out at a latticework of drying racks for meat and skins. The blood in the snow is a sign of life going on, of other life going on. Its presence is too often confused with cruelty.

I rest my gloved fingers on the driftwood meat rack. It is easy to develop an affection for the Yup'ik people, especially when you are invited to participate in events still defined largely by their own traditions. The entire event—leaving to hunt, hunting, coming home, the food shared in a family setting—creates a sense of well-being easy to share. Viewed in this way, the people seem fully capable beings, correct in what they do. When you travel with them, their voluminous and accurate knowledge, their spiritual and technical confidence, expose what is insipid and groundless in your own culture.

I brood often about hunting. It is the most spectacular and succinct expression of the Eskimo's relationship with the land, yet one of the most perplexing and disturbing for the outsider to consider. With the compelling pressures of a cash-based economy to contend with, and the ready availability of modern weapons, hunting practices have changed. Many families still take much of their food from the land, but they do it differently now. "Inauthentic" is the criticism most often made of their methods, as though years ago time had stopped for the Yup'ik.

But I worry over hunting for another reason—the endless reconciliation that must be made of Jacob with his brother Esau. The anguish of Gilgamesh at the death of his companion Enkidu. We do not know how exactly to bridge this gap between civilized man and the society of the hunter. The Afrikaner writer Laurens van der Post, long familiar with Kalahari hunting peoples as archetypal victims of our prejudice, calls the gap between us "an abyss of deceit and murder" we have created. The existence of such a society alarms us. In part this is a trouble we have with writing out our history. We adjust our histories in order to elevate ourselves in the creation that surrounds us; we cut ourselves off from our hunting ancestors, who make us uncomfortable. They seem too closely aligned with insolent, violent predatory animals. The hunting cultures are too barbaric for us. In condemning them, we see it as "inevitable" that their ways are being eclipsed. Yet, from the testimony of sensitive visitors among them, such as van der Post and others I have mentioned in the Arctic, we know that something of value resides with these people.

I think of the Eskimos compassionately as *hibakusha*—the Japanese word for "explosion-affected people," those who continue to suffer the effects of Hiroshima and Nagasaki. Eskimos are trapped in a long, slow detonation. What they know about a good way to live is disintegrating. The sophisticated, ironic voice of civilization insists that their insights are only trivial, but they are not.

I remember looking into a herd of walrus that day and thinking: Do human beings make the walrus more human to make it comprehensible or to assuage loneliness? What is it to be estranged in this land?

It is in the land, I once thought, that one searches out and eventually finds what is beautiful. And an edge of this deep and rarefied beauty is the acceptance of complex paradox and the forgiveness of others. It means you will not die alone.

❧

I looked at the blood in the snow for a long time, and then turned away from the village. I walked north, toward the spot where the gravel spit on which the houses stand slips under the sea ice. It is possible to travel in the Arctic and concentrate only on the physical landscape—on the animals, on the realms of light and dark, on movements that excite some consideration of the ways we conceive of time and space, history, maps, and art. One can become completely isolated, for example, in the intricate life of the polar bear. But the ethereal and timeless power of the land, that union of what is beautiful with what is terrifying, is insistent. It penetrates all cultures, archaic and modern. The land gets inside us; and we must decide one way or another what this means, what we will do about it.

One of our long-lived cultural differences with the Eskimo has been over whether to accept the land as it is or to exert the will to change it into something else. The great task of life for the traditional Eskimo is still to achieve congruence with a reality that is already given. The given reality, the real landscape, is "horror within magnificence, absurdity within intelligibility, suffering within joy," in the words of Albert Schweitzer. We do not esteem as highly these lessons in paradox. We hold in higher regard the land's tractability, its alterability. We believe the conditions of the earth can be changed to ensure human happiness, to provide jobs, and to create material wealth and ease. Each culture, then, finds a different sort of apotheosis, of epiphany, and comfort in the land.

Any latent wisdom there might be in the Eskimo position is overwhelmed for us by our ability to alter the land. The long pattern of purely biological evolution, however, strongly suggests that a profound collision of human will with immutable aspects of the natural order is inevitable. This, by itself, seems reason enough to inquire among aboriginal cultures concerning the nature of time and space and other (invented) dichotomies; the relationship between hope and the exercise of will; the role of dreams and myths in human life; and the therapeutic aspects of long-term intimacy with a landscape.

We tend to think of places like the Arctic, the Antarctic, the Gobi, the Sahara, the Mojave, as primitive, but there are in fact no primitive or even primeval landscapes. Neither are there permanent landscapes. And nowhere is the land empty or underdeveloped. It cannot be improved upon with technological assistance. The land, an animal that contains all other animals, is vigorous and alive. The challenge to us, when we address the land, is to join with cosmologists in their ideas of continuous creation, and with physicists with their ideas of spatial and temporal paradox, to see the subtle grace and mutability of the different landscapes. They are crucibles of mystery, precisely like the smaller ones that they contain—the arctic fox, the dwarf birch, the pi-meson; and the larger ones that contain them, side by side with such seemingly immutable objects as the Horsehead Nebula in Orion. These are not solely arenas for human invention. To have no elevated conversation with the land, no sense of reciprocity with it, to rein it in or to disparage conditions not to our liking, shows a certain lack of courage, too strong a preference for human devising.

❧

The farther I got from the village below Sevuokuk, the more exposed I was to the wind. I pulled my face farther into my parka. Snow squeaked beneath my boots. As I crossed from patches of wind-slabbed snow to dark cobbles, I wobbled over my footing. The beach stones clattered in the wet cold. The violet and saffron streaks of the sunset had long been on the wane. They had gone to pastels, muted, like slow water or interstellar currents, rolling over. They had become the colors of sunrise. The celestial light on an arctic cusp.

I stood with my feet squared on the stones at the edge of the ice and looked north into Bering Strait, the real Estrecho de Anian. To the east was America, the Seward Peninsula; to the west the Magadan Region of Siberia, the Chukchi Peninsula. On each were the burial grounds of archaic Bering Sea–culture people, the richest of all the prehistoric arctic cultures. In the summer of 1976, a Russian group led by M. A. Chlenov discovered a five-hundred-year-old monument on the north shore of Yttygran Island, on Seniavin Strait, off the southeast Chukchi coast. The complex consists of a series of bowhead whale skulls and jawbones set up in a line on the beach that is about 2,500 feet long. The monument is associated with the several stone and earth structures and also with meat pits. Many of the skulls are still standing up vertically in the ground, in a strict geometric pattern. Chlenov and his colleagues regard the area as a "sacred precinct" and link it to the ceremonial lives of a select group of highly skilled whale hunters, whose culture was continuous from Cape Dezhnev in the north to Providence Bay and included Saint Lawrence Island, where the cultural phase has been named Punuk.

Perhaps the Punuk hunters at Whalebone Alley, as it is known, lived, some of them, exemplary lives. Perhaps they knew exactly what words to say to the whale so they would not go off in dismay or feel the weight of its death. I remember the faces of the walrus we killed, and do not know what words to say to them.

No culture has yet solved the dilemma each has faced with the growth of a conscious mind: how to live a moral and compassionate existence when one is fully aware of the blood, the horror inherent in all life, when one finds darkness not only in one's own culture but within oneself. If there is a stage at which an individual life becomes truly adult, it must be when one grasps the irony in its unfolding and accepts responsibility for a life lived in the midst of such paradox. One must live in the middle of contradiction because if all contradiction were eliminated at once life would collapse. There are simply no answers to some of the great pressing questions. You continue to live them out, making your life a worthy expression of a leaning into the light.

I stood for a long time at the tip of Saint Lawrence Island, regarding the ice, the distant dark leads of water. In the twilight and wind and the damp cold, memories of the day were like an aura around me, unresolved, a continuous perplexity pierced here and there by sharp rays of light—other memories, coherence. I thought of the layers of it—the dying walrus moving through the chill green water, through the individual minds of the hunters, the mind of an observer. Of the very idea of the walrus living on, even as I ate its flesh. Lines in books about the walrus; walrus-hide lines tied to harpoons, dragging walrus-skin boats over the sea. The curve and weight of a tusk in my mind, from a head as dense with bone as a boulder. Walrus-meat stew is waiting back at the house, hot now, while I stand in this cold, thickening wind. At the foot of Sevuokuk, Lapland longspurs build their nests in the walrus's abandoned crania.

Glaucous gulls fly over. In the shore lead are phalaropes, with their twiglike legs. In the distance I can see flocks of old-squaw against the sky, and a few cormorants. A patch of shadow that could be several thousand crested auklets—too far away to know. Out there are whales—I have seen six or eight gray whales as I walked this evening. And the ice, pale as the dove-colored sky. The wind raises the surface of the water. Wake of a seal in the shore lead, gone now. I bowed. I bowed to what knows no deliberating legislature or parliament, no religion, no competing theories of economics, an expression of allegiance with the mystery of life.

I looked out over the Bering Sea and brought my hands folded to the breast of my parka and bowed from the waist deeply toward the north, that great strait filled with life, the ice and the water. I held the bow to the pale sulphur sky at the northern rim of the earth. I held the bow until my back ached, and my mind was emptied of its categories and designs, its plans and speculations. I bowed before the simple evidence of the moment in my life in a tangible place on the earth that was beautiful.

When I stood I thought I glimpsed my own desire. The landscape and the animals were like something found at the end of a dream. The edges of the real landscape became one with the edges of something I had dreamed. But what I had dreamed was only a pattern, some beautiful pattern of light. The continuous work of the imagination, I thought, to bring what is actual together with what is dreamed is an expression of human evolution. The conscious desire is to achieve a state, even momentarily, that like light is unbounded, nurturing, suffused with wisdom and creation, a state in which one has absorbed that very darkness which before was the perpetual sign of defeat.

Whatever world that is, it lies far ahead. But its outline, its adumbration, is clear in the landscape, and upon this one can actually hope we will find our way.

I bowed again, deeply, toward the north, and turned south to retrace my steps over the dark cobbles to the home where I was staying. I was full of appreciation for all that I had seen.

The Face in a Raindrop

✤

RICHARD K. NELSON

Grandpa William once told me: "A good hunter . . . that's somebody the animals *come* to. But if you lose your luck with a certain kind of animal—maybe you talk wrong about it or don't treat it with respect—then for a while you won't get any, no matter how hard you try."

I watch the deer bound away into a thicket, soft and silent as a cloud's shadow. And once again the old Koyukon Indian hunter's words drift through my mind. For several minutes I stand quietly, hoping to find the animal's shape somewhere in the tangle of twigs and boughs. But there is no movement, no shaking branch, no hint of sound. It's as if the moss and forest have soaked the deer up inside themselves, taken the heat of its breath, and nullified its entire existence.

A withering sense of loneliness fills me, but then Shungnak comes up and gently touches my leg with her nose. I rub her soft, warm fur, pleased that she stayed quietly behind while I stalked the deer. Perhaps she senses my disappointment, my sagging confidence, as yet another animal refuses to be taken. Though I've always been respectful toward deer, it seems as if they've shunned me during this long and luckless season. Now that it's mid-December, the hunting season is almost over, and if things don't change soon our family will run out of venison in the year ahead.

A short time later, we angle up a ridge, following a well-worn game trail. I force myself to keep it slow, needling my eyes into every dim pocket amid the trees and bushes, furtive, tentative, like a frightened animal searching for a way to escape. The rifle slung on my shoulder feels heavy and inert. Shungnak stays close behind, matching the pattern of her steps to my own, reaching from side to side with her nose, probing the air for scents. In one place, she pricks her ears and stares intently toward our left. Moments later, the sharp, sudden rasping of a squirrel on a tree trunk explains her curiosity.

As I cross a low swale, my foot sinks into the saturated moss and makes a loud noise when I pull it out. Trying to offset my clumsiness, I work carefully up the dry bank on the other side. If any deer are nearby, they now have their ears focused on us, tracing our every move, catching even the soft sounds of crowberry stems bending under our feet.

Then I make a bad mistake. Rather than stepping around a pothole where a bear dug skunk cabbage roots last spring, I take a long stride across it. And my heel snaps a twig on the other side. Cringing, I lift my guilty eyes and look into the surrounding woods.

Suddenly, a space in the thicket ahead is filled by a soft-edged shape, brown, tense, unmistakable, startling, alive. White-necked and funnel-eared, a large buck deer stands between two cedar trunks, like a shadow in a dim hallway.

I am pinched and off balance, but if I move my feet the deer will probably burst away. My whole body fills with insuppressible energy, my muscles tingle and tighten, and the cool confidence of other years is gone. Breathlessly, I raise the rifle, take aim through the tightly spaced trees, try to quell the heaving in my chest, and settle the bead on the narrow outline of the deer's neck.

Then, in the last moment before the rifle's jolt, a sudden, convulsed thought runs through me—that the animal will fall. A lie. The kind I tell myself to subvert my own misgivings.

The thought splinters my concentration; I blink, jerk the rifle to one side—and the deer spins away, untouched.

I watch the white tail flash through a scribble of brush and trees. Finally recovering, I fumble inside my pocket, pull out the deer call, and blow it sharply. Its feeble, reedy sound seems to evaporate into the forest. I stare into the tangled glade, feeling defeated.

But the deer startles me again, standing in a tight patch of trees, turned aside, his head and shoulder hidden from view. A second later he flips his tail and makes a series of powerful leaps in the direction of the wind. But when I blow the call he stops, now almost completely screened behind bushes. I have no choice but to move, and the noise sets him off as if I'd clapped my hands or shouted out loud. My heart is pounding. I am frustrated with myself for missing the first shot. Then, as though a sudden, painful stitch were running through me, I realize this might be my last chance for the year.

Again I blow the call, and to my surprise the deer stops. I move to the left, lean forward to brace the rifle against a slender tree, and wait until it stops swaying. The deer's head and neck are dimly visible in a cleft between huckleberry bushes. I lift my head to be certain of the shape, rest my cheek on the rifle, and take a deep breath.

The rifle's jolt seems to gather itself from my whole insides. But in the last tick before it comes, the buck leaps away.

The sound pours off into the forest, and we are left in an ear-ringing void.

In spite of what I already know, I dash over the hummocks and through the brush, with Shungnak whisking along beside me, to the spot where the deer stood and seemed to give itself, where now there is nothing except feathers of moss slowly springing back and hoofprints rich with scent that the dog alone can savor.

Shungnak prances back and forth, urging me after the deer; but I saw it move and know the shot went wide. It takes a few minutes to calm down and think the whole business through: first the sense of foolishness and error that comes from my own background, and then the deeper mysteries of luck that would give Koyukon people their explanation.

An hour later, Shungnak starts lifting her nose, as if she's caught a fresh scent. I find a likely spot by a grove of trees and stand for a long time, looking out over the brown grass, wishing for a movement or sound amid the stillness. The whole island seems inert, abandoned, lifeless, as fixed as a photograph. My tense anticipation slowly cools.

I take the deer call from my pocket, wait a few minutes more, then blow it several times. The pleading, high-pitched buzz seems to dissipate before it reaches the nearby thickets, like the beam of a flashlight with dying batteries. The fact that it sometimes draws deer out of the brush a hundred yards away attests to their marvelous hearing. Bucks in the rut and does with fawns are especially attracted by the call, though no one seems to know why. But at this time of the year, just after the mating season, deer are apparently so exhausted they seldom do more than pause to look when they hear it.

After another wait, I blow the call again. An oppressive, almost melancholy silence fills the air afterward. I am staring so intently that a moth fluttering against the black void of forest thirty yards away jars me like the flag-white of a deer's tail.

Moments later, there is an abrupt *whoosh*, like a thick rope whirling through the air overhead. A startled twang runs clean through my body. Then comes a loud, sharp, resonant, doubled yodel. I jerk my head up, and at the same instant I realize who it is.

The voice rings out again: *"gaaga . . . gaaga!"* A raven, shouting "animal . . . animal!" in the Koyukon language.

Another raven comes from the opposite direction, they meet above, and swing around each other like square dancers. *"Gaaga . . . gaaga!"* The same peculiar call from the same bird. Not a call, the Koyukon people would say, but a shout, a voice, a message—a sign. Grandpa William's words come back again, telling me about the raven's spirit and power, his special affinity with humans, and his willingness to help them in both small and great ways. Perhaps it's because the ancestral trickster-god Raven created humans to be most like himself; or it may be a kind of honor among thieves. If I have understood the elders, the raven is telling me there is game nearby.

And in case it isn't enough, the same raven adds another sign of luck. He tucks his wing and cartwheels in the sky, "dropping his packsack," the elders say, to give me a share of the meat and fat inside. Afterward, the two birds fly along the nearby wall of timber.

"Gaaga!"

Another cartwheel . . . and another. They perch in separate trees, squawking back and forth. Then one sails down and circles over me again.

"Gaaga!"

Nothing could be more black. There is no bird, only a shadow, a flat, soaring silhouette, a magic indigo hole contorting its way across the membrane of sky. I squint to catch any semblance of contour or roundness, but there is none. No silver glint from his beak or eye.

No fleck of color clinging to his feathers. If there *are* feathers. It's only a moving shade with a voice and a hiss like wind.

I look where the raven flies, where his beak points, for a clue. He settles in a band of trees that extends into the muskeg. Should I go there or keep on in the direction I'd intended? Does the raven really care about things, does he really know, does he move with the power Koyukon elders hold in such great regard? And would he manifest his power for me, or only for someone born into a tradition of respect for the spirit in nature? Then my wondering finds a new direction: if the raven has power, does he recognize it himself and use it consciously? Koyukon hunters say he does. If the raven brings you luck, it's to serve himself, because he will eat whatever you leave for him from the kill.

Accepting what the Koyukon teachers have said, I decide to take the sign of luck seriously and hunt with special care. But on one point I will yield to my uncertainty—I will choose my own direction. Instead of walking out toward the raven, I follow the muskeg's edge. Shortly, he flies my way again, then turns off toward the forest, where the other still sits. Easing through a glade of shore pines, I hear the distant voice once more: *"gaaga!"* And I think, he could be joking, playing with me, or reveling in my foolish ignorance. How I envy Grandpa William, Sarah Stevens, and the other Koyukon teachers for the surety and comfort of their knowledge, and for the gift of intimacy with nature that my own ancestors let slip away. I'm grateful for what little I've learned, but sad over what I've lost, and troubled by my abiding doubt.

Three hours later, exhausted from the strain of slow, tense, isometric stalking through the thickets and muskeg and forest, my questions have deepened. I've been as meticulous and attentive as I know how, yet haven't seen or heard a deer. Now that my energy and enthusiasm are about gone, I'm walking too fast, too clumsy-footed, thinking only about reaching camp, watching the ground rather than the unfolding patterns ahead. And then, perhaps, the raven winks his eye.

A quick tremor at the edge of sight. A series of deep, sharp thumps. By the time I react it's much too late, and I watch the deer bound over the tussocks, all four legs springing at once like a jumping toy, tail straight up, back arched, head erect, body tense and smooth-flanked and ruddy-brown, flashing between clumps of brush and skeleton pines.

I can only watch, stifling helpless frustration. But then the deer's vaulting flight suddenly stops. She is fastened to the earth, hard and motionless as the trees, her eyes and ears stitched on my impending shape. Our stares lock together, and neither of us dares to move. Finally I yield and very slowly straighten to a less awkward stance. As if released, she drops her tail and shakes it, moves her right front leg, and lowers her head for a better view. Conflicting emotions tangle inside me. First I feel as if the animal and I are absolutely engaged with each other, with this moment, and with this place. Then I am an invader and a craven predatory menace; I wish I could sink into the ground and be transformed into something that truly belongs here— a spider, a vole, a spruce needle, a clump of moss.

The deer takes a few steps toward us, snared by a curiosity that erodes the sounder judgment of her fear. Shungnak keeps flawlessly still as I crouch against a little mound covered with Labrador tea and bog blueberry. The rustling is so soft I can barely hear it myself; but for the deer, even forty yards away, it must sound like the clatter of a dropped plate. She catches herself midstep, off balance and ajar, lifts her head, and hones those magnificent ears on me. I feel that I've been caught by radar. I wonder if the doe hears the sound of my breathing.

Grandpa William often spoke of a rightness in this: the meeting of hunter and prey may be foreordained, a willful exchange of life, a manifestation of spiritual power, in a watchful world where little happens purely by chance. Looking at the deer, I can sense again the wisdom in his oft-repeated phrase: "Every animal knows way more than you do."

I gently lift the rifle and rest it in my hand, tilt my head to find the sights, and then bring them slowly down against the deer's shape. She turns her head toward me, then to one side, as if she's preparing to run. I am completely set, calm, but caught by my own ambivalence. I would never hesitate like this for a buck as large and heavy-bodied. She has come to me, but I want her to run. I wait a few seconds, then decide I must do what I came here for.

I hold my breath and steady the rifle.

But then, my eye catches an odd wavering in the meadow beyond her. A smaller deer, in plain sight this whole time, wonderfully

blended into the sere grass. My thoughts eddy and tumble. It's legal
to hunt any deer. The adolescent can easily live on its own. The season is near closing. But I have never knowingly taken a doe accompanied by her young one.

And I will not do it now.

My whole body slacks and loosens. The doe turns, switches her
tail, takes three or four gentle leaps over the clumps of grass, and disappears into the forest with the fawn flouncing delicately at her
hooves. A slender huckleberry branch waves back and forth where
they brushed against it. And the muskeg is empty of all except doubt.

A raven's call gurgles down from high against the bright mane of
clouds. Laughing at me again, I suppose.

I stand and turn away, look out across the meadow, and think
how strange it is to love so deeply what gives you life, and to feel
such pleasure and such pain in taking from that source. It's a difficult
thought, so I ease my mind away to other things. The clouds have
thinned and opened. This will be a cold night.

A still, brittle dawn. Frozen puddles inside the curled edges of fallen
leaves. Driftwood logs mantled with frost. Shore rocks shining at the
tide's edge. Haze above slick water in the strait.

I stand with Shungnak on a point near camp, watching the pale
orange sun rise above severed rags of cloud. A batch of harlequin
ducks sculls beyond the surge. Herring gulls perch on the shore and
drift in easy, aimless circles. A bald eagle soars along the treetops,
raven-black against patches of blue sky, head and tail bright as
clouds. The weather is almost ideal for hunting, but the muskeg will
be impossibly crisp, frosted, and noisy. Clearing sky gives some hope
for a thaw later, but boggy terrain often holds the chill as if it were re-
frigerated.

My solution is to work slowly back along a timbered ridge where
the moss is unfrozen, hoping I'll either stalk close to a deer in the
woods or call one in at the muskeg's edge. There is no sign until we
approach the place of yesterday's doe and fawn. Then Shungnak
veers off the trail, cocks her ears, lifts her nose against the drift of air,
urges me to follow her toward an impervious thicket. Her excitement means a deer must be close; but I see nothing. I hear a band of
teetering juncos . . . faint squirrel chatter . . . and then pounding

hooves. A big deer charges off, flashing through bars of light and shadow, and vanishes before I can tell if it's a buck or a doe. Within seconds, another bursts away into the woods farther on, and a dwindling series of thuds from beyond the screening brush sounds like two more. They've all fled downwind, into the thick of our scent, so there's no chance we'll come near them again.

The meeting ignites my optimism, while I also worry it might have been the only chance for the day. Just back from the muskeg's edge, I try the call. Shungnak is impatient; my feet are cold; nothing comes. Finally I decide to cross the opening and hunt in a band of forest behind Hidden Beach. The muskeg is half a mile wide here, reticulated with open meadows, thickets of prostrate cedar, and scattered copses of pine. We're surrounded by a field of sparkling grass, picketed with sharp-edged shadows from the bordering timber. Every footstep tinkles and glitters with frost. The snow-whitened crest of Kluksa Mountain shimmers against a blue dome of sky. I trace the curve of its peak, the sharp-lipped cornices, the long streaks of drifts, and wonder how it would feel to stand there now.

Shungnak wanders from side to side as we rattle across the meadow. Walking through the islands of pine forest is quieter going, but there is still enough frost so a deer would easily hear us. I have a feeling of helplessness, a sense that whether I see a deer or not is ultimately beyond my control. I can only move gently, watch carefully, and hope that an animal appears, waits, offers itself. This isn't to deny the importance of knowing about the animal, pursuing it skillfully, and having a keen sense for the woods. But on another level, everything is up to the deer, and I am beholden to its willingness. After this long absence of luck, I can't find any assurance, only a kind of hope that persists inside me, a desire as much from the spirit as the body. I want to return to the grace that gives life.

Thinking this, I remember an Eskimo man I often hunted with whispering beside an open lead in the sea ice: "Seal head . . . come, seal, show yourself." Twenty-five years later, I've begun to understand the deeper emotions behind asking the animal to come, and the wisdom of the humility in his voice.

We follow the edge of a small stream, jump across a pinched spot, and move through the middle of a pine glade. I look toward the muskeg ahead, making little effort to be quiet, focusing my attention on the walk rather than the hunt. In this most unlikely of situations, unexpected as a hot spark against bare flesh, a deer springs out from a patch of scrubby trees ahead. It looks at us and then slows to a half-alarmed strut, with its tail tensed straight out behind. A bright curve of antlers shows briefly as the deer turns toward the nearest cover.

I grope in my pocket for the call and give it a hard blow. The deer stops, his head and shoulder hidden behind two trees. I move quickly to the side and find an open view, brace the rifle on a pine trunk, squint along the barrel's shining edge, and fit my finger to the cold, curved trigger. My heart must be racing, but I'm not aware of it.

The deer jerks his head, turns aside, and walks in the nervous, almost mechanical way that often comes before the fluid explosion of a truly frightened animal. Perhaps Shungnak moved behind me; perhaps he caught our scent; perhaps it's this blurred business of luck. I grab the call again.

The wheezy phantom sound seems to catch the deer and turn him broadside. He takes two more steps, then stops directly behind a tree. Although the buck can't see me, he watches with his ears and keeps himself almost hidden. I can pick out an ear turning and flicking on one side of the trunk, and brown, bulging flanks on the other. My choices are to wait or move, and in either case the deer might run. Even in these concentrated moments my mind races through a vision of this all happening before—the missed buck on the ridge three days ago. The strings tighten inside me. I can feel blood rushing through my armpits, my wrists, my fingertips.

I decide to move. But my footsteps on a patch of frozen crowberries set the deer off again. Without slowing down, I blow the call, and the deer pauses just as I reach a bracing tree.

I lean the rifle against the cold, brittle bark. The metal and wood feel like ice in my hands and against the bare skin of my cheekbone. I fill my lungs and hold the air inside, bring the sights together, and try to steady them. The rifle makes a tiny jump every time my heart beats. Magnified over the distance between us, it could be enough to spoil my aim. I take another deep breath to relax myself.

When I focus on the close, sharp, gleaming edges of the sights, the deer's shape seems to dissolve into the mottled gray background. So I lift my head, etch the image clearly in my mind, then lean back and hold it.

And for an instant, everything is frozen, as if this winter morning is encased in clear ice. We could be discovered here a thousand years from now, a man with his rifle against a tree and a deer looking back, giving itself—the fusion of two lives.

The moment congeals in a lightning flash and thunder. The air parts and closes. The deer vanishes. I rush, breathless, over the crackling grass, with Shungnak bursting out ahead.

And it is there, on the jeweled and tinseled moss, perfectly still, like a precious and lovely thing laid in an opened hand.

I kneel down, touch the soft, moist, motionless membrane of its eye to be sure, and then whisper thanks for the life that has come to me. I am shivering.

Overwhelmed with gratitude and emotion, I feel myself crying inside. It is a buck deer, full and fat and heavy muscled. It is a buck deer and the island that made him—the muskeg, the forest, the high mountain meadows, the amber ponds and clear streams. It is a buck deer and the gray sky and rain, the rare sunshine, kelp eaten from the shore in the pinch of winter. It is a buck deer and all the seasons of four years or five, the bleating of fall, the supple does that moved beneath him and carried his fawns, and the moonlight and stars, the wind, the fretting of the sea we stand beside. It is a buck deer and it is me, brought together as flesh poured out over the island's rock.

I open the deer and clean out the insides, thinking of the many times I shared this work with Koyukon hunters who had killed moose or caribou. They were ever mindful of the demanding spirit that empowers an animal and remains with it, as its life slowly ebbs away. None of them had ever hunted deer, but their same gestures seem appropriate here: to treat the animal as a sacred thing, to speak of it only in respectful ways, to handle its remains with care, to use it thoroughly and avoid waste, to show appreciation for what is given, and to resist feelings of arrogance, power, or pride.

I trudge back toward camp, with Shungnak snuffling alongside. The deer's weight is a release far more than a burden. Sweating across the muskeg, I'm strengthened by the thought that my long siege of difficulty or ill fortune seems to have ended. The questions I had before remain unanswered, but I've also learned much, and in a way possible only through experience—that the hunter lives on a tenuous edge, that the power in his relationship to the world lies outside himself, and that cleverness, skill, and stealth are meaningless without harmony.

About the Contributors

❧

EDWARD ABBEY (1927–89) was an icon of southwestern literature, philosophy, and environmental thought and activism. "Cactus Ed" authored some two dozen books, including *Desert Solitaire, The Monkey Wrench Gang,* and *The Fool's Progress.* "Blood Sport" is excerpted from his final essay collection, *One Life at a Time, Please* (1988).

RICK BASS lives in Montana and is the author of several books of fiction and nonfiction, including *Winter* and, most recently, *The Lost Grizzlies* (1995). "An Appeal to Hunters" is adapted from an essay that appeared in the June 1995 issue of *Sports Afield.*

TOM BECK is the Colorado Division of Wildlife's bear biologist and a widely respected black bear field researcher. "A Failure of the Spirit" was adapted for this collection from a speech titled "The Amorality of Wildlife Management," delivered to a convention of professional wildlife managers in 1995.

STEPHEN BODIO is a magazine columnist, essayist, and author of five books, including *Aloft* and *Querencia* (both 1990). A slightly longer version of "Passions, Gifts, Rages" first appeared in the *Los Angeles Times Magazine.*

JIMMY CARTER was the thirty-ninth president of the United States and has written several books, including *An Outdoor Journal* (1988), from which "A Childhood Outdoors" is excerpted.

ANN S. CAUSEY holds degrees in philosophy, botany, and zoology. She teaches philosophy at Auburn University in Alabama and focuses her research on the ethical implications of natural resource management. "Is Hunting Ethical?" is adapted from a speech delivered to the first annual (1992) Governor's Symposium on North America's Hunting Heritage.

RUSSELL CHATHAM is an artist, writer, and wild game chef from Montana. "Dust to Dust" is excerpted from his essay collection *Dark Waters* (1988).

CHAS S. CLIFTON has been a newspaper reporter and magazine editor and now teaches writing at the University of Southern Colorado in Pueblo. "The Hunter's Eucharist" as reprinted here appeared in the October 1994 issue of *Colorado Central* magazine. The longer original version premiered in the fall 1993 issue of *Gnosis*.

DAN CROCKETT lives in Montana and is the editor of *Bugle*, the quarterly journal of the Rocky Mountain Elk Foundation. "All Birds Flying" was written for this collection.

PETE DUNNE is a conservationist with the New Jersey Audubon Society. "Before the Echo" first appeared in *Wildlife Conservation* and is the title piece for a collection of Dunne's nature essays published in 1995.

JIM FERGUS lives in Colorado and is a field editor for *Outdoor Life*. The essay used here is from Fergus's 1993 book *A Hunter's Road*, where it appears under the title "My Biologist."

MIKE GADDIS lives in North Carolina and has been an outdoor writer for more than a quarter of a century. "Taking a Life" appeared originally in the November 1990 issue of *Audubon*.

A. B. GUTHRIE, JR. (1901–91) received a Pulitzer Prize in 1950 for his novel *The Way West*. "The Blue Hen's Chick" is excerpted from his 1965 autobiography of that title.

JOHN HAINES is a two-time Guggenheim fellow whose poetry and essays arise largely from his two decades of homesteading in the Alaskan bush, as did "Another Country," which first saw publication in 1991 in *Witness*, under the title "Death," and also appears in his latest book, *Fables and Distances* (1996).

JIM HARRISON is a poet, novelist, essayist, and screenwriter who lives in Michigan, Montana, and Arizona. "The Violators" is from his essay collection *Just Before Dark* (1991).

RONALD JAGER is a former philosophy professor at Yale. He now lives in New Hampshire. He is the author of many articles and books on New England history, including the memoirs *Eighty Acres* and, most recently, *Last House on the Road* (1994). "Hunting with Thoreau" is a first publication.

M. R. JAMES is the founder and editor of *Bowhunter* magazine. He lives in Montana. "Dealing with Death" is excerpted from his book *My Place* (1992).

ROBERT F. JONES is a writer from southern Vermont. "It Wouldn't Be the Same" is adapted from an essay that appeared in the January/February 1994 issue of *Shooting Sportsman*.

TED KERASOTE lives in Wyoming and is a field editor for *Sports Afield*. His books include *Blood Ties* and the forthcoming *Heart of Home*. "Restoring the Older Knowledge" was revised for this collection from a speech delivered to an annual Governor's Conference on North America's Hunting Heritage.

BARRY LOPEZ won a Burroughs Medal for *Of Wolves and Men* and a National Book Award for *Arctic Dreams* (1986), whose epilogue is reprinted here. His latest book is the story collection *Field Notes*. He lives in the Oregon Cascades.

JOHN MADSON was a distinguished name in outdoor journalism. "Why Men Hunt" began as a speech delivered to the first annual Governor's Symposium on North America's Hunting Heritage in 1992.

PETER MATTHIESSEN lives on Long Island, New York. He is an explorer and natural historian whose books include *The Tree Where Man Was Born* (reissued 1995) and nearly three dozen other books. "Survival of the Hunter" is adapted from an essay that appeared in the April 24, 1995, issue of the *New Yorker*.

THOMAS MCGUANE is an essayist, screenwriter, and novelist. A dedicated conservationist, McGuane sits on the directors' boards of American Rivers and the Craighead Wildlife Institute. He lives on a ranch in Montana. "The Heart of the Game" is excerpted from his essay collection *An Outside Chance* (1990).

THOMAS MCINTYRE lives in Wyoming and is hunting editor for *Sports Afield*. His books include *Dreaming the Lion* (1993). "What the Hunter Knows" was adapted for this collection from an article published in the August 1995 issue of *Sports Afield* under the title "The Real Environmentalists."

CRAIG MEDRED is the outdoor editor of the *Anchorage Daily News*, where "Venison Sandwiches" saw first publication in summer 1990.

JOHN G. MITCHELL, of Maryland, has been published in many leading magazines. He is a former editor in chief for Sierra Club Books and science editor for *Newsweek*, and is now the environmental editor for *National Geographic*. "Moose and Mangamoonga" comprises two sections excerpted from his book *The Hunt* (1980).

JOHN A. MURRAY, now living in Colorado, spent six years teaching writing at the University of Alaska, Fairbanks. Editor of a dozen nature anthologies, Murray is also the author of eight books, most recently *The Sierra Club Nature Writing Handbook* (1995). "Climbing the Mountains after Deer" was written for this collection.

RICHARD K. NELSON is a field anthropologist who has lived among and studied native Alaskan hunter-gatherers for a quarter of a century. *The Island Within* (1989), from which "The Face in a Raindrop" was adapted, won the 1991 John Burroughs Medal for outstanding natural history writing. In 1995 Nelson received a Lannan Award for distinguished nonfiction.

DAVID PETERSEN lives in the San Juan Mountains of Colorado. "A Hunter's Heart" was adapted for this collection from an essay that appeared in the November 1995 issue of *Backpacker* under the title "Searching for Common Ground." Petersen's most recent book is *Ghost Grizzlies* (1995).

JIM POSEWITZ spent thirty-two years as a wildlife biologist in Montana, then retired to cofound Orion: The Hunter's Institute. His book *Beyond Fair Chase* (1994) has been widely adopted as a text for state-sanctioned hunter education courses. "The Hunter's Spirit" first appeared in the summer 1995 issue of *Northern Lights*.

C. L. RAWLINS, among other things, is the author of *Sky's Witness* (1993) and *Broken Country* (1996). "I Like to Talk About Animals" was written for this collection.

RUTH RUDNER, of Montana, is the author of *Partings: And Other Beginnings* (1993) and other books. "The Call of the Climb" first appeared in the summer 1991 issue of *Parabola*.

DAVID STALLING lives in Montana and is the conservation writer for the Rocky Mountain Elk Foundation. "Space Age Technology, Stone Age Pursuit" was adapted from an article that appeared in the winter 1995 issue of *Bugle*.

MARY ZEISS STANGE, PH.D., lives in Montana and upstate New York, where she directs the women's studies program at Skidmore College. "In the Snow Queen's Palace" is adapted from an article that appeared under the title "Little Deaths" in the November 1994 issue of *Sports Afield*.

GUY DE LA VALDÉNE lives on a quail farm in Florida. "For a Handful of Feathers" first appeared in the November 1994 issue of *Sports Afield* and is the title essay for his 1995 book.

GEORGE N. WALLACE farms and raises livestock in addition to teaching at Colorado State University, Fort Collins. "If Elk Would Scream" first appeared in the October 14, 1983 issue of *High Country News*.

TED WILLIAMS, of Massachusetts, is a columnist for *Audubon* and a frequent contributor to other leading magazines. (He is *not* a baseball player.) "Paying for It" appeared originally in the winter 1977 issue of *Gray's Sporting Journal*.

TERRY TEMPEST WILLIAMS is a native of Utah's Great Basin. Her books include *Refuge* and *An Unspoken Hunger*, in addition to the Southwest Book Award–winning *Pieces of White Shell* (1984), from which "Deerskin" is excerpted.

GARY WOLFE is a wildlife biologist living in Montana and executive vice president of the Rocky Mountain Elk Foundation. "When Not to Shoot" premiered in the spring 1991 issue of *Bugle*.

BRUCE WOODS is a poet and former editor of *Mother Earth News*. He now lives in Ohio. "The Hunting Problem" appeared originally in *Back Home*.

JOHN WREDE is a wildlife conservation officer for the South Dakota Department of Game, Fish, and Parks. "Dark Days in the Glass House" first appeared in the fall 1991 issue of *Bugle*.